Shakespeare and
the Problem Play

ALSO BY E. L. RISDEN

Heroes, Gods and the Role of Epiphany in English Epic Poetry (McFarland, 2008)

EDITED BY E. L. RISDEN

Sir Gawain and the Classical Tradition: Essays on the Ancient Antecedents (McFarland, 2006)

EDITED BY E. L. RISDEN AND NICK HAYDOCK

Hollywood in the Holy Land: Essays on the Film Depictions of the Crusades and Christian-Muslim Conflicts (McFarland, 2009)

Shakespeare and the Problem Play

Complex Forms, Crossed Genres and Moral Quandaries

E. L. RISDEN

McFarland & Company, Inc., Publishers
Jefferson, North Carolina, and London

LIBRARY OF CONGRESS CATALOGUING-IN-PUBLICATION DATA

Risden, E. L., 1957–
  Shakespeare and the problem play : complex forms, crossed genres and moral quandaries / E.L. Risden.
      p.   cm.
  Includes bibliographical references and index.

  ISBN 978-0-7864-7243-7
  softcover : acid free paper ∞

  1. Shakespeare, William, 1564–1616 — Tragicomedies. 2. Shakespeare, William, 1564–1616 — Criticism and interpretation. 3. Moral conditions in literature. 4. Ethics in literature. I. Title.
  PR2981.5.R535 2012
  822.3'3 — dc23   2012035339

BRITISH LIBRARY CATALOGUING DATA ARE AVAILABLE

© 2012 E.L. Risden. All rights reserved

No part of this book may be reproduced or transmitted in any form or by any means, electronic or mechanical, including photocopying or recording, or by any information storage and retrieval system, without permission in writing from the publisher.

Cover art iStockphoto/Thinkstock

Manufactured in the United States of America

McFarland & Company, Inc., Publishers
  Box 611, Jefferson, North Carolina 28640
  www.mcfarlandpub.com

To all the students and colleagues
who have studied Shakespeare with me,
and all those who will...

Table of Contents

Preface: The Idea of the Problem Play   1

1. *The Merchant of Venice:* Does Anybody Know the Quality of Mercy?   15
2. *Troilus and Cressida* and the Consummate Anti-Genre   42
3. *All's Well That Ends Well*: Not Really   66
4. Straining the Quality of Mercy: *Measure for Measure*   90
5. Comedic Problem Plays   113
6. Tragic Problem Plays   144
7. History and Romance: Problems of Love, Adventure and Language   177

Chapter Notes   205
Bibliography   219
Index   221

Preface: The Idea of the Problem Play

The "problem play" idea has sometimes helpfully, sometimes dubiously informed discussion of Shakespeare's plays, and though, along with much genre criticism, it has gone out of fashion now, it has figured periodically in the scholarship that helps us understand how the plays work technically.[1] *Problem play* as a term has aroused debate because in some ways it may seem to solve nothing: it leaves us with only a question about a play's genre, not with even a tentative guideline for reading such as we get from calling a work *comedy* or *tragedy*. But I believe it has value in that it suggests our discomfort with labeling a play according to traditional generic conventions. It hints at the value of a transgressive reading — and writing. As Harold Goddard wrote, we can find "nothing to indicate that Shakespeare's imagination ever allowed itself to be shackled by such prescriptions or definitions" (113); one of the few points that caused audiences of his own time to question his skills, his freedom with respect to Classical "rules" or transgressing genre expectations, allowed him to create plays that beg irresolution and thus continued meditation from his audiences.

Shakespeare scholarship generally could benefit, I believe, from our continuing discussion of this issue, because it connects us to fundamental concepts the playwright must consider in writing, directing, and producing plays: one must first get a stimulating script that either meets or exceeds — perhaps in a new and exciting way — audience expectations. And no one has yet approached how the problem play idea applies, if we read with genre problems in mind, to *nearly all* of Shakespeare's plays, not merely a few difficult-to-define outliers, such as those critics have occasionally called "problem comedies." After his earliest efforts in which he learned his craft, Shakespeare, I believe, wrote almost exclusively problem plays.[2]

In the 1987 film *The Princess Bride* (dir. Rob Reiner, from William Goldman's 1973 novel), the Spanish swordsman Inigo, hearing his employer once again inaccurately use the exclamation "Inconceivable!" observes, "You keep using that word. I don't think it means what you think it means." We meet something like that concern when we approach Shakespeare's plays with the term *problem*. This study of a number of Shakespeare's most difficult plays aims to apply the problem play idea better to understand how those plays work and, at least on some levels, to find what (and how) they "mean." Shakespeare's plays have such wonderful complexities and deal with so many excruciating problems that no single approach can sound the depths of what they do profess, as Marlowe's Faustus might say, but any serious and significant critical process attends to means of reading and analysis that complement other valuable approaches and contribute to fuller, more complete and satisfying readings. By *satisfying* I don't mean that we necessarily understand a Shakespeare play in full or that we're happy with the ending, but that we've got what the play does, how it works, and what problems he wanted us to think about. As David Bevington so aptly put it in *How to Read a Shakespeare Play* (Malden, MA: Blackwell, 2006), "Shakespeare does not answer such questions so much as he questions our answers" (2). Shakespeare apparently aimed to make them difficult and troubling.

While the notion of *meaning* has also fallen a bit out of fashion since Archibald MacLeish, Wimsatt and Beardsley, and postmodernism, artists of all sorts before Shakespeare's time, during his time, and for a good while after his time pursued unabashedly didactic purposes. They sought, in Horatian fashion, to delight — or at least emotionally move — and to teach their audiences. If we ignore those purposes, we misrepresent their art. One can find meaning and didactic purpose even in good writers pretty easily: they don't create "hidden meaning," but make it as plain as they can for all to see (and *feel*), since they create for that purpose. With some of the greatest writers, Shakespeare included, finding the meaning(s) creates bigger problems, not because Shakespeare had none in mind, but because he layered his work with all the confusing peculiarities of human nature. He gave us, though, plenty of structural, verbal, demonstrative, and allusive clues to work our way through what he had to say. As A. D. Nuttall has so aptly stated in *Shakespeare the Thinker* (New Haven: Yale University Press, 2007), "Shakespeare is fascinated by what could (just) be the case," by "exercises at the edge of human possibility" (382), and he didn't tend to bring them to ready resolution.

The term *problem plays* comes from F. S. Boas in *Shakespeare and His Predecessors* in 1896 (printed in the U.S. in New York by Charles Scribner's Sons, 1900): Boas used it to label those plays (such as *Measure for Measure*, *All's Well That Ends Well*, and *The Merchant of Venice*) that foreground perhaps unsolvable moral problems. More recently critics have used the term to indicate plays that defy easy categorization by genre, or literary type. *Genre*, a term that applies largely to the form and partly to the content of an artistic work (as in comedy, tragedy, epic, or novel), has much to do with how we read or view a work: if we attend a comedy or tragedy, we go with expectations about how we will find the work presented and how it will end. So criticism had already problematized *problem play* itself, since different critics have used it with different notions in mind. But it remains useful, I think, because it directs our attention to an immediate interpretive difficulty that we experience as soon as we study particular plays. I'm arguing here that the idea of the problem play applies to nearly all of Shakespeare's plays: what we call them does make a difference in how we read and interpret and play them, since labels (like titles) guide audience expectations and invoke interpretive strategies. When I see a tragedy, I expect scary things to happen to noble persons; when I see a comedy, I expect funny things to happen to ordinary or even "low-life" characters; a Romance should include adventures, exotic settings or elements (such as magic), and erotic features or incidents[3]; a history should at least nominally deal with characters and incidents from our past. If upon reflection I find no happy ending, and my jollity has faded to disgust with myself for laughing (cf. Keats's "Why Did I Laugh Tonight"), do I still have a comedy, and if I find no noble, self-destructive protagonist and experience no catharsis, do I still have a tragedy? Upsetting those expectations invokes difficulties — interesting and productive difficulties, one hopes — in the understanding and interpretation of a play.

A few significant books have appeared on this subject, but no one has dealt with it recently or completely, and no one has addressed how the question of problematizing genres affects our readings not just of "official" problem plays, but of the majority of Shakespeare's dramatic œuvre.[4] William W. Lawrence's 1931 *Shakespeare's Problem Comedies* (New York: Macmillan) suggests that the difficulty of the problem plays comes from Shakespeare's' increasing "maturity and insight" (2) as his work became more "serious and realistic" (3), attending less to the fantastic and more to the "darker complexities of human nature" (3). The book treats *All's Well That Ends Well, Measure for Measure, Troilus and Cressida*, and *Cymbeline*. Lawrence came to Shakespeare as I have, from medieval studies; I see the genre complexities or instabilities, though, as not coming later in Shakespeare's work, but as always having inhabited his plays. But, like Lawrence's, my approach to the plays shows the effects of observing them in part from a scholarly viewpoint tutored in an earlier age, one informed most by those works that most influenced Shakespeare, those that built the intellectual expectations of Shakespeare's time. Without substantial background in medieval and Classical literature and language, one can easily misinterpret what Shakespeare was doing. Many readers like to think of Shakespeare and his time as having begun the modern age, having broken away from a dark and dim past, but Shakespeare, like everyone else, read, studied, and responded to the work that preceded him — he simply did so more creatively and with less attachment to the details of traditional forms than had anyone who preceded him (or those who came in the next hundred or more years after him). That creativity — perhaps because he wasn't the university man the anti–Stratfordians so detest — led him to experiment more freely with genre than anyone else had. Those experiments incorporate interesting and powerful differences in content and construction, and they provoke different responses to the plays than they would had those plays more closely conformed to traditional generic expectations. Up to and for the most part within Shakespeare's time, writers adhered firmly to the practices audiences expected of the genres they attempted — all the more reason to attend carefully to exactly how Shakespeare flouts dramatic conventions, particular those of Aristotle's *Poetics*. Authors of his own time and for nearly two hundred years afterward expressed distaste at Shakespeare's tendency to mix genres — they did so based on their own adherence to Classical conventions — but that distaste hardly kept them from enjoying Shakespeare's work, though it did inhibit their potential to understanding them fully.

In 1949 E. M. W. Tillyard responded to Lawrence in *Shakespeare's Problem Plays* by returning to investigate those plays that Boas had addressed. But he immediately problematized the term, implying that the problem play rubric applies to plays we might call the author's "problem children," those that eschew the normal, that elude interpretation — not a bad use of the term, but one different from Boas's. So, then, any difficult play becomes potentially a problem play. In some ways that argument helps me in my approach, because it opens the field for re-examination, but it also makes the term more difficult to apply, because if it means "anything difficult" — it means almost anything worth studying seriously. I suggest that though the term has proven a little squishy and critics have defined it variously, we can still apply it productively: we can say that Shakespeare made his plays difficult to define by genre, thus urging us to read or view them as they are, with all their peculiarities, not simply as representatives of a type popular on the stage in his time or before him. By making his plays innovative and generically problematic, he pushed his audience not to rush to easy responses to complex compositions — what Keats identified as "negative capability" but which we may identify also as a positive urgency to allow and appreciate complexities, to leave audiences with more to think about than simple moral resolutions to real and difficult human problems.

The single most important subsequent work on this subject, *The Problem Plays of Shakespeare,* by Ernest Schanzer (New York: Schocken Books, 1963), treats *Julius Caesar, Measure for Measure,* and *Antony and Cleopatra*; it returns to those plays that raise or even create moral problems. Schanzer begins by disclosing that he wrote "out of a feeling of acute dissatisfaction—which I share with many students of Shakespeare—with the common grouping together of *All's Well, Measure for Measure, Troilus and Cressida*, and sometimes *Hamlet*" (ix) and concludes that *Antony and Cleopatra* best exemplifies the term and shows the most "consummate skill" (183) of all those plays so classified: it best combines, complicates, and realizes the value of problematizing genre. He finds the term *problem play* useful as long as we stop short of creating an "exclusive category" (186). The kind of genre freedom that we allow, even laud, in modern works such as Joyce's *Ulysses* we omit from consideration with the works of earlier periods. But from the productive, variable critical response that we get to Joyce, by means of opening the genre question we can open Shakespeare's plays to some new possibilities. A colleague who regularly teaches Joyce asserts that whatever we call *Ulysses*, it isn't a novel; I think it is a novel, though enormously innovative structurally, allusively, and linguistically. But reading it under another generic rubric, particularly, for instance, epic poem, opens different and fascinating possibilities, and so we should feel encouraged to do so.

More recently Susan Snyder in *The Comic Matrix of Shakespeare's Tragedies* (Princeton: Princeton University Press, 1979) has shown that Shakespeare often builds a tragedy from a structure that looks awfully like that of comedy; the turn to tragedy then heightens the powerful effects on the audience of the "fall" that occurs in the play. Unlike in comedies, characters in tragedies can't reverse or undo what they've done, though their actions, fun or foul, may look much the same, deepening the experience of the sense of the tragic. I see this structural trope as turning on Shakespeare's use of the Great Chain of Being, another metaphor that has passed out of contemporary criticism but that in his time informed the notions of how life works—whether a notion is out of fashion or not is not nearly as important as if it helps us understand how a play works.[5] All of Shakespeare's plays begin with or hinge on a break (or at least a dangerous weakening) somewhere in the Great Chain. Normally, if that break occurs fully and high in the chain, such as the murder of a monarch, the play will turn to tragedy; if it occurs lower on the chain and allows for fairly easy repair (such as the prohibition of a proper couple to marry), the play will turn to comedy. Thus the strange and problematic nature of *Romeo and Juliet*, for example: because of the simple and reparable nature of the problem, it should have turned to comedy, their happy marriage bringing familial peace. The families make peace, of course, but too late, and only at the expense of the next generation. The older generation resist peace and assert unyielding authority, and the younger generation act rashly, "falling" because of their parents' wrath and their own impatience.

In her 2004 book *Shakespeare After All* (New York: Anchor), Marjorie Garber explores the history of the term early in her chapter on *Troilus and Cressida* that

> nineteenth-century scholars invented a category they called the "problem play," a term borrowed from the works of dramatists of the time (Ibsen, Shaw, Strindberg, and others) whose plays were thought to engage with ongoing social problems (environmental issues, women's rights, venereal disease, prostitution). To those scholars, some Shakespeare plays seemed similarly preoccupied with issues of morality and public and private behavior ... plays ... sometimes categorized as "cynical," as questioning the possibility of noble or heroic ideals.... This grouping of the "problem plays" allowed for the segregation of those more troubled works from apparently more joyous comedies and allowed a deferral of the "problem" of their genre identification [537].

She adds that *problem plays*, along with *dark comedies*, began to fall out of favor as the critics began to find the "lighter" comedies just as dark[6]; I would add that we may see many of the tragedies and Romances as equally puzzling in terms of the modes of writing they use, the kinds of characters Shakespeare creates and what he does with them, and the ideas that emerge most clearly from plays of any sort.

Also, Leonard Tennenhouse in *Power on Display: The Politics of Shakespeare's Genres* (New York: Methuen, 1986) has shown that even when we agree on a "problem" label, we may not agree on exactly "what problem the play poses" or even the way it poses a problem (3). Tennenhouse argues that we must take care with generic labels and not detach the plays from their contemporary politics: each in its way deals with issues of government and power[7]— I find that point as true psychologically as politically. In one of the most critically acclaimed Shakespeare studies of the 1990s, *A Theater of Envy* (New York: Oxford University Press, 1991), René Girard treats several of the plays through a psychological method he calls "mimetic desire": we see what others desire and by displacement of attraction, or envy, we come to desire it too — that desire, Girard argues, initiates or even guides the action of most if not all of the plays. He uses the idea of the problem play twice in his book, accepting it as essentially a critical "given." He suggests that the idea of mimetic desire can help solve the problem of the problem plays by showing that uncritically adopting as our own desire what someone else desires creates grave difficulties for ourselves and others (5). He adds that we may reasonably call *Troilus and Cressida* a problem play because it creates so many unsolvable enigmas that it opens a nearly "inexhaustible" range of possible interpretations — and it so powerfully deals with problems of desire real or imagined. I prefer to apply the term or idea to a work not just because we find it elusive or difficult or because we must struggle to unpack its themes, but rather when we find difficulties in the play that inhibit us from understanding the generic clues that direct our emotional as well as intellectual responses. Comedy, tragedy, history, and Romance may all use the same themes (e.g., the need to understand and do our duty, the need to understand both the glories and limitations of honor, the foolishness of self-aggrandizement), but they evoke very different emotional complexes and produce very different emotional results in different kinds of plays. Genre *play* (in the Derridean sense of toggling or making space for adjustment or interpretation), either by expanding or collapsing boundaries, complicates how we understand, how we feel about, and maybe even how we respond to those themes. While Girard's notion of mimetic desire provides deep insight into many of Shakespeare's characters (and how the poet saw the problems of human action and character), alone it doesn't account for the complexities of structure, narrative, and theme that make Shakespeare Shakespeare. We need other supportive critical structures.

Aristotle defined dramatic genres pretty simply and directly: a tragedy is a serious play with a sad ending; a comedy is a lighter-hearted play with a happy ending—he doesn't address at length other forms of drama, but does briefly describe some other non-dramatic genres, such as epic. History plays, those that deal with events an audience accepts as past and true, and Romances, plays that deal with exciting (sometimes magical or supernatural) fictional adventures over an expanse of time or space, came later—Christopher Marlowe and Shakespeare gave them much of the shape that we recognize in them now, though they both borrowed from medieval prose models. While the Renaissance, the "rebirth" of Classical learning, idealized Classical models, Shakespeare more than anyone else played with them to create nuances of feeling and meaning that made them more difficult to label, but much more variable and often more powerful to experience and enjoy. Shakespeare didn't entirely abandon Aristotle—*The Tempest*, for example, nearly follows the "unities"—but he did find a means of structuring plays that he used consistently and that he must have found worked better for his audiences. As we do, and as medieval audiences had done with Romances, they could willingly suspend their disbelief and absorb themselves in the dramatic worlds Shakespeare created, with their spatial and temporal shifts, their parallel plots, and their ready movement from pedestrian to royal locales.

As we have seen above, not all scholars agree even on which plays to call problem plays; editors don't always know where to place them in collections, either. Recently, for example, Stephen Greenblatt in his critical biography *Will in the World* (New York: Norton, 2004) calls *The Merchant of Venice* a comedy, and even *Hamlet* has come into discussions as not fitting the pattern of traditional tragedy. In *The Merchant of Venice* only one character, Bassanio, has a happy ending, and he's a scoundrel, making the *comedy* label troublesome; earlier rather than more recent critics have had problems with what to call *Hamlet*, and I concur with the senior contingent: the play doesn't even nearly fit Aristotle's definition of tragedy, because the hero doesn't cause his own fall (his murderous uncle does), and given the fact that Claudius has murdered Hamlet, Sr., and will murder again if he deems the choice expedient, it ends about as happily as it possibly could. Such discrepancies in how we label the plays create difficulties (and possibilities) for how actors and directors choose to present the plays on stage or film, how teachers may best address them in the classroom, and how students and audiences may best understand, appreciate, and enjoy them. Perhaps we need not *label* any or all of the plays as exclusively problem plays — as if the term denoted an exclusive genre, rather than suggesting formal variety and emotional and intellectual uncertainty — but if we read any or all of the plays *as* problem plays, each one opens up with new and intellectually satisfying possibilities for understanding. Once we see how Shakespeare varied conventional genre, we have a means to understand our confusion over the plays and, at least in part, to resolve it. And the generic crux — where the play veers from generic expectation — often proves the very spot where Shakespeare raises the most complex and troubling questions.

Essentially, then, the traditional critical problems with the term *problem play*— that it doesn't answer any questions or help audiences solve the puzzles that the works present or that it has fallen out of use in a postmodern age that resists labels anyway — need not stop us from considering the usefulness it still may have if its application leads us to more solid, complete, trustworthy, or satisfying readings than we would otherwise achieve. And the problem behind the term remains present in the plays, regardless of whether we apply it: when Shakespeare swerved from traditional practices associated with the genres he used, what did his variations in form and content accomplish and how do they affect our readings of the plays both intellectually and emotionally? When he leaves us with discomfort over the resolution — or lack of it — at the end of a play, how do we respond interpretively to that discomfort? For students and teachers of Shakespeare's plays, that question represents an effective place to begin study, so I have chosen it as the focal point in this book: we always need new ways to bring new audiences to the great works of the past as more teachers — even somewhat educated ones — are trying to urge their irrelevancy to our time. Shakespeare's company, too, would have wanted from him not just a *play*, but a comedy or tragedy or Romance; readers who pick up a book want to read not just a *book*, but a novel or a biography or a history — and preferably a good one. How writers and readers situate a text, the expectations that structure and approach create and the effects that straying from expectations produces, powerfully affects how they create or recreate it, and the crossing of boundaries inevitably shunts one's creation of or response to a work from one stream of thought and feeling to another.

Each of Shakespeare's plays in its own way problematizes reading, so each resists simple readings based only on form, the social class of characters, and endings. The Romances present the easiest identifications: they have love, adventure, and some kind of magic, but they too present enormous difficulty in terms of our affective responses and interpretive schemes. They arouse moral or ethical problems that resist easy solution. Only one Shakespeare play fits the terms of traditional tragedy as they come from the Classics: *Macbeth*. Only two plays actually play out as comedies: *The Comedy of Errors* (which Shakespeare essentially "translated" from Latin) and *The Merry Wives of Windsor* (which he apparently created on demand).[8] In the history plays he adapted what he found in chronicle sources as he saw fit, but he still built into them the substance, emotion, and method of comedy, tragedy, and Romance: he aimed finally to build good plays, not simple fulfillments of generic demands, and to him "good plays" meant leaving his audience with points of concern to weigh and consider. A better means of describing the writing process may make use of Northrop Frye's idea of modes[9]: the writer may mix high and low mimetic elements, Romance or epic elements, tragic or comic elements — but the result, the play, remained a product that Shakespeare's company had to market on stage for an audience that came to see it with expectations for a kind of entertainment that they had come to know and enjoy.

In the chapters to come I'll treat the most troubling of the problem plays, analyzing them essentially according to how they use and revise genre and how they leave us with difficult problems to ponder.[10] Dramatic and critical movement based on the usual generic assumptions or classifications allows us also to follow how the critical cruces of the problem plays evolved, so that we may get a sense of what must Shakespeare have been thinking about as he created those emotional and interpretive conundrums and what they do as works of literary art. I'll begin with those works most commonly appearing in studies of problem plays, and I'll treat them in the order of how problematic I find them: *The Merchant of Venice*, *Troilus and Cressida*, *All's Well That Ends Well*, *Measure for Measure*. Next I'll move to the "comedic" problem plays, those we've most often identified as comedies or that particularly manipulate comic methods or expectations: *Much Ado About Nothing*, *A Midsummer Night's Dream*, and *Twelfth Night*. Third, I'll approach the "tragic" problem plays: *Hamlet* (which creates some of the most interesting genre problems among those plays we may term problem plays), *Othello*, and — the most difficult of all — *King Lear*. Fourth, I'll consider genre and interpretation problems in history and Romance for the issues they raise in love, adventure, and governance with stops at *Henry IV, Part 1*, *Henry V*, *Cymbeline*, *The Tempest*, and *Love's Labour's Lost*: they overlap in how they treat authority and adventure, and they all have curious implications with respect to love. I'll conclude that final chapter with some thoughts on others play that fall in or near the "problem" category and that will, I hope encourage further study. One play creates its own special problems by steadfastly resisting any efforts to focus on any serious dramatic problem: *Love's Labour's Lost*—it deserves more space than I give it, but one must stop somewhere. My remarks thoughout will address affective and aesthetic qualities as well as analyses of of structure, word use, character development, and especially the problems that the plays raise.

Through the work I've done on this project I've come to an even stronger sense that Shakespeare particularly sets in motion the modern democratization of drama, but with limits. Though we may like to call him modern, we can't at last call him Modern; however, we would probably have had a more difficult time becoming modern or Modern without him. He showed us how, at least in respect to many of the better ideas that *modern* and *Modern* imply.

So much Shakespeare criticism has appeared that no one can claim complete originality; any coherent reading will in part restate what others have already written. The critic, then, attempts to frame and detail an approach he or she has not seen fully exploited and that will help the reader with the practical concerns of studying, enjoying, appreciating, and teaching the text at hand. One may differ from the most accomplished critics without suggesting loss of respect for them or their approaches. For instance, while I admire all and agree with much of what David Bevington argues, I don't agree with his suggestion in the epilogue that students begin by seeing a play rather than reading it (*How to Read*, "Epilogue," page 155), particularly if the students are of college age or older. Seeing a play, whether on stage or on film, means seeing an interpretation — one interpretation — and that interpretation, in my own teaching experience, can limit students' subsequent responses to the play. The first performance they see becomes *the one*, the right one, and they often have trouble detaching themselves from the assumption that they already have it right so they can with open minds read the play and allow new (and often better, and often more accurate) understandings and interpretations of the play to arise as they read — we're working now with generations of powerfully visual learners, and we need to make sure they learn how to *read*. I believe students should read first, then see productions (as many and in what media they have available), and then read again — an ideal, perhaps, but practical to some extent in a Shakespeare course at the college level, where a syllabus may include multiple options for viewing.

In *Shakespeare and Christian Doctrine* (Princeton: Princeton University Press, 1963), Roland Mushat Frye, after much study and careful reasoning, comes to the conclusion that "the mirror of Shakespeare's drama was held up to nature, and not to saving grace" (267): while understanding Shakespeare's knowledge and use of Christian theology, we must understand his plays as first and foremost secular works, Frye argues. While I agree with that point in general, in some specific instances I find Shakespeare immerses himself and his audience in fully, specifically, and necessarily Christian experience: if we don't read Hero as Christ-figure in *Much Ado About Nothing*, the end of the play becomes monstrous, horrific, and if we don't read *Measure for Measure* as an allegory of divine mercy, the Duke and his Dukedom seem silly, mad, or worse—but more about that idea in the chapters ahead. Shakespeare's world was still an inescapably Christian world, however much he avoided doctrine in his plays. In both those above cases my disagreements are small, and I express them as alternatives to reading and teaching the plays: we aim to get the fullest, fairest, and most satisfying readings and interpretations of these incredibly rich texts that we can. However, while we must not exclude the possibility that Shakespeare used allegory—it had such great literary prominence both before and after him—we must avoid giving in too readily to simplistic allegorical reading, religious or otherwise. And as Frye so aptly points out, Shakespeare's awareness of theology doesn't make him in his plays theologian—or an allegorist. "[S]ixteenth-century theologians contended that the ethics relevant to the concerns of the secular order were not exclusively Christian, but universally human," Frye notes (8), and Shakespeare's time undertook literature as "independent of any specifically Christian theology and ... endowed with its own integrity" (8), yet while he stayed notably out of Christian debates or specifics of doctrine or Christian history, Shakespeare's world was dominated by Christian thought and a specific Christian experience of life only a little less pervasive than that of the medieval world and nearly impossible for us to understand today in our world of questioning and pluralism.

Much of the work I do in the following chapters will necessarily begin from, echo, or parallel that of other scholars and teachers — any honest readers working on the same texts must find much in common — but I hope in addition to the common ground to show the possibility of pretty complete and compelling readings through careful attention to the productive problems genre-reading creates, especially given Shakespeare's genius in manipulating them so intently.

As with all critics, I am making here an *essay*, an attempt, one informed and influenced by many excellent teachers and critics, in an effort to understand how and why Shakespeare so continually unsettles us. I owe a debt of gratitude to the professor with whom I studied Shakespeare, William Bache of Purdue University, who has since passed away. He taught us about tropes such as character doubles,[11] recapitulative scenes, offstage action, the importance of props (that sometimes do and sometimes don't actually appear physically onstage), and Shakespeare's use of verbal repetition and lists. Over time, through reading, teaching, and discussing the plays with many helpful colleagues and students, I have found attention to those tropes extremely helpful in grasping the number of aspects one needs to pursue to teach the plays honestly and effectively. But my understanding of them has evolved a bit. I see now character matrices, multiple parallel scenes or narremes, and inter- and intratextual echoes — not so very different, but more expansive, perhaps, infected with a touch of postmodernism. I remain enormously grateful for Professor Bache's introducing me to Shakespeare's strategies and structures, and I hope to build on them. Understanding strategies and structures, along with putting in the hard work of close reading (which often requires sorties into the sadly waning discipline of philology), wanting to understand, and having something to say have always proven the starting points for good reading and good writing, and they still do. Those methods along with all the criticism I have read and heard and the act of regularly teaching the plays — few experiences help more than teaching to direct, clarify, and specify one's thinking — have all inflected the genesis and development of this pursuit of the problem-play idea, which I hope now will contribute to other students' and teachers' quests into the dramatic world of our greatest and most renewably challenging English writer. We begin, as I once heard an elder colleague put it, by "grappling with his mind," and from there Shakespeare leads us to grapple with our own and with the troubling dissonances of human experience, with the many problems that come from the human penchant to transgress and to create.

From studying the problems of Shakespeare's problem plays we do learn something about Shakespeare as a thinker: a difficult task given that he never wrote any commentaries on his plays, his poetry, his methods, or his thinking. He turns out to be what in our time we'd have to call a social conservative: his plays tend to affirm old ideas of degree, of the importance of fidelity and duty, of a kind of private and personal versus public honor — many of the same ideas we see emerging from Chaucer's works. He has, though, a rather more refined sense of humor than Chaucer, surprising perhaps in a country boy as opposed to the urban Chaucer, London born and bred. But artistically and in terms of how he treats the human individual we must term him liberal: he takes the traditional, conservative stories, genres, and ideas and radically revises them for powerful and troubling effects: he never lets his audience off with easy resolutions or judgments or simple answers. He prepares us according to common expectations, and then he transgresses, breaking boundaries of form and technique and theme to push what drama can do and what the heart can feel. His creative application of the old ways makes him timeless; his transgression and even explosion of old limitations of thought with new language make him one of the greatest of poets; his sometimes painfully elastic metaphors and lively yet deeply troubling characters create the literary genius that we continue to admire above all others.

1

The Merchant of Venice
Does Anybody Know the Quality of Mercy?

Shakespeare's most transgressive and problematic play, and perhaps his most difficult to understand and most morally troubling, *The Merchant of Venice* defies classification. It usually appears in anthologies among "Comedies"; it certainly is not a comedy: it has little if any humor, and the only character for whom it has a happy ending, Bassanio, has shown in getting there nothing but selfishness and irresponsibility. "Every performance of *The Merchant of Venice* might well be heralded with the cry: *no comedy tonight*," wrote Harold Goddard (114) — nor tragedy, nor Romance, nor history, but something that, if you pay attention, will leave you feeling really disturbed, he might have added. If anything, in the last century, universally fraught with the plague of anti-semitism and the rise of Zionism, the play has got even more difficult to study and understand. It has become more a cultural test of a reader's feelings about Judaism than a play for study, discussion, and appreciation — I won't go so far as to say enjoyment, since I don't think Shakespeare had in mind pleasure as such when he wrote it.

Deconstruction has taught us the practical impossibility of separating our reading of a work from our own context, so, as time passes and the world continues to change, in many ways we get further from knowing exactly what Shakespeare wanted us to see and no closer to a reading free of prejudices. We pass judgments quickly and change our minds slowly if at all — probably humans have always done so. Even a critic such as Bernard Grebanier, who takes great pains to counsel us to avoid misreading and to stick to the facts of the play, can still nod, as when he asserts that Shylock "reveals himself as a harsh, brow-beating father and a miserly master" (7)[1]; Jessica's only real complaint is that she feels bored, and Launcelot hardly proves a trustworthy source of information: he plays a sick joke on his nearly blind father, and *if* Shylock tells the truth, he eats to excess (Shylock says that directly to

Launcelot, who does not dispute it, nor does Jessica, who in 2.3.2 calls him a "merry devil"), and we learn from Lorenzo that he has impregnated one of the maids.[2] Whom should we believe, Shakespeare asks, and how much do we trust reported events and speech? So we may also see Shylock as a concerned father or an untrustworthy daughter and a master troubled by a slothful, gluttonous, and lecherous servant.

A similar problem arises with what Shylock said when he learned of his daughter's elopement: we don't know what he said. We know what Solanio says Shylock said, and he isn't a trustworthy witness, since as a friend of Antonio's and a typical citizen of a biased Venice he harbors obvious prejudice against Jews. What Shylock actually says about Jessica doesn't imply he has greater interest in his money than his daughter; he says, "I would that my daughter were dead at my foot, and the jewels in her ear! Would she were hears'd at my foot, and the ducats in her coffin" (3.1.86–89). His desiring his daughter dead doesn't win him any sympathy, nor should it, but from his point of view (that of his own traditions and laws) she has already died when she betrayed him, robbed him, and left to convert and marry a Christian: she has broken the commandments to honor her father and to avoid theft, and having converted she has died to him. If he had the money she took, he says, he would bury it with her. Because of our modern particularly sensitive sympathy for children (abused or not), we may easily believe what unreliable opinions we hear. We may forget that we see him do her no harm, only try—raising her without her mother—to protect her from a dangerous society. Her escape to "freedom" may bring her more sorrow than the loneliness she suffered in their home. And by burying the jewels with her body he does more funereal honors than Bassanio would do for Antonio, were he the fatal subject of the court's decision. Shylock suffers an enormous amount of sorrow with which, because of his gruff manner and the relentless judgment others heap upon him, we may fail to sympathize: he has lost his last family member, his family has no future, he has no future, and his reason for acquiring wealth has vanished. We don't even know that Shylock is comparatively greedy: does he make more profit on loans than Antonio makes on goods? does he make more than Bassanio makes by borrowing from Antonio so he can look richer than he is or by marrying a rich women he barely knows? does *he show* any evidence of practicing particularly egregious usury, whatever others say of him? Assumptions die slowly even when one recognizes them as dubious or even moribund.

So much of the critical as well as an audience's aesthetic response to the play moves directly and passionately to Shylock that we can easily forget Shakespeare didn't follow Marlowe's model and call the play *The Jew of Venice*. He didn't do so because the play doesn't deal exclusively with Shylock, who

1. The Merchant of Venice

actually spends relatively little time onstage, or with Jewish issues: it deals with merchantry, an increasingly popular topic in Shakespeare's time with the continuing rise of a geographically spreading, wealthier, and more influential merchant class. A class of persons who up until the later Middle Ages hadn't a means of increasing wealth through regular business dealings had by Shakespeare's time expanded, and some of that class had begun to enjoy gaining wealth for its own sake as well as the newfound power and social mobility it has provided them: Ben Jonson satirizes one variety of them in *Volpone*. The larger group, including a range from dedicated merchants to dedicated con men,[3] became a topic of concern for writers as well as for the upper class who saw them beginning to intrude on traditional seats of power. Shylock belongs to that class; as for Antonio, we don't know much about his background, but we know he has many friends and a good deal of public influence because of his wealth, so he belongs by practice to the same financial class as Shylock, though a more powerful social one.

While Shakespeare by no means created a flattering or positive portrait of Shylock, neither did he create the negative one audiences often bring as an assumption to the play: he created a *sympathetic* one. His Christian Venetians, though, show little to recommend themselves, either. They prick Shylock, and he bleeds; they poison him, and he dies. They preach mercy, but fail to practice it; they speak as if they were rational, lawful, and generous, but they show little reason and twist the law to their advantage, and their generosity hinges on hidden, personal, and selfish motives. All the characters act, when we see them act, not like caricatures, but like real — and mostly bad — humans.

Shakespeare shows us how readily we fall into hypocrisy and cruelty — note the nearly unceasing nastiness of the "choric" figure Gratiano. Shakespeare uses him in the play for his voluble abuse, and he shows how readily we pass judgment on others, how seldom we look carefully at ourselves, and how easily we drift from our religious commitments. Whether Christian or Jewish, we assume others will either do the same to us or they will (and should) continue to allow us to get away with treating them badly. Gratiano uncensoredly speaks the prejudices of the Venetian Christians and the general human selfishness and tendency to rash and foolhardy judgments. Hardly "Shakespeare's Jewish play," as one will sometimes hear it called, *The Merchant of Venice* reads as neither pro– nor anti–Jewish nor pro– nor anti–Christian. Shakespeare did, though, make it a thoroughly Christian play in the same way many of the obviously Christian medieval cycle dramas serve as intense reminders of how Christians must avoid the pride of assuming oneself better than others: one has an obligation to God to avoid the bad and enact the good. Everyone in this play fails in that obligation. Morality plays may show bad examples rather than good ones. Hardly Shakespeare's "Venetian comedy," either, as one will also hear it called, the play undercuts any notion of a happy ending by showing that no combination of happiness and goodness lies ahead for anyone. No one has shown sufficient goodness to deserve, in a Christian sense — or a Jewish one — happiness, or salvation for that matter. And anything that look or sounds like humor (intentionally, I think) falls flat. Problems come about because the characters do what they want, often something bad, whenever they can, and they seek what they want regardless of their desires' effects on others — a good message for a Christian audience or for any audience about what to avoid.

We have got so accustomed to the general notion of ubiquitous anti-semitism in the European world of Shakespeare's time that audiences readily make assumptions about what Shakespeare must have thought about Jews, about what Shylock thinks and does, about the truth of what Christians say, and about how we as audience members must set our prejudice meter on high and prepare our high dudgeon to smoke it out and bring it to justice. As Martin Yaffe wrote so clearly, in opposition to much of the standard criticism, "I find no evidence to indicate that Shakespeare himself endorses the prejudices articulated by his characters who are unfriendly to Jews and much to indicate that he understands those prejudices fully for what they are, namely, as dubious and damaging opinions" (23)—close reading can relieve us of false assumptions even while it inhibits our urgency to draw simple and clear but limiting conclusions. In *The Merchant of Venice* Shakespeare leaves us with little that we *know* beyond a few verifiable events that we see onstage — determining the characters' emotions and intentions proves elusive, as we can see from the range of actors' and directors' interpretations. He dispenses with all Aristotelian precepts of play-making beyond imitation and the basic components of plot, character, thought, diction, music, and spectacle, even the idea of a beginning, middle, and end: the play has three endings. The play leaves us with problem after problem, doubt after doubt, and nothing in the way of assurance other than that we have seen a number of characters think poorly and act very badly — Shakespeare was above all the poet of real life, and this play gives us a large, nasty dose of it with all its hatreds, fears, ambiguities, and vagaries.

As Goddard points out, the play interlaces three common narrative motifs: the casket story, the bond story, and the ring story — all, especially the casket story, call attention to the "contrast between what is within and what is without," the bond story makes a "distinction between the letter and the spirit of the law," and the ring story deals with "the essence of a promise" (82). Each story, derived from folk motifs, makes us question what we can trust of what a person says and does. Each story, I would suggest, deals with insiders and outsiders, and each one begins with a bond: suggesting, making, and breaking bonds lies at the heart of the problems of *The Merchant of Venice*.[4] The folding, enfolding, and unfolding of bonds determines its structure, and I'll deal with this issue in the first part of the rest of this chapter. In the second part I'll look closely at two speeches that express the moral problem at the center of the play, speeches that I think are, while on the surface seemingly quite different, nearly interchangeable. Those two parts comprise the majority of my argument. "For all the power with which he claims our attention, Shylock at the end of the play is radically incomplete, denied a part in any realized action," Kenneth Gross argues[5]—far worse than that, I would say, since I believe they kill him three times over, and nearly every character succeeds in marginalizing himself or herself in the play. Only Bassanio really gets what he wants, and he deserves it less than anyone else we meet, since he more than anyone else embodies the mind-numbing selfishness that the play asks us to address—and avoid. This narrative course—the tension between getting what we want and finding ourselves marginalized by our society—shows the results of the unfolding of the problem of the play, and it will plot the course for part three to come. In part four I'll consider two subplots, Launcelot Gobbo's service and Jessica's elopement, that mirror major elements of the two main plots—an unusually complex structure even for a Shakespeare play—and show how they deepen rather than help solve the problems that have already arisen and how they leave the conclusion of the play even more ambivalent. Shakespeare remarkably enfolds all those elements in a thematic whole, all bent on the problem of our hearts not committing to the bonds we make.

Inside and Outside: Making and Breaking Bonds

The casket motif begins with a bond between father and daughter. Portia feels bound, or at least says she does, to execute her father's wish that she marry the man who solves the casket riddle. He left those directions, apparently, to discourage trivial suitors, since anyone who tries must promise to marry no other if he fails, and to try to find her a perceptive—and perhaps lucky—husband.[6] Someone of course might do it by guessing, but Portia gets from each man who tries a promise that if he chooses poorly, he will never marry—a deterrent at least to honorable contestants. The caskets bear clues not only in their color and substance—gold, silver, and lead—but also in their respective inscriptions: "Who chooseth me shall gain what many men desire"; "Who chooseth me shall get as much as he deserves"; "Who chooseth me must give and hazard all he hath." The rational contestant will consider all the clues, but reason alone will not give the answer, since the clues by themselves fall short of a solvable riddle: luck must also play its part.

Goddard finds alchemy as the metaphor that underlies *The Merchant of Venice*, the "art of transforming the base into the precious" (1:115). The caskets, inscriptions, and contents all have alchemical referents, as does the movement of the whole play — though in that case, in reverse. In alchemy, originally more of an esoteric philosophy of spiritual refinement than an actual attempt to make precious metal, gold represents not wealth, but purity of substance: one tries to turn the "base metal" or the body into the "gold" of the spirit. The person who in choosing gold aims at material wealth misses the point, just as the contestant who chooses the gold casket for the sake of wealth, "what many men desire," gets nothing but a *memento mori*. A sad psychological truth that Shakespeare understood that we don't often face is that while many persons do desire wealth, some — perhaps many — desire death or find it in some way alluring, as Freud would explain almost three centuries later. The risk of failure adds to the excitement of the casket game. Material wealth in no way implies spiritual accomplishment, nor does it imply love of another person, "this mortal breathing saint" (2.7.40), as Morocco calls Portia (he makes a common romantic error there, too, expecting the lady to conform to saintly behavior rather than that of a real, passionate person). Inside the box he finds a picture of a death's head, a skull, and a verse that explains, "All that glisters is not gold.... Gilded tombs do worms infold.... Fare you well; your suit is cold."[7]

Though Portia tells Morocco that his skin color makes no difference to her, and that he seems to her as "fair" a choice as anyone she has seen, she lies to him: in I.2 Nerissa mentions Bassanio, and Portia remembers him by name, and they both remark on his good looks. Once Morocco has failed and departed, Portia says, "A gentle riddance. Draw the curtains, go./ Let all of his complexion choose me so" (2.7.78–79).[8] She did not like his looks, and so she feels relief at his failure. That lie has some importance in how we view Portia and in how we perceive her participation in the casket game: it makes her less naïve and perhaps more involved in the process of the suitor's decision. She and Nerissa have also together berated all the suitors but the one whose looks she likes: she, too, undertakes a casket game with her suitors, judging the inside (character) by the outside (looks), and she ends up choosing, like all her suitors but one, poorly. She thus inflects the moral implications of the test and of the bond that go with the game.

In Morocco's case, as well as that of the other suitors, spiritual accomplishment fails, just as alchemy misunderstood fails. He shows himself not ready for the spiritual quest through his own pride: he brags about his looks ("this aspect of mine ... [t]he best-regarded virgins of our clime/ Have lov'd it too," 2.1.8–11), his courage and martial accomplishments (lines 25 ff.), and his degree (2.7. 25 ff.). The second suitor, Aragon, she addresses as "noble prince" (2.9.4), but when he fails, she happily if disgustedly exclaims, "O, these deliberate fools" (line 80)—a fool, yes, but one can hardly blame him for deliberating. He gets the point that he must not choose by "show" alone, but as with Morocco, pride gets in his way: "I will not jump with common spirits/ And rank me with the barbarous multitudes (32–33) and "I will assume desert" (51). He doesn't even observe common kindness and dispute when Portia names "her worthless self." He finds in the casket a picture of a "blinking idiot," and responds, "How much unlike my hopes and my deservings!" (57). We must wonder if anyone who enters the contest mustn't be an idiot, unless he has known Portia for a long time and has really had a chance to come to love her. The others choose by ego and for money and appearance. But spiritual accomplishment, like any wealth worth having and any true love, grows over time through effort and willingness to grow and change: Morocco and Aragon haven't the alchemy to succeed.

The problem comes, then, with Bassanio's success. How does he do it where others have failed? Portia wants him to succeed because she likes the way he looks. When he arrives at Belmont to attempt the game, as Act III, scene 2, begins, Portia begs him to wait a time before choosing. She says, "I would not lose you" (line 5), and makes clear her feelings, first suggesting a day or two and then a month or two: "I could teach you/ How to choose right, but then I am forsworn,/ So will I never be, so may you miss me./ But if you do, you'll make me wish a sin,/ That I had been forsworn" (10–14). She then berates him for gazing too intently at her, but obviously he is looking for the clues that she keeps hinting she may give—Bassanio doesn't show himself the type to feel thunderstruck by her beauty. While Portia goes back and forth between leading him to the answer and leaving him on his own, Bassanio hurries ahead to make his choice: not out of desperate love for Portia, but to hurry to get her money to replenish his coffers and save Antonio. He even begs her for hints: "O happy torment, when my torturer/ Doth teach me answers for deliverance!" (37–38). Nothing alchemical leads to his success, only the sexual chemistry that they share.

"If you do love me, you will find me out," Portia tells him, and "Nerissa and the rest, stand all aloof" (41–42): again she provides hints that may lead actors and directors to some interesting choices. Now only she and Bassanio stand by the caskets, and she suggests that the sacrifice will be hers, not his, if he fails. She asks for music, and what do they do?

While Bassanio overlooks the caskets, someone, perhaps Portia, sings a song. The first three lines end in the words *bred*, *head*, and *nourishèd*: each rhymes with *lead*, the substance of the correct casket. After the words "Reply,

reply," the next lines end in *eyes, dies, lies*, each assonant with *I*. Regardless of her fear of forswearing, she has hinted at — though not given — the answer. As the song progresses, Bassanio talks; he mentions the deceits of ornament, of corrupt legal argument, of heresy, of false bravado, of false beauty (using a chilling Medusa image). He even mentions "the dowry of a second head,/ The skull" (lines 95–96), as if he knew the contents of the gold casket as he looks at it, the "common drudge" of silver, used for coins, as he quickly passes by the second. The third he calls "meagre lead,/ Which rather threaten'st than dost promise aught" (104–105), and then adds, "Thy paleness move me more than eloquence;/ And here choose I." Does he mean the lead's paleness or Portia's? He doesn't even bother to read the inscriptions! He spends a little time lingering over the gold casket, moves briskly past the silver, and decides almost immediately on the lead. Perhaps he gets enormously lucky — a good trait in a friend or spouse. Most likely while he ponders, Portia stands by the lead casket waiting for him — she has sent away the others who attend the game so they can't intervene. Inside, of course, Bassanio finds Portia's picture and a rhyme proclaiming his success and right to a kiss. Portia answers that she wishes only that she had more to offer him than herself, her estate, and her fortune. Why? He hasn't proven himself worthy of anything and has probably won by Portia's breaking her bond with her father, in spirit and through hints if not through clear and simple verbal directions. Perhaps all along the game has merely provided Portia a means to choose the one she wanted without having to face too many suitors: few indeed would make the commitment that this game asks of them, success or a life of celibacy. Portia has won her man, and Bassanio has won his fortune, but, sadly, their alchemy has failed: they have won material ends, but not spiritual ends: they chose by making bonds and breaking them: Bassanio chooses with help the other suitors lacked, and the real bond that drives him isn't a love for Portia, but a desire to save Antonio, whose life he has put at risk — hardly a bond any decent person would make. Bonds that come from selfishness and looks alone lack the chemistry — or spiritual alchemy — to survive and thrive.

Bonds of all sorts, making and breaking them, create the foundations of the action. What bond holds Antonio to Bassanio? The play begins with Antonio feeling sad.[9] Salerio and Solanio try to amuse and comfort him, but without success. They guess he worries about his ships and his merchandise, but Antonio says no; they posit that his is in love, and he answers, "Fie, fie"— not exactly "no," but no real answer. Antonio himself says in the first line of the play, "In sooth, I know not why I am so sad," and adds, "I have much ado to know myself"—I find either hard to believe. He wants sympathy, but doesn't want to say why. When Solanio announces that Bassanio, "your most noble kinsman," has come, they depart: "We leave you now with better company" (lines 57 and 59). Later, in II.8, Solanio observes that "I think he [Antonio] only loves the world for him [Bassanio]," so he and Salerio seek Bassanio to bring him to Antonio to treat his sadness. Why can Bassanio alone ease that sadness, since he beyond any person (other than Antonio's own risky shipping transactions) has contributed to Antonio's financial woes and has got him into a bond with a man he hates? In IV.1 Antonio says, "I am a tainted wether of the flock,/ Meetest for death," and adds, "You cannot better be employ'd, Bassanio,/ Than to live still and write mine epitaph" (lines 114–15, 117–18): he calls himself a castrated ram and again begs for sympathy rather than help or love. He has lost himself in self-pity. When he claims himself ready for the knife to fall, in a "final" speech, he declares, "Commend me to your honorable wife./ Tell her the process of Antonio's end,/ Say how I lov'd you, speak me fair in death;/ And ... bid her be judge/ Whether Bassanio had not once a love" (lines 273–77). Is he suggesting that Portia doesn't really love Bassanio, while only he does? Why would he want her to hear such words? Does he hope to inspire her to love more strongly or to love at all, or would what he says actually make her wonder if she had married appropriately?

We know from the reaction of Portia and Nerissa that Bassanio is a handsome and charming fellow, but he's also an abusive friend. He admits he has already borrowed a great deal of money from Antonio, but he returns not for Antonio's sake, but to borrow more. Is Antonio in love with Bassanio? Or does Bassanio, as a friend with youth and potential, appeal to him as a source of vicarious success and pleasure? Is Antonio simply a kind and generous man who joys in helping a friend and kinsman? Do we know how closely they are related? Does Antonio serve as a kind of foster father or *in loco parentis*, perhaps at Bassanio's parents' request? What of Bassanio's parents? Have they died, have they abandoned or disowned or simply dismissed their son, or does Bassanio keep them ignorant of his troubles to stay out of greater trouble with them? Could Antonio be Bassanio's mother's brother—a position of importance in raising a child—or even his real father, so he feels responsible for the young man's well-being despite his willingness to waste all the money he has and gets? The play gives us few hints about the nature of the relationship, but clearly Antonio's happiness hinges on Bassanio's happiness, or at least Bassanio's presence. Bassanio himself worries more about Antonio than he does about Portia—though not much about either, and Antonio clearly gains more from Bassanio's presence and affection than from anything else in his life, including his business concerns.[10]

Does Bassanio show any real regard for Portia, and do we believe his promise at the end of the play that he will henceforth keep his fidelity? In Act I, scene 1, he admits his prodigality and preference to repeat old ploys, and he seeks money to dissemble, to look as though he has wealth when he hasn't. When he returns to Belmont after the courtroom scene, though Portia knows he has given away the ring, she says, "You were to blame... To part so slightly with your wife's first gift" (5.1.166–67). Aside he says, "I were best to cut my left hand off,/ And swear I lost the ring defending it" (lines 177–78): he will already lie to her, even mutilate himself to avoid getting caught, but even that he wouldn't matter: he promised to lose it by no means. When he can find no way to deny it and admits its absence, Portia says, taunting him, but in fact quite rightly, "Even so void is your false heart of truth" (189). In his next speech, five straight lines end with the word *ring*, Bassanio repeating it annoyingly as if to taunt Portia in return over a trivial matter, and the final line of the speech ends with the word *displeasure*: both hers and his, certainly. In Portia's speech immediately following, five of her lines end with the word *ring*, including the final line "I'll die for't but some woman had the ring," which of course she knows to be true, since she has it. The repetition may call to mind for more recent audiences Edgar Allan Poe's poem "The Bells," using *ring* much as Poe uses *bells*. Do the bells toll for a marriage or for a death — or for the incumbent death of a marriage? Bassanio begs forgiveness twice, which Portia grants, and Antonio interposes that "I dare be bound again,/ My soul upon the forfeit, that your lord/ Will never more break faith advisedly" (249–51). This time he offers his soul, not his flesh, as surety — not a good deal given Bassanio's track record — and Bassanio may break faith unintentionally, or he may do say intentionally and say he didn't, and still keep the bond — again not very good for Portia. Whatever he may say, Bassanio has shown no ability to keep his bonds.

If we hadn't already enough reason not to trust, Gratiano as Bassanio's double makes the same promises — he ominously has the last word in the play. In I.1, nominally trying to alleviate Antonio's sadness, he says, "Let me play the fool,/ With mirth and laughter let old wrinkles come" (lines 79–80). He does show his foolishness, but not in the fashion of the Shakespearean wise fool: he talks too much, has nothing useful or funny to say, and directs his words mostly to insults. Even Bassanio must admit "Gratiano speaks an infinite deal of nothing, more than any man in all Venice" (lines 114–15), but keeps his company anyway. The play gives us no means to understand how he woos Nerissa in the brief time he has with her, other than perhaps as Bassanio woos Portia: by looks alone. He makes the same error Bassanio makes in giving up his ring, but with no reason or provocation whatever: Nerissa as "Balthasar's" assistant simply asks for it, and he gives it up probably because Bassanio gives up his. He concludes V.1 by saying how eager he feels to get Nerissa to bed and urges that "while I live I'll fear no other thing/ So sore, as keeping safe Nerissa's ring." Who cares? What a silly, anticlimactic ending! The play ends focusing not on Shylock's disaster or even Portia and Bassanio's reconciliation, but in the untrustworthy words of a minor (and perpetually irritating) character double. Gratiano even misses the point: he should protect not the ring as such, but the promise of fidelity it represents. He uses the metaphor, but misses the meaning.

Shakespeare takes this narrative turn, I think, for much the same reason as he places the Porter scene after the murder of Duncan in *Macbeth*: as Thomas DeQuincey wrote, the enormous contrast of the off-color humor of the Porter, punctuated by the repeated loud knocking at the gate, creates a stark contrast with the horror of the murders and jerks the audience from silence to full realization of the enormity of the violent deed. The inappropriate lightness of Gratiano's speech contrasts with the merciless dismissal of Shylock, and it shows how little any of what has happened has meant to the participants: they have learned nothing, haven't changed at all. They remain selfish and trivial. Even Portia's apparent mercy to Bassanio — like Nerissa's to Gratiano — means nothing, because they have learned nothing from it, and we have no reason to believe they will behave any differently in the future: there we come to the thematic crux, the philosophical problem of the play. What can we do about those who practice abuses and refuse to learn better? Shakespeare seems to answer: nothing. The poet can attempt to write moral and instructive work, just as life provides opportunities for one to gain experience and wisdom, but even the best poets have no power to break through willful ignorance and meanness of experience — a problematic rather than hopeless ending disguised, in this case, as a series of "happy" marriages.

The exchange between Jessica and Lorenzo at the beginning of V.1 foreshadows the troubled faith that ends the play. Instead of a good Christian with his happy converso, they have become a niggling couple already devolving to sarcastic quarrel. Jessica shows no remnant regard for her father — wouldn't a kind person show at least some concern over her parent, even if she didn't love him, especially since we get no evidence of his having abused her in any way? As Jessica and Lorenzo talk, they rehearse a brief series of allusions to tales of love gone badly, either through infidelity or rash choice: Troilus and Cressida, Thisbe and Pyramus, Dido and Aeneas, Medea and Jason. Lorenzo then says rather indelicately that Jessica has robbed her father and departed with an "unthrift" love (line 16, a pun that implies she has acted prodigally and has married an unthrifty man — both true). They pursue then a genteelly spoken but snarky quarrel. Jessica hints that though Lorenzo claimed he loved her, he may not really, and that he has stolen her soul and won't keep faith: her father's fear, certainly, and one she apparently insufficiently considered. Lorenzo counters that she, "like a little shrew," has slandered him, though he forgives her: the move to name-calling hasn't taken long. The appearance of a messenger stops them as Jessica claims she would beat him at that game, barring interruption. At this point in the narrative they have spent all they've stolen — has this relationship any hope of surviving, or will they spend the additional inheritance they'll get from Shylock and return to quarreling, ending with one of them leaving or both of them dying, the result of a marriage not based on love? This relationship serves as a double for that of Portia and Bassanio: the husband has married for money, the wife seemingly for love, but with haste and insufficient knowledge of the proposed mate. Shakespeare hints thereby, as he often does by paralleling relationships, that the marriage of the main plot hasn't much hope, either.

Portia will begin and end as an insider, and she has brought Bassanio with her to the de-centered of the world of the play. The move from Venice to Belmont gives the couples a potentially new narrative start, but unfortunately they have the same characters they had before. Jessica, who had been an outsider, has become at least temporarily an insider, but for how long will Lorenzo find her interesting and lovable — perhaps until they run out of their most recent monetary windfall? The play foregrounds both willing relationships and unwilling relationships to stress the problem of trying to get from the outside to the inside. When Antonio seeks Shylock for the loan, Antonio insists, "If thou wilt lend this money, lend it not/ As to thy friends... But lend it rather to thine enemy" (1.3.133–36): he will continue to abuse the person of whom he has asked help when others will not give it. Shylock, despite Antonio's many insults and abuses, offers it without interest as an act of friendship: "Why, look how you storm!/ I would be friends with you, and have your love,/ Forget the shames that you have stain'd me with,/ Supply your present wants, and take no doit/ Of usance for my moneys, and you'll not hear me./ This is kind I offer" (lines 138–42). Bassanio turns to Antonio, "This were kindness," and Shylock continues, "This kindness will I show.... [A]nd in a merry sport/ If you repay me not on such a day ... let the forfeit/ Be nominated for an equal pound/ Of your fair flesh" (144–52). "Content, in faith, I'll seal to such a bond," Antonio immediately decides; Bassanio briefly and weakly tries to dissuade him, but they take Shylock's money and terms, whatever the extent to which Shylock may mean them. Bassanio would accept the friendly offer; Antonio will not, and he gets instead a horrifying bargain that he expects never to need to keep, but that Bassanio believes Shylock will readily enforce.

Why would Shylock make that bond?[11] Partly because by doing so, he has been the most hated of outsiders in Venice becomes an insider: he plays with a Venetian merchant at his own game. As a hated outsider, he has no chance of winning. He believes the laws of Venice really will apply to him equally, if he needs them, but they won't: the court and the people will always see him as an outsider. The terms of the bond, though, allow the bond to take place: Antonio will accept no friendly terms, only those that express his own hatred. The bond fits Antonio, who has already done the moneylender repeated violence, more than it does Shylock. It comes with a psychological horror that echoes what a Christian of the time expects of a "Jew," but that more accurately reflects the treatment of Jews by Christians, who might well and legally show violence to Jews even after their conversion, when they could force it. The forming of any kind of bond with Antonio gives Shylock an opportunity. He must fully expect Antonio's ships to return and for him to pay off the loan easily. Once that has happened — and at no interest — perhaps Antonio would come to see Shylock as a source of help, if not fully as a friend, and ultimately as a "useful" and therefore tolerated if not welcome citizen of Venice. A high-interest loan wouldn't have had any chance of moving Antonio in that direction; Shylock had to offer a bond Antonio would take — and he would take only an unfriendly one — and one that had a good chance of gaining profit in the long run. If Shylock has any sort of approval from Antonio, the merchant mighty well recommend his friends and business colleagues see Shylock also. The ultimate outsider moves a bit toward the inside.

But Shylock didn't expect Jessica would leave him to marry a Christian. That incident more than any other tears out his heart, drives him to madness, and moves him toward revenge — it makes him, in his own mind, even more an outsider than he had already been. Because she is beautiful and brings wealth with her, her suitor and his friends draw her from the locked "casket" of her home. Can we trust Lorenzo to continue to love Jessica? Do we know that he loves her at all, or do we see him as an adventurer, much like Bassanio, who wants a wealthy and pretty wife out of selfishness rather than for their mutual good? That question may seem an anachronism when we ask it about a time of arranged marriages, when matches had more to do with familial and financial alliance than romantic love. But Shakespeare pushes us to ask it repeatedly in this play, not just with respect to the marriages that occur, but also with those that don't: we must remember the motivations of Portia's failed suitors as well. Does anyone here make a good marriage bond? Shakespeare hints not — the best may have been Shylock and Leah's, and she has died, leaving her husband one step further toward disaster in a merciless world.

What the court shows to Antonio on making him free of his bond is not mercy, but blind and one-sided clemency. Concentrating on punishing Shylock, everyone forgets the point on which Portia agrees: Antonio has willingly made a bond, he fails to keep it, and he owes Shylock repayment. Of course he never does, and he even gains access to half of Shylock's wealth: he gains from his failure to repay the bond. Ironically, if Shylock were to keep his bond, the one on which he claims to have made a holy oath, he would be the only character in the play to do. What does that fact tell us about what Shakespeare thought of bonds? I suspect he wants to show us to make them on very carefully and very thoughtfully: they tend to create problems later on, and breaking them, even with arguable good intent, may still bring about suffering and trouble.

Our third motif, the ring tale, shows a bond that fails with amazing speed. Both Bassanio and Gratiano have sworn they will never give them up, but they do so at the first opportunity — and not even with particular urgency. How many of us would give away our wedding ring and our solemn marriage bond at someone's odd whim, even if that someone had done us or a friend a good — or great — turn? We would think it a thoroughly inappropriate, even an impudent or insulting request. Antonio urges Bassanio to give it up. It seems to him — to him — little more than a replaceable trinket, because Bassanio's bond to Portia means nothing to him: he apparently cares rather to feel he has dispensed his own debt to "Balthasar," as little as that payment costs him after he has had his life returned to him by the Venetian court.

Portia forgives Bassanio and welcomes Antonio to her home. Metaphorically she does more than forgive Bassanio: she has resurrected him. Bassanio says, "But when this ring/ Parts from this finger, then parts life from hence;/ O, then be bold to say Bassanio's dead!" (3.2.183–85). He overstates his trustworthiness, which he well may do, since Portia has already given him lordship over her and all she has, "This house, these servants, and this same myself.... I give them with this ring,/ Which when you part from, lose, or give away,/ Let it presage the ruin of your love/ And be my vantage to exclaim on you" (lines 170–74), and her threat should he fail amount only to that she'll reproach him. We can show mercy to those we love, if not to those we hate, the play suggests. But mustn't she have gained an awareness and concern that her husband feels a deeper and more important bond to his friend than to her and that he may not deserve her trust? She has traded a husband-to-be for a disaster-to-be. We may easily enough assume that Bassanio has learned his lesson and that he will choose better in the future, but he nearly lies to her about what has happened to the ring, and he has already told us that he often shoots and arrow where he has previously shot one, to determine whether and where the first has landed. As he returns to Antonio for more loans, why should we believe he won't repeatedly return to Portia for forgiveness after more transgressions?

The ring story recapitulates the casket and bond stories: one makes a choice, one forms a bond, one acquires a duty to keep that bond. The fact that in the ring story both men fail so completely and fall into that failure so easily and willingly again shows the problem of bad bonds. As the particular symbol of a wedding or sexual bond, it also shows that Bassanio and Gratiano offer little better likelihood of fidelity than Shakespeare's Cressida, whom we'll consider in the next chapter: one may swear, but if the first opportunity to stray or fail results in capitulation, what hope have the characters of happiness? The sexual bond becomes more source of failure and dishonesty than of joy and completeness. Marriage in the world of *The Merchant of Venice* suggests neither comedy, a happy ending, nor tragedy, the fall of worthy persons guilty of mistakes, only another source of problems.

Two Speeches, and Two Sides of the Same Problem

Two speeches most stand out in this play underrated for its vagaries (but not vagueness) of emotion, nuances of staging, and verbal fireworks: Portia's on the quality of mercy and Shylock's on a Jew's right to revenge. They may appear as opposites, expressions of kindness and wickedness, respectively. But they do nothing of the sort, and together, essentially interchangeably, they take us to the most difficult — but hardly the only — problem of this big, ugly, powerful two-hearted play. They show us the diseases, parallel to those in *Troilus and Cressida*, that are consuming the world of the play: selfishness, free-floating wrath, and lack of compassion.

Though it comes later than the other speech I'll treat here, I'll begin with the speech on mercy that Portia delivers to Shylock and to the courtroom in Act IV, scene 1, because it explicitly raises the central concern of the play. This speech should come from Shylock, not from Portia. In a world with any kindness, one where Shylock had any hope of integrating in its society, he would have the opportunity to address those characters who trouble him and teach the need for mercy. But the Venetians suffer from such embedded cruelty, and Shylock has acquired such deeply roiling anger and in response to it, that the speech shifts to someone whose veneer suggests the possibility of mercy, but who uses the appearance of gentle rationality to strip any hope characters or audience may have of a merciful result for anyone. Judgments in this world will prove harsh and unyielding to enemies and insipidly generous to friends — exactly the point at which Shakespeare aimed, I think.

Taking Portia's speech at face value creates great difficulty, because she is dissembling when she presents it, and Shakespeare through the course of his œuvre repeatedly warns of the dangers of dissembling. She has come to court in disguise with the purpose not of seeking justice or even mercy, but to save one man she has never met at the expense of another she has never met. Shakespeare loved to use and show the problems of disguise and misdirection, even when someone does it with good intentions (not entirely the case here). Portia seeks to help her husband (whom she barely knows) based only on a brief description of circumstances (which she should not trust).

Readers have tended to laud the quickness and wit with which she helps Bassanio and Antonio, but they less often regret the ease with which she dispatches Shylock. She has even suborned the perjury of her friend, the "learn'd Bellario," posing herself as a youthful but accomplished advocate. She begins by asking a curious question: "Which is the merchant here, and which the Jew?" (line 174). How could she not know? Antonio and Shylock would have dressed differently — clothing styles and colors would have indicated race and class — even if they showed no signs of ethnic difference. Perhaps she experiences nervousness once she actually enters the court and must speak, but she shows no signs of that once the legal business begins. She has already called herself an "unlesson'd girl" (3.2.159), but no one who hears her speak will believe that. Perhaps she simply doesn't look, gazing on Bassanio instead or sizing up the Duke, who holds court, or her position in the courtroom. Most probably Shakespeare has her provide through the verbal uncertainty a visual and moral pun: who is the merchant, the nominal good guy, the one for saving, and who is the Jew, the bad guy, the one to punish? She doesn't know, and, ethically or ideally, in the courtroom we shouldn't know, either. Shylock, as moneylender and thus a kind of merchant, pursues the only business Venice will allow him; it would have excluded him from other means of making a living. Antonio, a businessman, lends money, too, but without interest — he can do so because he has other means of income. He makes that income by trading, by getting others to pay more for goods than he has paid for them: a kind of interest permitted the Christians permitted themselves but not Jews. Shakespeare urges us to conflate the occupations as well as the characters. Portia's failure to distinguish the two men makes us focus on the fact that they differ only insignificantly, not as men, not as humans, not as persons with problems, only as culturally dictated and defined entities. Portia digs herself as deeply into the cultural exclusion as any of the other characters in the play, and she does so by preying on Shylock's experience and expectations.

Having asked if Antonio confesses the bond, she asserts, "Then must the Jew be merciful" (line 177). Shylock takes exception to the *must*, and Portia answers at length:

> The quality of mercy is not strain'd.
> It droppeth as the gentle rain from heaven
> Upon the place beneath. It is twice blest:
> It blesseth him that gives and him that takes....
> It is enthronèd in the hearts of kings,
> It is an attribute of God himself;
> And earthly power doth then show likest God's
> When mercy seasons justice. Therefore, Jew,
> Though justice be thy plea, consider this,
> That in the course of justice, none of us

1. The Merchant of Venice

> Should see salvation.... I have spoke thus much
> To mitigate the justice of thy plea,
> Which if thou follow, this strict court of Venice
> Must needs give sentence 'gainst the merchant there [lines 184–205].

She argues, of course, for mercy as a divine gift, as godly in humans, as essential to human salvation. But she believes in neither mercy nor justice, and she practices neither. Her speech sets up not an act of mercy, but one of deadly vengeance.

Mercy should come naturally, Portia says, but it doesn't: she asks for it, but offers none. It may bless twice, but it must occur first, and in this play it doesn't appear at all. Shylock answers, "My deeds upon my head! I crave the law,/ The penalty and forfeit of my bond" (206–207). He means, of course, that he accepts responsibility for claiming his bond: he will verbally accept the consequences as well — the judgment less of the court than of the interested Christian players will give him no choice. He does occasionally use odd syntax, part of what separates him linguistically as well as by religion, dress, and profession from other Venetians. Literally here he calls upon himself the punishment of the court, a penalty, and the forfeit of his bond: not what he means to ask them, but what he gets from them, and what they can hardly wait to give him. The court will force him to forfeit his bond, and it will give him the penalty: they will take his life. "You take my house when you do take the prop/ That doth sustain my house; you take my life/ When you do take the means whereby I live," Shylock says (4.1.375–77), and with the court's judgment he declares himself content and begs leave: "I pray you, give me leave to go from hence;/ I am not well" (lines 395–96). Anyone who doesn't understand that Shylock will not live very long and that the Venetians have killed him hasn't paid any attention. They practice merciless mercy.

Mercy should come with tears of kindness — that gentle rain — and should temper justice and mirror grace. Portia warns Shylock, though of the strictness of the court — and then she lies again. She says, knowing better, that the court *must* rule against Antonio. In those words she speaks rightly, but not truthfully, because the court will not and does no rule against Antonio. Portia has shown an extraordinary cruelty and cunning in getting her adversary "on the hip" to throw him into the abyss; she eggs him on, begs him, pushes him toward vengeance, and misleads him to the point where the law places him in equal danger with Antonio: she brings him to a threat of death. The court, with urging of the other principles, rules against Shylock, but against neither Portia nor Antonio for the same offense. Shylock doesn't count, because to them he is Jew, not a real Venetian, so the law of endangerment applies to him and not to them. Portia's speech on mercy means nothing to her beyond its rhetorical capability to bring about the end she wishes; it exhibits a profound and light-hearted hypocrisy.

As Yaffe asks, "Why does the court ignore Shylock's repeated subjection to publicly tolerated harassment concerning both his religion [and one may also say his ethnicity] and his means of livelihood" including "spontaneous Jew-baiting outbursts" from those in attendance who don't even have anything to do with the hearing? "And why does the court fail," he adds, "to warn Shylock about the imminent likelihood of self-incrimination" (2). On the first point the court does so because the ruling Duke has the same prejudices as the other dominant Christian citizens, though without their influence he would judge more mercifully. We don't hear as abuses utterances that fall in with our own prejudices: they appear as truths instead, and so one need not censor them. We learn thereby that Shylock has no chance of getting "fair" treatment in court: his nominal and repeated insistence on the bond only confirms for the court their prejudices and, if possible, closes their minds more completely. On the second point we must assume that the Duke and anyone else in attendance with legal knowledge feels so appalled by the circumstances that they fail to think of it, which would show them ineffectual and simple-minded, or they simply don't know or don't remember, which would show them horrifyingly unqualified to conduct legal business. In either case the incident reflects worse on Venice than it does on Shylock: their court, which claims to stick to the law and treat each case fairly according to its merits, provides no more than a sham. As to why Portia holds back the information that Shylock has already placed himself in danger, Goddard's proposes that she wanted a "spectacle" (1:109) and John Lyon that she was gathering evidence of Shylock's "malevolent intent" to strengthen her cause in the legal debate (105); Yaffe suggests she was offering Shylock "every opportunity to render a spectacular act of mercy so as to render nugatory the law under which she alone knows he stands guilty" (8). She doesn't tell us what she was thinking, but all of those possibilities may be true, though we don't know where Portia would have gained such detailed knowledge of Venetian law and such powerful debating skills unless from careful consultation with the learned Bellario before she arrived in court or unless she had at one time studied both in detail.

For me the important point lies in the fact that she doesn't allow Shylock the opportunity to show that spectacular mercy: she stops him just before the opportunity to show it arises. I think more likely than Portia's creating a spectacle, the incident may involve Shylock's failed attempt to create that spectacle. We don't *know* Shylock's intentions; we assume them from what he says, that he wants the yield of his bond, the pound of Antonio's flesh, despite Jewish law's forbidding such an action every bit as much as does Christian.[12] What if Shylock really intended to "teach the Christians a lesson" from his point of view: to strop the knife, grin and growl, even place it against Antonio's breast — and then walk away? What if he had created a plan not to speak mercy, but to show it at the most dramatic instant? What a point he would have made!

Of course I have no way to prove that he had such a scheme: no textual evidence shows it. But Shakespeare does provide evidence that at least at first Shylock doesn't desire the pound of flesh: he wants his money back and a better relationship with Antonio. When the first (ultimately spurious) news of the loss of one of Antonio's ships arrives in III.1, Shylock says, "There I have made another bad match" (line 44), suggesting that he first wanted his money back. What good would the flesh do him, Salerio asks, and Shylock responds, "To bait fish withal" (53): since he doesn't fish, it will do him no good but to "feed my revenge" (53–54), that is, no good at all. The actual statement of revenge comes only after Jessica's elopement. "Devil" Solerio and Solanio both call him — they also serve as choric characters to provide the audience with current knowledge and public opinion — but then they ask and expect his mercy. The Christians, though, have already consumed Shylock's flesh: "You knew, none so well as you, of my daughter's flight," and then "I say my daughter is my flesh and my blood" (lines 24 and 37) — interesting that he makes the distinction between flesh and blood that Portia will make in the courtroom later and that he makes no mention of the valuables Jessica took with her, only of her rebellion against him in going. Most likely by the time of the trial Shylock has gone mad at the horrible treatment he has received — in a modern court, that might excuse him — but those events have given him all the more reason to prove he is not like the Christians, but better than they are, that he can scare them as they have scared him, then spare one of them where none would spare him. But, as Shakespeare knew, reason can fail us in times of great stress: if we understand Shylock's stress and at least attempt to sympathize with it, the play becomes a clearer if greater problem.

When the court's judgment (unlike mercy) rains down on him, Shylock reacts first with backpedaling and then with what seems to me a curious docility. He has already rejected payment even ten times in excess of the bond, so he hasn't come with the intention of making money — so much for the idea of simple greed. When Portia turns the tables on him, he asks, "Is that the law?" knowing immediately he has lost. He asks then three times the amount of the loan, then only the principle itself, and then says only that he will leave the courtroom: whatever his true intent, he tries to leave the debacle with something. Hearing the threat of his own death sentence, and the "reprieve" the court, driven by Portia and Antonio, offers him, he says, having reached despair, first "Nay, take my life and all! Pardon not that!" and with their final judgment simply "I am content," which of course he is not. He has already lost Jessica, his flesh and blood, and now he has lost his living, his possessions, any chance for either vengeance or to grant mercy, and the religion with which everyone, including he himself, identified him — thus his heart and soul also. He leaves the courtroom a dead man thrice over, in legacy, in profession, in spirit.

How exactly to understand Shylock and what Shakespeare tells us through him: that remains a great though hardly the only problem in the play. The most damning evidence against Shylock comes when the Duke, having addressed him as seldom happens in the play, by name rather than race, "Shylock the world thinks, and I think so too,/ That thou but leadest this fashion of thy malice/ To the last hour of the act, and then 'tis thought/ Thou'lt show thy mercy" (4.1.17–20), but Shylock answers that "by our holy Sabaoth have I sworn/ To have the due and forfeit of my bond./ If you deny it, let danger light/ Upon your charter and your city's freedom!" (36–39). Has Shylock sworn so, or has the Duke uncovered his actual intention and spoiled Shylock's surprise? Would a sane and lawful Jew swear so? Does the additional courtroom antagonism push him to forget his intention to give mercy, or has he created a scenario in his mind that requires the ultimate suspense before he relieves it, and must he speak so as to frighten his audience for it to have full effect? Shylock must not be stupid or cowardly, or he wouldn't have succeeded in acquiring the wealth he has in a market full of hatred for him, and he wouldn't walk in the Rialto except when he couldn't possibly avoid it.

The cannibalism motif, which appears in III.1 as I mentioned above, occurs several times in the play. It reinforces the ferocity of the characters, the degree to which they all figuratively feed on one another: Shylock to the least extent, through usury; Antonio, in his enervated love for Bassanio; Jessica in her filial impiety toward her father, and Launcelot in how he feeds on his master; Portia, perhaps most sadly and sickeningly, on the love for and immediate indulgence of someone hardly worthy of her potential gifts; Bassanio worst of all, on anyone who will let him. In our time, and were he female, we would call Bassanio a gold-digger — the fact that we don't attests unfortunately to a lingering sexism in how we read and understand Shakespeare and humans in general.[13] Shylock's non-idiomatic usages of "Your worship was the last man in our mouths" (1.3.60) and "I'll go in hate, to feed upon/ The prodigal Christian" (2.5.14–15) stand out most obviously and call our attention to directly and uncomfortably to Shylock, but the way the other characters feed on one another metaphorically creates for more disturbing results — exactly what the play directs us to see. Shylock clarifies directly to the audience that he hates Christians (1.3.42), but no more than they hate him; they call him devil, and they treat him exactly devilishly: they to get him to bring about his own fall. They succeed. When Shylock recounts the

1. The Merchant of Venice

Laban story from Genesis 27–30, Antonio remarks that the "devil can cite Scripture for his purpose," but in doing so he also quotes Scripture for his own purpose (Matthew 4:6). Perhaps we have devils fighting to devour one another, or more likely we have men who have either chosen or felt forced into horrifying behaviors. Notably, Shylock says non-idiomatically that Antonio was in both their mouths, his and Bassanio's, and Bassanio doesn't deny it: he has cannibalized Antonio as well, taking money with no real intention of paying it back and allowing his benefactor to enter into a dangerous bond rather than accepting that danger himself. He aims, of course, ultimately to cannibalize Portia instead: as husband he will gain control of her wealth and property, and she will have made a bond that not partially (as in the casket game that her father created) but fully subjugate her to a man — in this case, though, one who can ruin her rather than make her wealthy.

Antonio, unlike Shylock and Portia, will not only get free of the bond he readily made, but he will benefit from having failed in it. Shylock will suffer a penalty greater than what Antonio, according to the bond, should have paid if he were to pay in full: he must give up the religion that would have served as the only remaining anchor of his life. He accomplishes neither what he said nor what he meant: he gets far more in worldly goods. Portia, on the other hand, enacts not what she says, but what she means: either Shylock will grant mercy to Antonio, or he will be given by the court no salvation, no mercy. They see him grant no mercy, so she asks the Duke to grant none. When she asks Antonio what mercy he will grant, he takes more for himself beyond the money has already accepted — we must now say stolen — from Shylock, which he keeps, gratis. Portia encourages more crime where crime has already occurred and no mercy from those who claim to have sole (and soul) commitment to its practice.

Portia adds next that mercy comes from kings and from God; whether it will come from God to such characters as we meet in this play, who knows? But it will not come from the Duke. He seems at least partly disposed to offer it, but the others in attendance won't allow him to carry it through. "Earthly power" will not prove like heavenly, since it does not temper justice with mercy, nor does it practice justice: it continues to practice abuse and retribution even for "crimes" that have not occurred. The idea that no one should find salvation based on justice, but only by mercy has long hung about the center of Christian eschatological thought, and Shakespeare expresses the idea elsewhere, though in a more secular context. When the players arrive at Elsinore, Hamlet asks Polonius to take good care of them. Polonius replies that he will treat them according to their deserts. "Better, man," says Hamlet: "Treat each according to his deserts and who shall 'scape whipping": the point has, of course, obvious Christian as well as social implications. We want and hope for not justice, but mercy, not mere lodgings, but eager welcomes. But we live in a world that seldom offers either justice or mercy, where we seldom live up to our promises or our bonds. The ironical "happy" ending of the play shows just how badly our plots can turn out: they may like good, but born of dissembling, rash decision, and selfishness, they acquire an unstable foundation that will allow them to topple at any subsequent tremor.

Everything in a Shakespeare play has a kind of simultaneity and synchronicity, especially after one has read it several times. The second speech I'll treat here, Shylock's outburst on revenge in III.1, argues nominally for revenge, but begs tacitly for mercy: Portia will invert it in IV.1. Asked by Salerio what good a pound of Antonio's flesh will do him, Shylock answers:

> To bait fish withal — if it will feed nothing else, it will feed my revenge. He hath disgrac'd me, and hind'red me half a million, laugh'd at my losses, mock'd at my gains, scorn'd my nation, thwarted my bargains, cool'd my friends, heated mine enemies; and what's his reason? I am a Jew. Hath not a Jew eyes? Hath not a Jew hands, organs, dimensions, senses, affections, passions ... warm'd and cool'd by the same winter and summer, as a Christian is? If you prick us, do we not bleed? If you tickle us, do we not laugh? If you poison us, do we not die? And if you wrong us, shall we not revenge? If we are like you in the rest, we will resemble you in that. If a Jew wrong a Christian, what is his humility? Revenge. If a Christian wrong a Jew, what should his sufferance be by Christian example? Why, revenge. The villainy you teach me, I will execute, and it shall go hard but I will better the instruction.

This speech comes right after Shylock learns of the elopement of his daughter and her theft of a good deal of his wealth, including a keepsake ring that his now dead wife had given him — to see it out of that context can create a gross misunderstanding of it. It also directly follows the announcement in Belmont that Bassanio has arrived to attempt the casket game and try to win Portia. Portia's loss of herself to Bassanio will parallel Shylock's loss of Jessica to Lorenzo: the women of play all choose to place themselves in the hands of untrustworthy men. Both Portia and Jessica (Nerissa falls readily into the same error, following poor example) feel as though they have employed their freedom and gained thereby, but they have both lost irrevocably, just as Shylock has. What Shylock says about himself seems perhaps not to apply to Jessica because her husband and his friends deny her Jewishness: her beauty and wealth briefly blind them, but how long will that last, especially once her money has run out?

The speech begins with a repetition of the cannibalism motif: Shylock will use Antonio's flesh to catch fish, which he will then eat. He then expresses legitimate complaints against Antonio, but they lose force because of that first metaphor, whether we confront it directly or whether it sink into the subconscious. He aims then to show his auditors his their mutual humanity and his own suffering, but they will not hear it, especially if he expresses it with anger or vehemence — he can hardly do otherwise in his current state of mind. The poison image has particular force, since medieval legends of Jews poisoning Christians abounded and remained current in Shakespeare's time — though Shakespeare's audience would have had little if any acknowledged contact with actual Jews. He accuses the Christians, though, of poisoning him, which in spirit if not physically they have done. Their unceasing ill-treatment has poisoned his thoughts, his business opportunities, and even his soul: we don't know if he has even maintained the human capacity for mercy that they ask of him but never grant him. I suspect that he has kept it, but bungles the possible attempt to display it, probably out of frustration, anger, and an overwhelming sense of loss. He never has the opportunity to laugh: in this world no one tickles; they kick, they spit, they insult, they threaten, they steal, they kill. Having been refused entry into the "inside" of Venetian society, he vows to make himself an insider by the means they allow him (he says what they have *taught* him): vengeance. If he can't act like them in other ways, he can in that way, he believes — but of course they deny him that means as well. Shakespeare's Venetians will accept no similarity of any sort: they will simply use their superior position to feed on whom they can and will. The similarity to the Christians that Shylock accepts is their mutual indulgence in villainy: a sad identity for them and a disastrous choice for him.

Getting What We Want and Ignoring the Rest

Perhaps the real merchant of the play isn't Antonio, but Bassanio: of all the characters in the play, he alone gets what he wants. He uses himself as commodity, his friendship to buy loans from Antonio and his looks and charm to buy love from Portia. Neither seems to mind; in fact, they seem eager to do it. They trouble themselves with no examination of his character for worthiness. They forgive him readily and give him exactly what he wants despite his inability to manage money, to keep his bonds with them, or to trouble himself with their welfare. He has gained a wealthy, beautiful, and clever wife: he calls her virtuous as well, but given what we see her do in the play, I have my doubts. Bassanio makes clear his goals in wooing Portia: "In Belmont is a lady richly left,/ And she is fair and, fairer than that word,/ Of wondrous virtues. Sometimes from her eyes/ I did receive fair speechless messages..." (1.1.161–64). Following his own order, he feels attracted to her money, her beauty, and her virtue (either the likelihood of her faithfulness to him or the chance that he feels as though he had better describe her as virtuous to satisfy Antonio or to follow convention and not praise her money and looks exclusively). He also believes he has perceived something in her looks that leads him to think her attracted to him, so he has a better chance of winning his goal. But how much if at all does he actually love her, and once they have married, how will he treat her?

Portia, too, we may want to assume happy, since she has married the man she thought she wanted without — at least vocally — breaking her bond with her father. But how happy will she be with Bassanio?[14]

Antonio will find himself relegated to the role of occasional guest in Portia and Bassanio's home — will that role make him happy? How will he deal with the feelings he has for Bassanio, whatever they may be?

Shylock hoped for a friendship or at least an alliance that would grant him more freedom and opportunity; barring that, he hoped for revenge for all the ill treatment he has suffered. He gets worse than nothing: he gets stripped of all he had, and departs the courtroom and the play as an empty shell with nothing but sorrow and death ahead of him. No one, not even his daughter — and I wonder about audience members — mourns for him. He disappears entirely from the last act.

Jessica has married her Christian suitor, but will they find happiness together? They have already shown themselves prodigal to the point of silliness — they trade her mother's ring for a monkey? — and by the beginning of Act V they are already quarreling and insulting each other.

Can anyone imagine Gratiano happy except in insulting someone, and whom will he insult now that he has married a woman he hardly knows and who has publicly shown him untrustworthy? Launcelot is simply a lower-class Gratiano: he will always indulge in scurrilous behavior until any master throws him out, despite any dutiful and loving ministrations by his caring but hapless father. Nerissa, stuck with Gratiano, whom she thought she wanted, will get what he has shown everyone else every time he appears in the play: insults, flippancy, prejudice, and irresponsibility. Many of the characters get — or nearly get or think they get — what they want. What good will it do them? They choose based on selfishness, not based on genuine, earned love and regard for others — sadly, often, the general state of the human condition.

So what kind of happy ending concludes this play? None at all: it directs itself into the mode of anti-comedy. It raises the problem of a play with no humor, no happy ending, little hope for satisfying Romance, suffering without anyone learning any lessons from it, titles and wealth with no actual nobility of thought or deed. Cleverness and good looks win, but they don't last very long.

1. The Merchant of Venice

Launcelot and Jessica: The Failure of Bonds of Duty

Two subplots enhance our understanding of the play and contribute to its difficulty and its troublesome qualities. We must take care not to take Launcelot and Jessica at their word — the play has shown us to take no one at his or her word — but to observe what facts or other perspectives we can find in the play to test the truth of why they do what they say but what we see of what they do.

The scene with Launcelot and his father fills the spot that Shakespeare usually allotted to his choric or thematic comic sketches, such as the gravedigger scene in *Hamlet*. But the scene in *The Merchant of Venice* does something even graver: it also unearths a *memento mori*, but instead of a kind of earthy wisdom, it shows the pointless meanness that distinguishes the characters of this play. Launcelot plays a trick on his nearly blind father, disguising his voice and telling him that his son is dead. The old man, kind and needy, replies, "God forbid! The boy was the very staff of my age, my very prop" (2.2.66). Launcelot then identifies himself and adds wryly, "It is a wise father that knows his own child," and, Hamlet-like, "murder cannot be hid long; a man's son may, but in the end truth will out" (lines 76–79). I can't imagine even the lowest of Shakespeare's audience finding that funny, since it shows filial impiety not against a bad parent, but against one who is trying to be a good one. It does, though, echo the Christians' desire to believe Jessica doesn't come from Shylock, but from a Christian father, and illustrates Shakespeare's interest in bastardy, which appears as a motif in several of the plays, most notably *King Lear*. The Christians in this play raise the issue not so "the truth will out," but as an excuse to "liberate" her from her father, and to liberate him from some of his wealth. Launcelot's sad joke foreshadows the sadness of the daughter's deserting and stealing from her father. It also gives us every reason *not* to trust anything Launcelot says or does, perhaps confirming Shylock's opinion of him and undermining anything he may say against his master.

We have already considered Launcelot's service to Shylock. Why does he leave to serve Bassanio instead? He believes he will get better pay and more privileges, and he will serve a Christian rather than a Jewish master. Old Gobbo must have tried to place his son with Shylock for some reason, and he brings Shylock a gift, evidence that he believes Shylock is at least not abusing Launcelot and probably treating him pretty well. We may also suspect that he knows he must do something to encourage a master to keep his prodigal son employed.

At first Launcelot appears to have made a stupid choice — even Bassanio tepidly warns him against it, but doesn't entirely turn him away, since he may gain from the appearance of having servants—since he has shifted from a fairly wealthy employer who can afford to pay, house, and feed him to one who can't. In the long run, he may have got lucky: by the end of the play his new employer has a wealthy wife and an estate. But if he falls into the behavior of which Shylock has accused him, laziness, overeating, and seducing the other help, one suspects that Portia won't tolerate him for very long, and Bassanio, having no real attachment to him, will do little or nothing to keep him.

Launcelot fails in what Shakespeare's time would have seen as natural duty to his father, to his employer, and perhaps even to God: if he has fathered a child on one of Shylock's other servants, he has failed in his Christian duty of pre-marital chastity and in the parental duties he will avoid as well. Launcelot thus casts in relief the problem of good parenting versus bad, and even good mentoring versus bad. If we see Antonio as Bassanio's mentor, he has got the young man money, but has helped him learn nothing toward becoming a better person, the far more important duty.

But Launcelot's failure serves only as a parallel to the greater failure, Jessica's when she breaks her bond and leaves her father and converts for the sake of marrying a man she doesn't know very well. Jessica and Lorenzo have that telling argument at the beginning of Act V, suggesting that her elopement has brought her change, but not happiness. Worst of all, she has died to Shylock, and he has died to her: she will have no recourse, should she ever feel regret, to return to her father to re-establish their bond. And while the Christians claim to Shylock that he has no right to a daughter like her—what they mean, of course, is a beautiful one, since she doesn't show virtue in leaving her father—will they ever forget that racially, ethnically, she too is a Jew, regardless of her conversion? *Conversos* didn't always fair well in Shakespeare's time; Queen Elizabeth, for instance, had her Spanish Jewish physician horribly executed on dubious charges of treason while all the while he claimed his innocence and stuck by his Christianity.

The Jessica subplot reflects the Portia subplot: if Portia helps Bassanio by anything from song lyrics to body language, she has probably cheated her bond with her father. As Jessica and Lorenzo argue in Act V, Portia is preparing to confront Bassanio with the failure of his bond. Jessica becomes a temporary insider, but will she remain one permanently, however Portia may claim to welcome her, even if Lorenzo tires of her and leaves her? Has Portia, the ultimate insider with wealth, position, desirability, and pretty fair control of her own circumstances, made herself an outsider by forgiving a bad husband and turning all she has over to him, even wishing she had more to give? Has she sacrificed wisdom for cleverness, and by her decision lost the value of both? Has her failure of duty cast her into a position of unhappiness and loss?

1. The Merchant of Venice

Shakespeare took ideas of duty seriously: through the range of his plays his characters consider a subject's duty to the king, a monarch's duty to God, nation, and righteousness, a general's duty to military action, a soldier's duty to his leader, any person's duty to spouse or family or friends, one's duty to a community or to keep one's commitments, and he shows without telling us our duty to God. *The Merchant of Venice* throws a good deal of weight upon the problem of making and keeping bonds, of establishing and fulfilling one's duty: that encumbrance falls not just upon monarchs, dukes, and civil officials, but on everyone, and failing creates not tragedy in the Classical sense, but something more insidious and more generally, deeply, humanly troubling. As in the Middle English Romance *Sir Gawain and the Green Knight*, when we fail in our *trawpe*, our troth or fidelity, we fail our companions, ourselves, and our God, and we have little if any opportunity to win our way back to righteous behavior. The world seldom gives us second chances; it offers little if any mercy, and if we break with our faith, we have nothing left but, depending on luck, either a long or a short road to despair. Sadly even a brief and silly failure, such as King Lear's temper tantrum, or what may have been failure to act quickly and clearly enough in a world that may give no more than one opportunity, as with Shylock, the failure of duty brings a stiff sentence: death, social, physical, spiritual, with no reprieve.

The Merchant of Venice concludes with a series of problems still wafting like troublesome odors from the stage to the London streets: can we accept Shylock's forced conversion and Antonio's benefiting from failure to keep his bond? Can we accept two dubious marriages that begin in greed, lust, and lies, especially when one, the main one of the story, has undertones of a greater passion that may undermine it, and when the second mimics the irresponsibility of the first? Can we accept a comedy without real humor, a tragedy with no noble protagonist to fall, a Romance — or anti–Romance[15] — with no dependable love or illuminating adventures, a history that turns to multi-leveled exemplum rather than actual events? We have instead a perfect example of Shakespeare's ability to mix genres (and modes) to create uncertainty and uneasiness, to resist catharsis and trouble us long after: the perfect problem play.

2

Troilus and Cressida and the Consummate Anti-Genre

In *Troilus and Cressida* Shakespeare used the degradation of character, manipulation of beginnings, middles, and ends, and the undermining of possibilities for humor to create the ultimate anti-genre play. He aimed at the disruption of notions of romance, fidelity, and honor and, of course, to transgress artistic boundaries and bring us to a troubling distrust of stories—and he succeeded.

Acid Character, a Trojan's Trumpet, and the Problem with Problems

In *Shakespeare's Problem Comedies* W. W. Lawrence suggests that the "acid brilliancy of its character drawing" in part "compels instant attention" to *Troilus and Cressida* (122). He finds Troilus and the Greek chieftains "powerless ... before egotism, selfishness, and lust" (165), and he sees in the play Shakespeare "rather analyzing life than satirizing chivalry" (170)—I'd lobby for both. What G. Wilson Knight called the "hate-theme" in Shakespeare—"cynicism toward love, disgust at the physical body, and dismay at the thought of death ... [and] a revulsion from human life (15)—I will call here, following Lawrence's image, "acid character": the problem of the affective qualities of all the characters in the play leads to the greatest difficulty in how to read and understand it. The play has too limited a scope to express a general hatred of life, but it does collect a cacophony of "bad" characters none of which earns audience sympathy, and the lack of ending produces little more than disgust.

David Bevington observes that Shakespeare "approaches genre in a protean fashion, mixing comedy and tragedy as appropriate and using (even helping to invent) generic forms like the English history play and tragicomedy" (105)—we already had the mix of comedy and Romance, as in Chaucer's "Tale

2. Troilus and Cressida *and the Anti-Genre*

of Sir Topas" and perhaps the fourteenth-century *Land of Cokaygne*, the fifteenth-century *The Wedding of Sir Gawain and Dame Ragnell*, and the turn-of-the-fifteenth-century *Sir Gawain and the Carle of Carlisle*. Bevington adds that *Troilus and Cressida* "ends anticlimactically, in utter disillusionment, with the senseless death of Hector, the drifting apart of Troilus and Cressida, and the continuation of the war in a spirit of blind fury"—worse, perhaps, as Troilus laments, "The bonds of heaven are slipp'd, dissolved, and loos'd" (Act V, scene 2, line 156): the setting and content of Romance have lead to nothing, or something worse than nothing, in that the characters learn nothing, gain nothing, and can hope for nothing (Bevington 147). We lack the happy ending of comedy, the cleansing ending of tragedy, the instructive ending of Romance; we conclude in the *-anti*.

Those "acid" or bad characters in *Troilus and Cressida* repeatedly hoist any expectations of worthy or honorable behavior, and they take the play out of any milieu in which comedies and tragedies with firm didactic elements keep safely to themselves. Worse yet, they corrode any other characters with whom they come in contact: no one in the play makes anyone else any better, and nearly everyone makes other characters worse. The reputation not only of Cressid, but of nearly every character in the world of the text plunges, and Bevington asserts that "Shakespeare's task, as dramatic artist, is to deal with this fallen reputation" (34). The problem then arises of how to make fallen reputation into some kind of valuable play. If the characters lack sufficient grandeur, it doesn't make for tragedy or Romance; if they're not funny or nasty it doesn't make for comedy. In the simplest terms, tragedy is scary, Romance is exciting, and comedy funny: this play offers none of those options.[1]

Shakespeare often affirmed Horace's notion of poetry as "sweetly useful" regardless of the weightiness or lightness of its plot, but sweetness of poetry and depth of thought often mix with bitter truth and scurrilous actions. Anne Barton has observed that "its unconventional form, neither comedy, tragedy, history, nor satire, its intellectualism, savagery, and disillusion speak forcefully to contemporary audiences naturally skeptical about ideas of honor, nobility, and military glory" 443)—notions and practices common enough in modern or postmodern art—but Shakespeare's audience still devoured work that taught the value of moral lessons, patient suffering, redemption, exemplary behavior, even if cast in relief by their opposites. And they and the next few generations firmly believed in following traditional form and genre: note for instance that Dryden called Ben Jonson the more correct poet because he more exactly followed Latin models, and Samuel Johnson condemned Shakespeare's pleasure in puns regardless of the vehicle. Regardless of the topic or mode of his plays, Shakespeare, particularly as he grew as a playwright, mixed generic elements more commonly, more confidently, and more profoundly—

he must have known from experience that his audience cared more about the complexity of thought and character than they did about Classical correctness.

In the *Poetics* Aristotle established some pretty simple and usable notions of genre. Besides definitive verse forms and the difference between imitation and narration, he notes that among dramas tragedies have serious actions, characters of more noble rank, and unhappy endings, and comedies have characters of lower rank and happy endings plus a lighter tone. Tragedy creates a catharsis of such emotions as pity and fear, and comedy — well, no remnant text of Aristotle's tells us that, and if Umberto Eco is right, we probably won't find it, but we may guess that Aristotle suspected comedy should also purge emotions that in excess inhabit clear thinking and action. With the exception of Thersites Shakespeare uses noble characters in *Troilus and Cressida*, but they think poorly and act badly, and we don't see their endings — Chaucer shows Troylus dead but happy, and Henryson shows Cresseid alive but diseased and rotted beyond recognition. The rascally Thersites serves better than anyone else as a voice of wisdom in the play, but his wisdom suffers from cutting cynicism, perpetual cowardice, and the tendency to shape all commentary on character and the world in the form of insults. Those insults may seem funny until we realize they are both really mean and largely true, slicing the noble heroes down to violent, arrogant, adolescent bullies and tarts, sarcasm rather than satire because the characters are so bad the audience can hardly use them as a means to improve our own moral fiber.

Chaucer treats Criseyde's character a good deal more gently and sympathetically than does Shakespeare: Troylus must win her, and she hasn't quite the rapid and obvious responses to him and to the Greeks as does the seventeenth-century Cressida. While not *saying* strictly so, Chaucer depicts Troylus both in action as a liar and by metaphor as a rapist (*raptus*), a hawk that grasps an innocent lark in its talons (Book 3, lines 1191–92). He shows Criseyde's problem largely and to some extent reasonably as *fear*, which more than any other thought or emotion guides her actions. As the Romance ends, she is in the process of failing in both loyalty and chastity. Troylus acts, though, on what we may call violent attraction: having at the beginning of *Troylus and Criseyde* made fun of love and lovers, he falls irresistibly for Criseyde, achieves her body in an image of violence, and dies in the mindless violence of battle; the hopeful lesson rests, of course, in Troylus' looking down from heaven and laughing at the sad absurdity of human folly.

Henryson's *Testament of Cresseid* deals with the aftermath of what both Chaucer and Shakespeare show us: Troilus has recovered a bit of his soul if not his heart, while Cresseid has lost heart and body and retains only the merest hold on a thread of soul: the gods punish her for failing to sacrifice to

2. Troilus and Cressida *and the Anti-Genre*

Venus and Cupid and for bewailing how they have failed to reward her devotions. They curse her with leprosy, and so she loses both the quality that attracted Troilus to her in the first place and any hope that the Greeks will give her further notice. Henryson's Cresseid has failed in troth, chastity, and piety, and that sad warning, in her former lover's failing to recognize her when he sees her, constitutes the moral power of the poem: for divine and human alike, she has dissolved away.

Where Shakespeare takes up the action, Troilus and Cressida have already fallen in love: Troilus is mooning and complaining over it, and Cressid refuses to admit it. But quickly we learn that neither has a particularly admirable character, and neither attracts much sympathy. Shakespeare packs the play with nominally comic scenes, but they only throw dark light on the scenes that precede them. The Prologue identifies the "princes orgillous" (line 2), recalling Spenser's prideful giant in Book 1 of *The Faerie Queene*, and notes how "their high blood chaf'd" has caused the circumstance of war. After we meet an unappealing Troilus and Pandarus, scene 2 shows Cressida repeatedly saying insulting things about Troilus as Pandarus tries to broker their love, and Cressid even calls Pandarus a "bawd" (line 281). The third scene takes us to the Greek camp and Ulysses' overzealous defense of degree: we learn that Patroclus does funny imitations of the Greek commanders, that Hector has medievally challenged the Greeks to send a single combatant against him, and that Ulysses will adopt wiles similar to those Pandarus uses to win Cressid for Troilus so he can help the Greeks get Achilles back into battle again.

Act II begins with Thersites railing at Ajax, literally proclaiming him "fool" (line 25). In II, 2 Hector argues that the Trojans should simply let Helen go and so end the war, but Troilus argues him into believing that honor should prevent them from doing so — even Cassandra's warning cries don't reach through their courtly dispute. The third scene again features Thersites railing, this time at Achilles and Patroclus rather than at Ajax, and Ulysses whips up Ajax's anger at Achilles' pride. Act III, scene 1, begins with silly "comic" dialogue between Pandarus and a servant and continues with a sickeningly satirical exchange between Pandarus and Helen and Paris that in the course of a little over a hundred lines uses the word *love* eighteen times and the word *sweet* nineteen times. The scene ends with the opposition of love and thought, one of the themes of the play, I think. In III, 2, as Pandarus conduct Troilus to Cressid, Troilus asks of him, "O, be thou my Charon,/ And give me sweet transportation to these fields/ Where I may wallow in the lily-beds/ Propos'd for the deserver!" (lines 10–13) — an odd metaphor for someone supposedly preparing to meet his beloved. We haven't seen anyone who has behaved well enough to deserve something good, and we know from the tradition of the story that Troilus, who is clearly thinking of himself and not Cressid here, hasn't long to live. Pandarus even begs, or requires, of Cressid that "if my lord get a boy of you, you'll give him me" (lines 104–105), as if he were some sort of Merlin preparing for Troy's better future. Cressid admits that "to be wise and love/ Exceeds man's might" (156–57), reinforcing the theme of the previous scene. Scene three shows Calchas arranging for the exchange that will bring Cressid from Troy and the Greek princes showing their mock-scorn for Achilles; Ulysses observes that virtue is its own purpose — odd, since hardly anyone in the play shows any. That scene and Act III conclude with Thersites joking about Ajax to Achilles and Patroclus.

Act IV begins with dialogue between the Greeks and Trojans about the exchange, including jokes about Helen as whore and Menelaus as cuckold, and pretty clear indications from Aeneas that everybody already knows about Troilus and Cressida's "secret" romance. IV, 2, has Pandarus joking with Cressid even as she's about to be exchanged and Paris in a horrifying irony telling Troilus he should willingly give up Cressid for the good of Troy. Just in case we didn't get the irony, in scene 3 Paris hurries Troilus to give her up and adds, "Would, as I shall pity, I could help" (line 11): of course he could! In IV, 4, Troilus repeatedly exhorts Cressid to fidelity, and she him, and they exchange favors in a reverse of chivalric tradition: he gives her a sleeve, and she gives him a glove. They reverse roles, and Troilus will later see Diomed with that sleeve, sparking in him a monomaniacal hatred. The glove, normally a symbol of the knight's strength and martial endeavor, serves here as a symbol of Cressid's pledge of fidelity — which immediately fails. The sleeve, normally a sexual symbol in that it shows the woman's devotion to the man, passes from the sexually faithful man to the disruptor of fidelity, Diomed. And even though we must call Troilus sexually faithful to Cressid, he still exploits her and turns from her directly to battle with greater fervor than he showed in love: everything in this world turns to emptiness and chaos.

The scene ends as Hector approaches the Greek camp for the aforementioned single combat with Paris calling out that he hears "Hector's trumpet" (line 140), setting up that nasty pun in scene 5 on which, I believe, the interpretation of the play hinges. The notorious scene 5 shows Cressida arriving at the Greek camp and immediately exchanging kisses with the Greek princes. "[H]er wanton spirits look out/ At every joint and motive of her body" (lines 56–57), Ulysses observes, and eight lines later, at the sound of a second trumpet flourish, all the men exclaim together, "The Troyans' trumpet," an obvious and raucous suggestion to the audience that they all see Cressid as Troy's strumpet, their lower-class version of Helen whom they'll pass around as they please, a narrative turn that Henryson makes poignantly and, in a modern sense, tragically. Hector arrives for single combat with Ajax: they make but one pass, Hector doesn't try very hard, and Ajax appears to be winning — he even says that he would willingly have killed his adversary — when Hector stops the fight, arguing that cousins shouldn't harm one another. Once Achilles has sized up and threatened Hector, they all repair to dinner except for Troilus, who asks Ulysses to take him to see Cressid at Menelaus' tent.

As Achilles plots Hector's death for the next day and Thersites rails against Patroclus, Achilles, Menelaus, and even Cressid (the "Troyan drab," he calls her in 5.1.96), Diomed is already seducing Cressid with Troilus and Ulysses looking on — and Ulysses fanning the flames of Troilus' jealousy. Even Cressid notes that "the error of our eye directs our mind (line 110), and Troilus in a long lament suggests that "this is, and is not, Cressid!" (line 146): she is herself, not his idealization of her, and we must note that hers is also himself and neither her nor his idealization of Troilus. Even as Diomed seduces her, Cressid laments that the mind is too easily swayed by the eye — an excuse for her own choice of infidelity — and even as Troilus hopelessly suggests that the heart must believe despite the evidence of the eyes and ears, Ulysses offers nominal comfort that one must suspect serves rather as part of his plan to weaken another of Troy's greatest soldiers. Scene 3 shows Andromache and Cassandra uselessly trying to get Hector to avoid battle that day, and Troilus receives through Pandarus a letter from Cressid that he shreds without reading in a line that recalls Hamlet: "Words, words, mere words, no matter from the heart" (108). He gives her no chance, and she probably deserves none, but he also undermines all the words he has spoken of his own love and care for her: he fails to recognize that she is living in a hostile camp and has no control over her own circumstances. In a brief scene 4, Thersites on the battlefield continues his torrent of insults, is confronted by Hector, and begs off fighting because he is only a "filthy rogue" (line 29). In scene five Diomed has won Troilus' horse on the battlefield and, speaking to his servant, reveals that he know of Troilus' love for Cressid. In scenes 6 and 8 Hector and Achilles meet in battle, and Hector gains the upper hand, but when he pauses to rest, the lurking Achilles and his Myrmidons slaughter Hector; those scenes sandwich another of silly comedy with Thersites again begging off battle, this time because he has met a "bastard" like himself, and bastards should stand up for one another. Scenes 9 and 10 show the retreat from battle, the spreading news of Hector's death, and Troilus' dismissal of Pandarus with a slap — Pandarus gets the last word, bequeathing to all who like him "trade in flesh" — and perhaps to the audience in general — his "diseases." Any audience — not just those with sexually transmitted illness — who believe in the glories of battle, the acceptability of faithlessness, the propriety of secret love affairs, the willingness to put aside honor for political purposes, and the value of the humor of scurrilous insult suffer from the diseases that Pandarus bequeaths. Those diseases plague the world of the play, and Shakespeare makes them matter for plain and public discourse.

The unyieldingly coarse humor of the play, that greater cruelty than Chaucer's tale — and Shakespeare devotes a great many of his scenes to that humor — turns on the pun that identifies Cressid as strumpet. Cressid becomes a woman ruined not by reasonable fear and impossible circumstance, but because of her own acid character, which doesn't in itself ruin Troilus, but certainly does him no good, corroding whatever limited ability he may have had to see clearly and act reasonably. Thersites has verbal wit and identifies the problems of the world — he serves a purpose, but wins no sympathy; Hector's death at the hands of a dishonorable Achilles and his mob undercuts any humor in Ulysses' plots or Ajax's proud and stupid ravings, because it brings to the forefront the destructive horrors of one's believing in honor as a reason for battle: if we fight, we fight well only in defense of ourselves and of what good we can find in the world, not for a vague sense of our own vanity. Once we believe Cressid a simple strumpet and no more, we lose Romance, we lose tragedy, and we lose comedy: why make fun of something sickeningly sad? The *-anti* of the play comes to a head here: all we can do is, with respect to ourselves and others, try to behave more bravely and generously, stay truer, avoid dissembling and others' wiles. The play, which severs itself from all genres, tells us that in a world of problems we can't avoid confronting them, and we may not have the strength even to mitigate them; we can only prepare for them and resist giving in to them.

In a recent and excellent book on Henryson's *Testament of Cresseid* and its analogues, Nick Haydock observes that "no work among Shakespeare's extant plays so tempts the critic to Polonius-like torrents of genre amalgams as Troilus and Cressida ... (247)." He also finds in Shakespeare's play, as I do, an "elimination of catharsis" (249), terms it "antiromance" (254), and calls attention to its "degrading [of] rank and deflating [of] overblown egos" (263); in the term *problem play*, though, he finds a "suppression of the distinctiveness inherent in particular examples of generic errantry" (247).[2] There, with respect to Shakespeare's plays, I find the term's particular virtue in this case: *problem* urges us to find where the problem lies and exactly what it does in any particular case, and it accounts for why so many of Shakespeare's plays prove troublesome emotionally as well as interpretively: he never leaves simple happy endings, seldom leaves simple sad ones, and occasionally, as in *The Winter's Tale*, undercuts his own undercutting of Romance. Louis Wright and Virginia LaMar assert that "the Elizabethans, who thought of the Trojan War as a genuine episode in ancient history, probably regarded *Troilus and Cressida* as a chronicle play" (255), but Shakespeare charts such a different emotional course and includes such different incidents than his sources that he moves his Troy

2. Troilus and Cressida *and the Anti-Genre* 49

play from the realm of the historical to that of the darkly, even brutally inventive. This antitragedy, anticomedy, antihistory, antiromance forcefully undermines any generic identification: it urges us to find and confront the *problem* of problem play. Harold Goddard notes its "debunking" of the heroic and romantic as appropriate to its audience (probably the "barristers at one of the Inns of Court") (2), suggests the "annihilating power of this play" (3–4) as well as its "aphoristic" power (2) and calls it "the most intellectual play he ever wrote" (4) and, along with *Measure for Measure*, one of only two Shakespeare plays we may call "didactic" (3) — I see no problem in finding didacticism in Shakespeare's plays, despite our time's distaste for the term and the notion, but whatever *Troilus and Cressida* teaches, it does so in a peculiarly difficult way. It certainly deals with out-of-control excesses, making it antiphilosophical — and in some ways typically Ovidian — as well: philosophy has no place in a world where thought and wisdom take as their substance naughty jokes and insults, and faith honor and give way to the weakest cajoling. Its closest generic analogue, Romance (Chaucer serves as the major source), disappears in the language of lies and vituperation: railing replaces love-language, and convenience replaces love.

If we call it anti–Romance, what do we gain thereby? It undermines the genre staples of adventure, the glories of battle and love, and the power of magic in the world for good or ill. No real adventure occurs, the soldiers bollix the battle scenes and the lovers undercut the love scenes, and this world has no magic of any sort — it has no religion at all — so perhaps with nothing left of traditional Romance, it isn't even anti–Romance, a send-up of the genre. Instead, it shows the problem of an empty world with nothing worth doing, no one worth loving or fighting, and no means to transcend the horrors of quotidian life: the problem's the point, to catch the conscience of its audience — a less than joyful diversion, but a powerful comment on the value of living in a world with the potential for so much more. If we call the play an anti-tragedy, we simply note that it lacks or minimizes the self-wrought fall of a noble character. Neither Troilus nor Cressida acts nobly. Even Hector, a pretty minor player in the plot, fails his own sense of honor, and he dies, after stupidly disarming to rest right in the midst of the battlefield, mangled by gang-tackling Myrmidons. Cassandra warns characters of their danger and folly, but they ignore her — their tragedy more than hers. Anti-tragedy brings no catharsis, so it has no purpose beyond making fun of tragedy, a silly pursuit for someone who was still successfully writing them. And what can we say of anti-history? Shakespeare doesn't follow any of his "historical" sources, and we "adapt" history to make tragedy, comedy, or Romance, not just to get history wrong. To anti-comedy we can perhaps say yes. The almost exclusively scurrilous humor shows how joking doesn't fit the seriousness of the subject matter: prolonged war, dishonorable behavior from nearly everyone, destruction, infidelity, extreme egotism, and loss followed by loss. In terms of "moral" or an overall reading of the play, the notion of anti-comedy gives much the same reading as anti–Romance: a diatribe against war reckless selfishness, and folly — in short, satire, which in Shakespeare's time is more mode than genre. And why do a comedy to make fun of comedy? Comedy at least is fun, and should a writer undermine fun for its own sake? Only if he's a Puritan, perhaps.

We return to the possibility that Shakespeare wrote the play to create a *problem*, something that, like life, remains difficult to inhabit, difficult to understand, full of irrationality and largely irritating, full of danger and enormous potential for more danger yet, but thus also full of opportunity for hope, heroism, and love. Sadly, though, he shows, we take insufficient advantage of those potentials for good, but we can begin by recognizing them and looking them squarely in the eye.

Evolving Shakespeare's Troilus and Cressida: *Beginnings, Middles, and Ends*

The movement of the Troilus and Cressida story from Chaucer to Henryson to Shakespeare produces not only the obvious changes in genre, plot, and tone, but also a notably evolving series of tensions as the tale moves through affectively distinctive beginnings, middles, and ends. With broad emotional shifts, even something as simple and direct as theme or didactic purpose changes significantly, though each of the three texts retains a full diapason decrying a pusillanimous heart and a failed *trawþe*. Most importantly for interpreting the movement toward and in Shakespeare's play, the developing dramatic tensions and their building intratextually as well as intertextually produce in *Troilus and Cressida* a discrete and especially disturbing emotional and aesthetic experience.

Shakespeare of course does far more than recapitulate his sources, but he does move further in a direction they point. Attention to a pattern as simple as Aristotle's awareness of beginnings, middles, and ends highlights the major dramatic vectors and uncovers how Shakespeare used and disrupted form to turn the intellectual and affective qualities of the story in a very different direction. Together the three pieces yield an unexpected but certainly a worthy consummation to thoughtful explorations into how broadly a single story can change in the smithy of writers with the same material in hand but different motivations at heart. Given a genesis in sexual frailty, a subject as sure to raise consternation in Shakespeare's time as in Chaucer's, the Troilus and Cressida Romance begs mimetic and autobiographical readings even as it deconstructs courtly love expectations, but most importantly for Shakespeare's purposes it allows him to leave his audience with quite a number of moral, aesthetic, and philosophical problems to solve.

The "story" begins properly but minimally with Benoît de Sainte-Maure's *Roman de Troie,* but it gains no significant steam until Boccaccio's *Il Filostrato,* where a strong autobiographical influence of youthful disappointment laces it with male complaint at female infidelity — a product far less worthy of detailed attention in its simplicity and relative puerility than Chaucer's more compassionate version. Its focus and rhythms change markedly in subsequent incarnations, Chaucer's by far exhibiting the most varied and generous sympathies and most thorough and nuanced character development.

Chaucer's characteristic undercutting of simple readings laces his refiguration of Boccaccio with emotional incongruities, a turn that Shakespeare will later intensify. As he begins, Chaucer's narrator observes (Book I, lines 13–14 and following) that it suits well "a woful wight to han a drery feere,/ And to a sorwful tale, a sory cheere": a woeful person will probably have a gloomy companion and a sorrowful tale shall have a sad tone. He purposes to tell Troilus's "double sorrow," yet asserts that if his telling may "don gladnesse/ Unto ony lovere," that Cupid has his thanks. The Muse he invokes, oddly enough no Muse but the Fury Tisiphone, "the punisher," in Greek myth, sees to it that spirits enter the Underworld, particularly Tartaros when appropriate — an authorial choice that better fits a curse than a request for aesthetic inspiration. "By his contrari is everything declared," says Pandar," and the tale functions by a series of opposites, doubles, comparisons, reversals. Weakness tames pride, and the plot turns on no emotion so much as fear: Troilus fears telling his love, Cressid fears returning it, Pandar fears if she doesn't, Cressid fears the Greek camp, Troilus fears she won't return — one has a hard time believing that Calchas has left Troy for the sake of prudence rather than fear. Chaucer begins with a symbol of terror and turns a would-be love story into a debacle of loss and adolescent melancholy.

The middle of Chaucer's tale, Book 3, invokes a seemingly likelier Muse, Venus, and then follows with a second, of Calliope, the Muse of Epic poetry — an odd second choice, even as Troilus begs only a kind glance and Cressid's willingness to accept his service, and Cressid begs that Troilus respect her honor. Odder yet for a Romance, the whole of Book 3 leads through male trickery to what amounts essentially to Cressid's rape. She then ironically pledges her fidelity; by the end of Book 3 one has a hard time retaining sympathy for anyone in the text: the love affair has reached physical consummation, but at the expense of everyone's honor. As we move from the effects of the "middle" of the tale towards its crisis, Book 4 begins with a turn of Fortune's wheel. Again the narrator invokes Furies — all three this time — as well as Mars, Venus' less appealing consort, as the plot prepares Cressid's exchange for Antenor, who according to medieval tradition later betrayed Troy. Cressid will fall to infidelity through fear, and Troilus will tumble into despair through loss, both damnable sins to Chaucer's audience, and we find no respite in love from the general infidelity of the world that tolerates if not glorifies the kidnapping of Helen.

Troilus and Criseyde ends, of course, with a further downturn of Fortune's Wheel: Hector is killed through Achilles' treachery, Cressid fails to keep her troth, shame silences Pandar, and Troilus also dies at Achilles' hands, only to ascend improbably to the happy Seventh Sphere of Heaven, where he looks down on the vanities of human life and laughs.[3] "Go litel bok," says the narrator, in both a tonal and factual irony, as he asks that God send him a comedy instead of a tragedy to write. Seek divine rather than human love, says the voice — fidelity to either seems to produce desirable results in the next life if not in this one. The peculiar, jovial catharsis at the end of the poem turns about-face from the narrative and emotional trajectory that has come before — even the brief love scenes lack any sort of emotional satisfaction, because they derive from schemes and pimping rather than any dependable demonstration of love. But, for all that, Chaucer manages sympathy for everyone: he explicitly excuses Cressid because of the obvious difficulty of her circumstance — how could anyone feel anything but terror there, a lone woman being turned over to a camp of bitter, angry, lonely soldiers? He shows Pandar recede into his own shame; he redeems Troilus despite his dishonorable wooing. The same loopy congeniality of the *Canterbury Tales'* narrator appears in the Romance, omitting Boccaccio's bitterness and falling well short of Henryson's stricter moralizing. Chaucer aims at our consolation through the sharing of the mutual sadness of living and hope for release and redemption after.

Even Henryson's unabashed didacticism gives way, however, to hints of compassion, though their emotional effects evoke a stony hardness of spirit. The sorrow of the final confrontation between the two former lovers places the poem emotionally midway between Chaucer's and Shakespeare's, without Chaucer's explicit urging to forgive, but short of the general condemnation Shakespeare demands. Critical responses to "The Testament of Cresseid" have varied widely, particularly to the harsh judgments of the pagan gods, their responding to Cressid's complaints by infecting her with leprosy. We may read the disease allegorically as punishment for blasphemy, or more simply as a typical medieval response to sexual excess, or even as Cressid's failure to accept fully the sacrament of confession: as Robert Kindrick observed, Cressid "does not look inward to find the cause" of her woes.[4] Henryson begins by asserting that "ane dooly sesoun to an cairfull dyte/ Suld correspond"— a

2. Troilus and Cressida *and the Anti-Genre*

mournful poem should fit a sad season — and he proclaims his poem a tragedy. The narrator reflects for a time on the nature of romantic love, especially for old men, though he claims to know well what it means to both old and young. He sits by the fire and takes a drink of "spirits," reads first from Chaucer's *Troilus and Criseyde* and then from a second book, "In quilk I fand the fatall desteny/ Of fair Cresseid, that endit wretchedly," and he begins the narration with how Diomed satisfied his appetite for the lady, then sent her off, after which she became a "court commoun." Henryson takes a page from Chaucer, both literally and figuratively: the sorrowful one finds comfort in a sorrowful story. Unlike Shakespeare, who begins with trepidation and moves to romantic passion, Henryson begins in sorrow, after his characters have used or been used up. Mood and tone echo, as Shakespeare might say, more in sorrow than in anger, and we find ourselves in the midst of a sequel, though a sequel with the same ostensible purpose as its source and its progeny, to lament infidelity, the personal sorrows wrought by war, and sad afflictions that life casts on the weak and fearful.

The middle of the poem only increases Cresseid's misfortune. "Quha sall me gyde?" she asks, then curses the gods: "O fals Cupide, is nane to wyte bot thow/ And thy mother, of lufe the blind goddess!/ 3e causit me alwayis understand and trow/ The seid of lufe was sawin in my face.... Bot now, allace, that seid with froist is slane..." (ll. 133–39), and of course she sets up the curse that follows. In nearly the exact center Saturn and the Moon reply: "For the dispyte to Cupide scho had done/ And to Venus, oppin and manifest,/ In all hir lyfe with pane to be opprest,/ And torment sair with seiknes incurabill,/ And to all louers be abhominabill" (304–308). They have no need to "change her mirth to melancholy," since she already faced rejection and scorn, but to her shame the gods add more. The middle of the poem adds no tension here, as it does in Chaucer, nor a lampoon of lust and faithlessness, as it will in Shakespeare, but instead simply more sorrow to attract more pity and reinforce the need for the patient suffering that must follow sin and misfortune in this transient world.

Naught for Cresseid, then, but wandering and suffering ... until one day on the field Troilus passes her and other lepers, who call out for alms.... Neither recognizes the other, but Troilus sees something in her face that reminds him of Cresseid, and so "for knichtlie pietie[5] and memoriall/ Of fair Cresseid," he tosses her a small purse of gold. Cressid must ask of another there the name of the soldier, and when she learns it, she bewails her woe, "O fals Cresseid and trew knicht Troylus!" She makes her testament, her corpse to the worms, her gold to the lepers, her ring to Troilus, and her spirit to Diana — chastity at last. Troilus learning of her death, builds a tomb and inscribes it with the words "Cressid of Troy, once counted the flower of womanhood, under this stone, late a leper, lies dead"—succinctly put, somewhere between merciful and unfathomably cold. Critics argue over whether or not we may consider Cressid redeemed by her last speech; Henryson omits Chaucer's scene of a redeemed Troilus. Denton Fox suggests that Henryson "takes a weak, selfish, and unfaithful, even lascivious, woman and manages to make her into such a pathetic and much-abused beauty that we are tempted to comfort her"[6]— but I'm not sure that he wants us to experience that desire to comfort so strongly that we forget to judge the actions. We can say at least this much about the end: it reflects the decay not only of beauty but even of our ability to recognize one another in our sorrows; the narrator need pass no moral judgment, since the penalties of the gods and the passing of time have done so themselves, swelling the waves of human sorrow into pitiless breakers. That ending more than Chaucer's foreshadows the direction Shakespeare will take with his re-vision of the story, where, unlike his two major predecessors, Cressida will lose what sympathy the audience has for her.

"Shakespeare's play," Heather James argues, "systematically repudiates its predecessors"; it "exhibits an exasperating pleasure in rousing audience expectations based on an anticipated genre or text"[7]—it certainly builds on entirely different emotional constructs. Shakespeare's Cressid calls to mind his Joan of *1 Henry VI* in her oddly willful turn to wantonness, and perhaps for similar dramatic reasons: the emotional effect of the *turn*, Joan from proclaimed holy warrior to wanton and Cressid from faithful lover to wanton, directs the audience away from sympathy we might otherwise experience. Both cases suggest wry, satirical if not misogynistic readings, both warn of dubious loyalties in love and war, and both lead us to feel wary of identifying with potentially romantic figures. Troilus ends the play a mad, friendless combatant lusting only for blood, and Pandar wills the audience the diseases happily enough distributed by the children of his profession—the affective moralizing hits as hard as or harder than Henryson's explicit morality. Shakespeare's tendency to the more widely sweeping Renaissance humanist sympathies dies away in this play, replaced by disgust and futility.

Shakespeare begins quite differently than does Chaucer, with the latter's call upon the Fury; Shakespeare's Prologue brings immediate focus to the Greek princes' pride, which in an ancient setting has positive implications, but for Shakespeare's Christian audience implies deadly sin. As I mentioned in part one of this chapter, he recalls Spenser's giant Orgoglio of Book 1 of *The Faerie Queene*, who nearly manages to destroy the Redcrosse Knight: only Arthur and Una's help save him from living death in a dungeon that clearly symbolizes hell—in this play we inhabit a kind of hell populated with infidelity, cruelty, violent arrogance, and mean jokes. Shakespeare's Prologue reads:

2. Troilus and Cressida *and the Anti-Genre*

> A prologue armed, but not in confidences
> Of author's pen or actor's voice, but suited
> In like conditions as our argument,
> To tell you, fair beholders, that our play
> Leaps o'er the vaunt and firstlings of those broils,
> Beginning in the middle....
> Like or find fault, do as your pleasures are,
> Now good or bad, 'tis but the chance of war [lines 23–31].

The Prologue, unusually for Shakespeare, almost scorns audience approval as out of his control, a matter of the fortunes of war rather than something in his or the author's hands. So we begin more akin to epic, or at least Epic Romance, *in medias res*, specifically in the midst of *war*—but in anti-epic as much as anti-Romance, because we don't see any productive heroism or any laudable actions. Contrary to a likely epic move, Act I takes us immediately not to war, but to nominal (if not actual) love: Troilus, unlike in Chaucer, has already fallen for Cressid (no disdain of love here). "Why should I war without the walls of Troy,/ That find such cruel battle here within?" he asks, making the love/war equation explicit rather than implicit. Of course we haven't epic here, or comedy—where editors often place the play amidst Shakespeare's *oeuvre*—nor even quite tragedy, though something closer to that. If Shakespeare knew Henryson, that echo may have made tragedy impossible, and we find in the play a Cressid even influenced more by lust than by fear. We haven't even Romance: love fails quickly, and no magic saves it or anything or anyone else. The world of this text hinges on monstrous self-indulgence and explosive arrogance. "I tell thee I am mad/ In Cressid's love," says Troilus in I.1.51–52, foreshadowing his and the general madness at the end of the play, and then "she is stubborn-chaste against all suit," he adds in line 97, his mode of sexual attack already abrupt. In I.2 we learn in a soliloquy that Cressid conceals her love for Troilus, and in III.2.117–18 she admits, "I was won, my lord,/ With the first glance"; war may produce impatience, but encourages honor in love no more than in battle. So the "beginning" of the play concludes by entirely undermining the love motif just as it will continue to undermine the heroic battle motif.

In III.1, as we move into the middle of the play, Pandarus, in an exchange with Helen and Paris, uses the word *fair* or *fairly* ten times in five lines; shortly he uses the word *sweet* ten times over the course of fifteen lines, then five times more before the scene ends. In scene 2, as Troilus stalks Cressid's door, he asks Pandarus, "O, be thou my Charon," to beg admission—Charon, again, conducts souls not to Paradise, but to the Underworld, the land of the dead, and, if Shakespeare thought of Dante rather than the Greeks, to eternal torment, a torment that souls in the *Commedia* seek willingly. The middle of the play conducts us not to Purgatory, but further into Hell. When the lovers do meet, between them they use the word *fear* six times in eight lines, and over forty lines Troilus, Cressida, and Pandarus use the word *faith* five times, and when Cressid pledges, she uses *false* or *falsehood* eight times in twelve lines: the verbal echoes convert quickly from fair and sweet to fear and faith and then to false: what begins as sexual attraction turns quickly to fear of faithfulness and simple falsehood at last. "Well, uncle, what folly I commit, I dedicate to you" (III.2.102–103), warns Cressid, and soon come the famous echoes in their pledges "As true as Troilus" (line 182) and "As false as Cressid" (line 196), again foreshadowing the conclusion, yet overstating Troilus' faith. Troilus' second sorrow, the treacherous killing of Hector by Achilles and his Myrmidons, trumps his loss of Cressid and turns any remnant claims of friendship with Pandarus to scorn — no one keeps faith long in this world, but the world upends everything worth living for if one remains fixed on what one has rather than how well one thinks and acts.

As we move further into Act III, Troilus and Cressida meet and agree to a "bargain," as Pandarus puts it, "to press it [a bed] to death"; in III.3 Ulysses arranges a single combat between Hector and Ajax, with the intention of inflaming Achilles with the desire to fight so that the Greeks can have hope of victory. The parallel events show the mischief of plotting and dissembling in either context. Ulysses acts as pander for a false fight designed as another kind of wooing. The fight, in Act IV, ends "sweetly," with no bloodshed because Ajax and Hector are cousins, but it does help move events toward Hector's death and in a sense toward Cressid's departure from Troy: Act IV begins with Diomed's arrival in Troy at night to receive her in exchange for Antenor. Anything resembling love takes place offstage, and the onstage exchange takes place in the dark, lit only by torches — another symbol of the covert nature of action in the play. In III.3 Ulysses observes, "Beauty, wit,/ High birth, vigor of bone, desert in service,/ Love, friendship, charity, are subjects all/ To envious and calumniating Time": the characters need very little time for all such virtues to fail them. "I care not to be the louse of a lazar, so I were not Menelaus," says the scurrilous Thersites in V.1, perhaps echoing Henryson, but certainly verbalizing the sense that the world of the characters has been decaying long before the events of the play began. He decries lechery and refers to Cressid as "the Troyan drab" in V.2, echoing Ulysses' sentiments and Troilus' worst fears; far worse for Troy, in V.3, asserting his honor, Hector departs Troy for the battlefield despite the pleas of Cassandra and Andromache, and in V.8 he foolishly disarms on the battlefield, allowing opportunity for the treacherous Achilles. "Hope of revenge shall hide our inward woe," laments Troilus, who has become little more than a berserker, in V.10, before turning over the stage to Pandarus, whose final words dispense

2. Troilus and Cressida *and the Anti-Genre*   57

disease and dis-ease generally to the world — no other Epilogue eases the conclusion of the play, whose echoes sneer with decay, ruin, and scorn — and leave the audience with no relief, no catharsis, from a world that declines from bad to worse to uninhabitable by any sane creature. The end of this problematic play offers no respite, simply an overwhelming sense of impending, unyielding, and unnecessary loss brought about by the human tenacity for self-serving, disgraceful rascality.

The closing tone contrasts starkly with Chaucer's and Henryson's: Chaucer hints at redeemability in the desire to love faithfully and in the opportunity to gain distance from and perspective on the folly of human experience; Henryson has Troilus build a marble tomb for his dead sometime-love, his narrator warns women of deception, and he hints at respect for even the dishonorable departed ("Sen sho is deid, I speik of hir no moir"). Shakespeare leaves us in disgust.

Shakespeare's sonnets have often encouraged readers to find in them autobiography, but I find such readings dangerous and intrusive and difficult to defend: they come more from a desire to know more about the poet than from anything we actually know about his life, circumstances, preferences, or character. Dare one hazard, then, anything about what the later variant versions of the Troilus and Cressida story say about their authors? Chaucer's narrator in the early poems particularly claims sleeplessness and sorrow in love: "For both I hadde that which I nolde,/ and I ne hadde that thing that I wolde,"[8] probably a characterization to attract sympathy to the narrator in a courtly love–influenced world, but also perhaps a state of mind that leads to both lament and consolation for lost love real or imagined. We know so little of Henryson, yet his narrator also claims the pains of love-longing, perhaps in honor and echo of his beloved mentor, but perhaps because he felt the same sorrows and so dealt with them through similar themes, in this case enhancing the suffering of the faithless woman — Boccaccio reputedly wrote *Il Filostrato* as a response to spurned love. Of Shakespeare's feelings we know nothing — Keats's negative capability stands between Will and us — but we need not stretch too far to guess, accurately or not, about a marriage to a woman already pregnant, some twenty years spent away from her and their home, and the bequeathing, not of disease, but of nothing beyond the infamous "second best bed." Any story takes a coloring from its author, and the *Troilus* bears three quite different spectra from its most famous British incarnations, the last of the three bearing the darkest cast.

More importantly, and I hope more usefully, a simple comparison/contrast based on structure and emotional flow shows us quite different affective responses to the horror of loss that comes not merely by chance, and not merely by war, but also by the rapidity with which we often give in to weakness.

Surprisingly, at least for me, Shakespeare treats the subject with the least compassion and humanity: perhaps he decided that his predecessors had sentimentalized the story and so weakened its effects on an audience still needing its message. Perhaps he struggled more than did Chaucer or Henryson with the fear and loathing associated with pledges of truth and subsequent infidelity, a theme that pervaded his world politically as well as individually. The evolving story of Troilus and Cressida provides an adjustable lens, in this case a trifocal, back to the times and authors who incarnated it, hinting at the balance — or imbalance — of passion and anger that led them back to this troubling tale. Shakespeare concludes it with a strong sense of irresolution, and he uses it to address a painful matrix of life-lessons and to leave his audience troubled by providing no simple solutions to the problems of bad thinking, bad choices, and bad actions.

Thersites the Anti-Ass: Humor and Other Themes of the Play

Thersites takes up quite a good deal more of this play than he deserves. While he may bray insults at other characters, and while he may utter truths about the problems of the world, he never does anything to make the world or its characters better. They listen when they find him witty and ignore him if they find him right. Only Cassandra actually tries to help, but she appears only briefly, and no one pays her any attention. Thersites' humor adds no insights that we didn't already have, and it entertains others in the play only briefly, until he turns his poniard on them — and a pretty weak poniard at that, since it brings no one greater self-awareness, nor does it change any behavior, falling into sarcasm rather than satire. Two other characters, Cressida and Pandarus, also provide humor in the play, but their humor, too, causes more annoyance than pleasure, and even an audience who responds briefly to it will quickly see its emptiness.

Shakespeare uses humor in his plays — humorous characters, language, situations, repartee — not for that silly cliché notion of "comic relief," but to reveal aspects of character and clarify and deepen his themes. In *Much Ado About Nothing*, Dogberry, insulted by the villain Conrade, who calls him an ass, insists that the insult become part of public record: "O that I had been writ down an ass!" (5.1.87). Dogberry, guilty of all sorts of hilarious malapropisms and perhaps even of some degree of cowardice, actually serves, along with his fellows among the Watch, as the *ass* of the play: he carries the burden of truth and justice in the world of the play. Leonato, as Governor of Messina, should do that: he should interrogate the prisoners and discover who has tried

2. Troilus and Cressida *and the Anti-Genre*

to ruin his daughter and why. Don Pedro, as the single most powerful character in the play, should also carry some of that burden, but he does not: he falls for his brother's ruse and participates in a cruel public shaming of an innocent young woman. Shakespeare will often shift the burden of wisdom or action from the person who should bear responsibility to a clown, a fool, or someone of less nominal power who, at some intellectual distance from the problem, can at least think clearly or act directly.

In *Troilus and Cressida* Thersites should serve that purpose, but he doesn't. I can't even tell exactly what he's doing in the Greek camp. Certainly no soldier, he begins as a kind of "voluntary" servant to Ajax, with whom he immediately trades insults and whose company he leaves for that of Achilles and Patroclus. Achilles, hearing part of the exchange of insults, calls him "fool"; Thersites replies, "Ay, but that fool [i.e., Ajax] knows not himself," to which Ajax responds, "Therefore I beat thee" (2.1.65–67). Thersites' humor should help Ajax know himself, as that of the Fool in *King Lear* does for Lear, but it doesn't. Ajax remains strong and stupid—if anything, he gets worse, becoming more proud and dull. Ajax doesn't learn; he beats. With Achilles and Patroclus he does the same thing: instead of calling a traditional curse upon Patroclus, "thyself upon thyself!" he shouts, "The common curse of mankind, folly and ignorance, be thine in great revenue!" he adds (2.3.27–29). That curse comes true for all the characters in the play: they condemn themselves to foolish and ignorant behavior throughout. In the dialogue following among Thersites, Achilles, and Patroclus, the word *fool* appears ten times in the course of thirteen lines: anyone listening or reading carefully at all will notice that Shakespeare calls our attention to the mutual foolishness we see throughout the play, from the most noble to the most ignoble. In *Lear* the Fool at least does the king some good; in *Troilus and Cressida* Thersites can point out others' foolishness, but fully participates in it himself, showing no greater purpose than the fools around him and not even giving the audience something we need to understand the play: we can see well enough the ubiquitous foolishness without him. This play doesn't have the ass it needs to carry the events to some sort of useful resolution. Even Troilus, who has at least some good traits to recommend him in Chaucer's poem, and Aeneas, usually a positive figure for English poets, lack a sense of the seriousness of their situation: In Act I, scene 1, when Aeneas returns from the field of battle to report that "Paris is gor'd with Menelaus' horn," and adds, "Hark what good sport is out of town today" (i.e., the fighting), Troilus responds, "But to the sport abroad—are you bound thither?" (lines 112–15): to them the war implies not the struggle for the survival of their city, but sport.

The nominal comedy begins in Act I, scene 2. Cressida, having observed to her servant that the behavior of Ajax—no small enemy—should produce smiles rather than anger, engages in a long dialogue with Pandarus: he tries to win her to Troilus' love, and she fends him off, even though we learn later that she loved him already. "I swear to you, I think Helen loves him [Troilus] better than Paris," Pandarus, obviously lying, asserts, and Cressid replies, "Then she's a merry Greek indeed" (lines 107–108). She makes fun nominally of Helen, but really of both Pandarus in his praising and Troilus in his loving, ironically since she has fallen for Troilus easily enough and will do the same again with Diomed — the humor turns quickly from witty to sad and embarrassingly ironic. Pandarus suggest that Troilus esteems Helen "no more than I esteem and addle egg," and Cressida replies, "If you love an addle egg as well as you love an idle head, you would eat chickens i' th'shell" (lines 130–34): both Pandarus and Troilus suffer from an idle brain — neither Cressid nor Troilus nor anyone else will think too clearly or effectively anywhere in this play.

In Act I, scene 3, Ulysses delivers his famous "degree" speech. Whether Shakespeare intended it as honest comedy or the statement of an outdated, lampoonable position I don't know: like Chaucer, he seems in his work to believe in a natural social order. Ulysses claims that Troy hasn't yet fallen to the Greeks because "[d]egree being vizarded/ Th'unworthiest shows as fairly as the mask./ The heavens themselves, the planets, and this centre/ Observe degree, priority, and place" (lines 83–86); the solution, he argues, comes in exploding Achilles' pride and getting him back to his proper place leading the fighting. But he makes more a practical than a philosophical argument, since he will soon plot with Nestor to accomplish that end by dissembling rather than by convincing Achilles of the truth of that assertion. Then, almost as a response to Ulysses' speech, in 2.1, 2.3, 3.3, 5.1, 5.2, 5.4, and 5.7 Shakespeare unleashes Thersites, who in Don Rickles–ish fashion insults anyone he meets. He proclaims Ajax a fool and a dog, and won't even stop when Ajax beats him: "no man is beaten voluntary," suggests Achilles after Thersites insists he serves there of his own will, but rather than answering Achilles he simply shifts his service to him and Patroclus instead. Apparently we do take voluntary beatings, and the audience may see the whole of the Trojan War as such an instance: neither side should be there fighting, and yet we see them so. Thersites' soliloquy begins II.3; he says that the walls of Troy will fall by themselves before Achilles and Patroclus can get the job done. As so often happens in Shakespeare's soliloquies, the character speaks as he believes, and he happens to be right: neither Patroclus nor Achilles will bring down Troy; only the Trojans' own foolishness can do that. Thersites continues to call Patroclus, Agamemnon, Achilles, and even himself a fool: they all serve unreasonably, partly because the reason for the war, "a whore and a cuckold" (72–73), hardly merits their suffering and certainly does not deserve the name of

2. Troilus and Cressida *and the Anti-Genre*

honor. Why do we fight? makes an awfully compelling question, but nobody bothers to answer it, and nobody changes anything in his or her behavior — except to get even worse.

In III.3 Patroclus urges Achilles to fight, "Sweet, rouse yourself" (line 222), and Achilles, with a "sweet Patroclus" (*sweet* appears enough in this play to remind one of the sonnets), observes selfishly in reply, "I see my reputation is at stake,/ My fame is shrowdly gor'd" (lines 227–28). *Shrowdly* puns, as a portmanteau, on *shrewdly* and *as if in a shroud*: Ulysses has acted shrewdly to try to get Achilles to fight, and his reputation has nearly died, since he has done nothing to keep it alive — degree, as Ulysses has warned, is failing.[9] Thersites then appears to comment on Ajax's behavior as he prepares for the one-on-one combat with Hector, but his lines apply equally well to Achilles: "if Hector break not his nick i' the' combat, he'll break it himself in vainglory" (258–59), and "I had rather be a tick in a sheep than such a valiant ignorance" (311–12). He is, essentially, a tick irritating the Greek soldiers as he lives on their blood. Having observed Cressida with Diomed in V.2, he says that the gossipy Patroclus "will give me any thing for the intelligence of this whore," and he concludes, "Lechery, lechery, still wars and lechery, nothing else holds fashion. A burning devil take them!" (lines 192–96). There he defines the dominant passions of the play, lechery and battle-lust, largely for their own sakes, not for anything productive.

In V.4 Thersites, again in soliloquy, this time right before he convinces Hector not to fight with him, refers to Nestor as a "stale old mouse-eaten dry cheese" and to Ulysses as "dog-fox," to both Achilles and Ajax as curs, and to the Greeks in general as barbarians (lines 1–16). He even calls himself "a rascal, a scurvy railing knave, a very filthy rogue" (28–29). Hector immediately replies, "I do believe thee," and leaves him alone. In V.7 he begs off another fight — one wonders what he is doing on the battlefield at all — with Margareleon, who appears in the play only for this instance, arguing that as bastards they should respect each other and do each other no harm. Margareleon calls him "coward" and curses him, but also leaves him alone; Thersites serves there only to call the attention of the audience to the fight between Menelaus and Paris: "The cuckold and the cuckold-maker are at it. Now, bull! now, dog!" (lines 9–10). Once again none of the ostensible humor enlightens the characters, but it does tell the audience something about the world of the play: Thersites largely tells the truth, if mean-spiritedly: this world offers us little worth respect or admiration.

Pandarus, the remaining focal point of humor in the play, offers little more: his humor falls flat, and in the last lines of the play it turns into sarcasm and curse. In I.2, as he tries by his charm to win Cressida for Troilus, he mentions an incident where "there was such laughing," but apparently Pandarus has no talent for telling jokes: he actually says nothing funny to make Cressida laugh, and she lampoons his ineptness with her own jests. In III.1 Pandarus is attempting to get help from a servant of Paris, but the servant jokes at Pandarus' expense; Pandarus misses the content of the jokes entirely, "Friend, we understand not one another; I am too courtly and thou too cunning" (lines 27–28). When he does meet Paris and Helen, he addresses them with a nearly incoherent mix of courtliness and familiarity—he even calls Helen "Nell," reducing her to little more than a typical servant girl, and they make fun of the silliness of his locutions. In III.2, having just come from Paris and Helen, he taunts Troilus and Cressida for their blushing and their hesitancy to jump into bed, suggesting they get busy and "press it to death" (line 209). They can't see the danger in kind of precipitous act of lechery that Shakespeare, through Thersites' speech, pairs with war in V.2. An odd, though traditional and ubiquitous pairing, Shakespeare suggests, war and lust: in this thoroughly Ovidean trope Shakespeare embodies the great problem of the play, this blending of excessive and incongruous passions. They don't mix well and in fact produce explosive volatility that subsumes any hope of the characters' learning better. Perhaps lechery comes along as a byproduct of the stresses of war, but in this case the excess of lechery has produced the war to begin with. War we can see as the ultimate horror of excess. Both the Troy story generally and its Troilus and Cressida byproduct foreground those excesses and the typical human inability to reason ourselves out of either once they've begun.

Whether ironically or directly, Shakespeare also filled the play with maxims, many of which clarify or state outright themes or subthemes of the play. In 1.1.14–15, Pandarus, brokering Troilus and Cressida's meeting, adjures, "He that will have a cake out of the wheat must tarry the grinding," obviously counseling patience. Troilus should certainly be willing to show some patience (not to mention *love*) in winning Cressida, but the world of the play as a whole doesn't need patience alone: it needs a sense of right and wrong and willingness to do the right thing.

In a soliloquy in Act I, scene 2, Cressida makes this point to herself: "Therefore this maxim I teach:/ Achievement is command" (lines 292–93): once one has given in to love (or sex), one has lost control of one's body and one's life to the other. Therefore, we must take care to whom we submit. Even knowing better, Cressid does not take sufficient care, and she and Troilus both pay for her (and his) overeagerness. In I.3 Nestor makes a similar point: "choice.../ Makes merit her election" (lines 348–49): we give someone or something approbation or value when we select it—we must therefore take great care in whom and what we choose, because we may not have the opportunity to return and change our choice.

"[P]leasure and revenge/ Have ears more deaf than adders to the voice/

2. Troilus and Cressida *and the Anti-Genre* 63

Of any true decision," says Hector (2.2.171–73): our desire for pleasure or revenge — in Christian if not ancient terms, and so for Shakespeare's audience, a particularly evil kind of pleasure — often closes our minds to clearer thoughts or better choices. Hector makes this point as the Trojans consider returning Helen to the Greeks, which would constitute both a moral and sane choice, returning her to her rightful husband, ending the war, and saving Troy and many lives on both sides. But his point immediately and ironically proves true: the desire of some to keep Helen and of others to avoid dishonor in returning her (and lose the honor of fending off the Greek heroes) outweighs the clarity of thought in which Hector has just argued for her return. His true maxim fails entirely. Shakespeare attacks not the maxim, but our unwillingness to follow wisdom even when we find it before us in the clearest possible terms.

In II.3 Ulysses, as the Greeks try to find a means to get Achilles back on the battlefield, asserts, "The amity that wisdom knits not, folly may easily untie" (lines 101–102): that maxim proves true repeatedly throughout the play. If we fail to apply wisdom to make a friendship work, or if that friendship isn't a wise one to begin with, it will fail: our subsequent foolishness will undoubtedly ruin it. That point proves true: Troilus and Cressida's relationship will fail just as Paris and Helen's will, and Cressid's realignment with Diomed has no hope at all; Pandarus' services to Troilus have immoral bases, so they must lead to no good; Hector and Ajax's friendship is weak and useless to begin with, and any interactions between the warring parties, however courtly, merely provide means for treachery and invasiveness or invasion. "He that is proud eats up himself," Agamemnon says at the end of the scene, ostensibly about Achilles, but it applies to nearly everyone in the play: their proud eats them all, either their honor, their hope of achievement, or their lives. "He will be the physician that should be the patient," Agamemnon adds in III.3.213–14, referring this time to Ajax, just as proud as Achilles but — if we can imagine it possible — even less self-aware. Those points, too, bring to the surface layers of meaning built into the foundations of the play: we must learn to choose friendships and alliances wisely and avoid the pride that will destroy them, and if we would find and cure destructive faults in others, we must excise them from ourselves first.

In III.2, as Cressida prepares to meet Troilus, "giddy" with expectation for their sexual encounter, Troilus warns her, "This [is] monstruosity in love, lady, that the will is infinite and the execution confin'd, that the desire is boundless and the act a slave to the limit" (lines 81–83): he warns her that a man's performance often doesn't live up to a woman's expectations or to his own promises even before they have made love. Ironically deflating and sadly true, that, and equally a warning to all of Shakespeare's audience ... Cressid has already prepared herself, though: "To fear the worst oft cures the worse" (line 73): she hasn't awfully high expectations for their relationship even as it has barely begun. Shortly she will make that point even more clearly: "to be wise and love/ Exceeds a man's might; that dwells with the gods above" (lines 156–57). The first part of that maxim identifies the cause of the war in the play, and the second part rings hollow, as we get no proof for it at all — better, as we saw in Act II, to seek wisdom first and hope for the best in love later.

In III.3 Ulysses uses two maxims to try to win over Achilles, first that a "man ... [c]annot make boast to have that which he hath,/ Nor feels not what he owes, but by reflection" (96–99), and second, that "no man is the lord of any thing.... Till he communicate his parts to others" (115–17). The first makes much the same point as we saw in *The Merchant of Venice*, that nothing has meaning of itself, but rather we come to understand it by perspective: we must see one compared to another to know its value; the second says that someone may something may have skills or intrinsic value, but no one will know about it until we see that virtue on display. Here we get a curious thought with theological implications that actually stands up to critical Christian analysis, and Milton will echo it in *Areopagitica*, a defense of at least limited freedom of the press: virtue comes not merely in thinking about good and right actions, but in doing them. In the Fallen world tests separate assumed virtue from demonstrable virtue. Ulysses will second these thoughts with "Perseverance, my dear lord,/ Keeps honor bright (150–51), and third it with "Love, friendship, charity, are subjects all/ To envious and calumniating Time" (173–74), then to make sure in Nestorian fashion that he has thoroughly pelted Achilles with apothegms, he fourths and fifths him with "The present eye praises the present object" (180) and "things in motion sooner catch the eye" (183). With elements of both the medieval and the modern world, Ulysses not so subtly asks Achilles, "Look, time passes to nothing before you know it, and so do we, so what have you done for us lately?" Later, in Act IV, scene 5, Hector will recapitulate the sentiment: "The end crowns all,/ And that old common arbitrator, Time,/ Will one day end it" (224–26). I don't think Shakespeare was suggesting to his audience that they arm and hurry off to war, but that they make the most of the virtues given them, and that sooner rather than later, an echo of the Parable of the Talents. Later yet in Act III, Patroclus sadly warns Achilles, "Those wounds heal ill that men do give themselves" (229), deepening and adding credence — because he delivers it more out of love than utilitarian purpose — to Ulysses' advice.

In Act IV, scene 4, Troilus warns Cressida, as she is about to leave for the Greek camp, that "sometimes we are devils to ourselves,/ When we will tempt the frailty of our powers" (95–96) — he ruefully notes a point that proves true of nearly everyone in the play and nearly everyone in life, that we believe ourselves stronger than we really are, and we would do better to avoid temptation than to test ourselves with it. Hector tests the frailty of his own powers when he arms to fight despite the warnings of Cassandra and Andromache right before Achilles' men will kill him on the battlefield. "Mine honor keeps the weather of my fate," he proclaims, and "Life every man holds dear, but the dear man/ Holds honor far more precious-dear than life" (5.3.26–28): Hector echoes traditional notions of honor, and quite sententiously at that, but the speech does him little good, it leads to disaster for his family and Troy, and Shakespeare may well have wanted his audience to wonder about it, too. Honor, of course, has great value, but one must know how to separate it from pride and foolhardiness.

Finally, as early as Act I, scene 1, Troilus observes, "Fools on both sides!" (line 90). That is the clearest and most exact statement of the situation of this play, and it specifies the problem that makes *Troilus and Cressida* a problem play: when we watch or read, we inhabit a world of fools from whom we learn or gain nothing. The humor fizzles, the characters fall short of tragic nobility, and the adventures turn sordid. We have neither the joy of comedy, the relief from tragedy, the excitement of adventure, nor illumination of major events of our past. We depart with doubts about heroism, love, honor, fidelity, truth and wit — just as Shakespeare wanted us to do.

3

All's Well That Ends Well
Not Really

It isn't, you know.

That's where the problem comes in: how we get to an end — or anything in between — makes all the difference. Any Christian audience (or ethical person of any stripe) will know that immediately. The means matter, in fact, more than the ends, since short of death our stories don't end: exactly the point toward which Shakespeare directs us in *All's Well That End's Well*. The problem in this play comes from a series of dubious means, leading to unstable and unsatisfying ends. The play follows youthful searches for honor and love, and it begins and ends (and largely indulges throughout) in irony.

Interpretations of *All's Well That Ends Well* vary greatly, particularly with respect to how we should understand Helena and Bertram. With whose troubled and troubling relationship we must begin.[1] The play works with the problem of who has power over another person, how and why he or she gets it, and what results come from such power struggles. Harold Goddard wondered if we may consider the driving vector of the play Helen's and Parolles' struggle to possess Bertram, Helena's tenacious action versus Parolles' empty verbiage. Yes, Helena wins. We could then read allegorically (Shakespeare never resorted to simple allegory, but he allowed himself to suggest it at one level of reading, as it remained a significant mode of literature through and after his time): a true, courageous, romantic love ultimately overcomes a false, cowardly, parasitic love. Much too easy, that.... Or we could say that diligent pursuit of romantic love trumps a dishonorable pursuit of honor — also pretty weak.

But, also allegorically or in terms of character comparisons, we may suspect part of Parolles remains in Bertram.[2] Bertram, whatever one's final judgment of him as character, has not only a soldier's courage, but also unappealing Parollian aspects of the self-important wit and the seducer: he speaks readily and pointedly if not volubly, and he tries to "court," and then to seduce,

3. All's Well That Ends Well

Diana in Florence soon after he is technically (if not happily and willingly) married to Helena. He hardly mourns Helena's absence, and he has no respect for Diana, whatever he may say in passing. We find him subject to the typical sins of a promising and driven but privileged and selfish youth. His courage hardly forgives his arrogant dismissiveness.

Eager to leave his mother's perhaps overbearing influence, he readily places himself under the King's, then resists his King's command as well — anyone around twenty years old (or who can remember what being twenty felt like) will sympathize with his feelings if not the way he acts on them.[3] Those actions, along with Helen's, paralleled by Parolles' and Diana's, drive the thematic tension of the play and take us right to the problem. They don't deal with comedy in any way, but they do move toward Romance — sadly, Romance built on dubious judgments and dangerous feelings. Helen, like Portia in *The Merchant of Venice*, desires a man she believes perfect because of his looks and manners; she doesn't really know much about his character, and any character flaws he reveals don't deter her from pursuing possession of him. Bertram, like Bassanio, pursues what he wants without any real concern for what others around him want or need. If we view them coolly, we must admit that though we understand both of them, and we can admire their energy in pursuit of their goals, we must have a hard time liking either of them. Both allow selfish and unrealistic desires to overwhelm them and to trap them in a nearly solipsistic world of their own. Each readily dissembles to reach the desired end, and each will expect others to participate in dissembling so he or she can get it — and Shakespeare always warns us about dissembling even for what the characters may consider the best of purposes.

More reasonably than we may argue for the power of romantic love or the pursuit of honor, and more convincingly, I think, we can suggest the play shows us that any sort of relationship that aims at possession will (and probably should) fare badly. Dogged insistence on gaining one's beloved without mutual commitment may look for a time like a good idea, in the belief that we may thereby earn love and deserve it by our patience and persistence, but it has unhappy prospects. Similarly, one's search for honor while displaying dishonorable behavior and lack of compassion leads only to cold bitterness, and honor without love leads to an empty life. Romantic relationships — or friendships — require honesty, courage, self-knowledge, knowledge of the other, and equal partnership if we wish them to offer anything stable, dependable, lasting, real, good. Honor through valor requires commitment to a worthy cause, not simply fighting for fighting's sake, because it implies friends and colleagues who observe, share, and value that honor. And such relationships prove hard to come by: most of us, not the human beings we should be, pursue relationships out of selfish motives. We use them to get what we want regardless of what others want, and Shakespeare takes pains to make sure we see the dangers of acting on such wanting.

This play more than any other in Shakespeare's *œuvre* shows the playwright working on that element of our experience, the problem of how we think about and how we try to get what we want. The "happy ending," as in so many of the problem plays that we often call comedies, rings hollow: anyone who believes Bertram has honestly committed to change his feelings and love Helena probably also believes in *Deus ex machinis* and has simply forgotten his behavior through the rest of the narrative. Even if Bertram himself were to think he has changed, why should we believe him, or he himself, without evidence? When Helena returns before the King and court, pregnant and with Bertram's ring, he doesn't beg her pardon and commit himself; he speaks conditionally, and to the king, not to Helena: "If she, my liege, can make me know this clearly/ I'll love her dearly, ever, ever dearly" (5.3.315–16). He has made his promise to her once before the king and abandoned her; what has suddenly changed him now? Has he leaned fidelity by his discovery of Parolles' lack of courage and faith, by his own experience in battle, by simply becoming older and more mature, or does he use an accustomed ploy to get himself out of the commitment that Helena wrung from him with two ploys of her own?

Much of the bad behavior that we see in the young characters comes from poor guidance or lack of guidance: Helena's father has died, and she has no mother or mentor to whom she can go for advice and help except the Countess of Rossillion, and as the play commences she has no reason to believe the Countess will help her in her goal — one would expect rather than opposite because of their different status — though we learn different as the action proceeds.[4] Bertram wishes to get out from under his mother's influence and even the King's, either of whom would at least give caring advice, and he falls instead under the worst possible influence, Parolles', given the nature of his desires. We can easily enough forgive Bertram for falling under the sway of an older, seemingly suave courtier, and we can forgive Helena for having to rely on her own untested resources, but both of their own accord fall into dissembling[5] with the goal of placing others under their control. Shakespeare seems not to like that sort of thinking any more than we do: from Shakespeare's time onward much of our philosophical, political, and economic thought has gradually come around to issues of freedom of thought, speech, and action.

Shakespeare loved to exploit trickery and misdirection and all their effects, how even when we do it with what we identify as the best of motives, it inevitably creates unstable results or relationships. The King concludes the play, "Yet all seems well, and if it end so meet,/ The bitter past, more welcome is the sweet": it may *seem* well, but we don't know if events will go well.[6] Any evidence the play has shown us up to the end suggests it won't and perhaps even shouldn't: however much we may admire Helena's persistence, cleverness, courage, and fidelity, do we want persons to pursue us unceasingly even after we've repeatedly told them we have no interest in them? In our time, don't we call that harassment, and wouldn't Shakespeare's audience have seen that kind of behavior particularly inappropriate in a woman, but nearly as much so in a man as well? While someone must make the first move, real love comes from mutual engagement, not from one person imposing an obsession on another. So, as with *The Merchant of Venice*, "no comedy tonight...." And as David Bevington concludes, "This is not a comedy about the heady pleasures and risks of young love" (91). As in The *Merchant of Venice* and *Troilus and Cressida*, Shakespeare makes sure the humor falls short of jollity and the end falls short of settled and anything desirable.

Because this play ends with the affirmation of a marriage[7] that the partners are willing to express in language we can construe as happy, with authority still in place and properly obeyed, and with the authorities having uncovered for the youth the bad behaviors that could corrupt and ruin their lives, *All's Well* moves close to comedy, but it lacks the fun and lightness that makes a comedy work as such on the stage. As I consider what lies ahead for the characters, I find it quite a mixed situation indeed. The ending leaves both the audience and the world of the play full of uncertainty, I would say even with a fair degree of sadness, but the play certainly falls short of tragic. Having no historical basis, it focuses on the pursuit of marriage and honor rather than on any persons or event we need to know. Of all the standard genre options, it comes closest to Romance. But again, as in *Troilus and Cressida* and to some extent *The Merchant of Venice*, the unstable ending and the means of reaching that ending undermine Romance and turn the play once again toward the *anti-*genre rather than into the midst of a tradition. The anti–Romance elements and the questionable characters of the combatants-at-love create the play's problems: petulance and obsession don't lead to useful resolutions, but to the consideration of how to deal with the problems they raise.

The biggest problem with the play comes from its title: "All's well that ends well" has the force of cliché, something we may often express and accept without questioning it and that may or may not hold up to actual experience. But we meet nearly as big a problem when we consider the ending and our response to it: do we really feel happy with it? Does it cleanse our emotions or add to our concern for how humans treat one another in the world? And we must ask not only whether the title proves true in the play: does it ever prove true in art or in life?[8] We can too easily take the title as an assertion about the meaning of the play without considering its ironic implications both in the play and in actual experience. Does anyone really believe that, in any endeavor, if we get the result we set out to get, the means, processes, pathways, and all the good and bad things we did on the way to that end don't matter, that we may or even can forget them as insignificant? Can we justify in any reasonable way the similar notion that "the ends justify the means"? We may at times forgive ourselves for acting poorly on the way to getting what we want, but we seldom fully forgive others who have trodden over us on the way to what they want. Both the title and the end of the play urge us to ask what we believe about those questions, and the means in the middle suggest we had better not to readily rely on cliché.

Also, though not one of Shakespeare's more powerfully poetic (in the sense of *lyrical*) plays, *All's Well* does repeatedly hinge on odd and intense turns of language, troublesome exchanges, rhetorical devices, and problematic utterances: in some ways one could call it a *language play*, since not much action occurs on stage, and the play of words makes the biggest impact on how we understand the process and product of the narrative. So in the remainder of this chapter we'll look first at anti-Romantic unfolding of character, much as Shakespeare does it in *Troilus and Cressida*, and second at the anti-comic web of language. The play doesn't stray into the realm of tragedy (unless one considers a bad marriage a tragedy) or history, though it frequently echoes motifs of filial disloyalty and the selfish use of others that drive many of the tragedies and histories. It does, typically for a Shakespeare play, readily undercut popular if sentimental notions of comedy and romance.

Replacing T & C with B & H, with P Thrown in for Bad Measure

All's Well comes from around the same time as *Troilus and Cressida*. They precede the plays that we may more willingly posit as proper Romances, and they share a tendency to undermine the essential notions of Romance by troubling notions of how we may gain honor and honorable love. We can do a pretty interesting and helpful reading of *All's Well* if we think of Bertram and Helena as replacements for Troilus and Cressida (not exclusively) and Parolles as a replacement for Pandarus. Helena, like Troilus rather than Cressida, represents a kind of (that not necessarily appealing) fidelity. Parolles seduces Bertram into battle as Pandarus helps Troilus seduce Cressida into bed. Neither Helena nor Bertram experiences fear the way Chaucer's Cressida does, but each makes a commitment to "battle" as Troilus does generally. This kind of reading has the virtue of showing how in *All's Well* Shakespeare continues working with the some of the same themes and concerns that appear in *Troilus and Cressida* and a number of the other plays from around the same time: the importance of recognizing what *honor* really means and not falling into false, misleading notions of it; the dangers of failing in our promises of fidelity or in our vows or commitments to family, friends, and ideals; we must all hope that the presence of *mercy* has greater strength than the trouble we create by our own errors (even if that mercy will not at last appear with sufficient strength to save us in this world); when we take chances and place our desires ahead of our reason or our compassion for others, we beg for our own destruction.[9] Quite a powerful list, and Shakespeare returns to them often and insistently.

If we think of Bertram as a version of Troilus, he begins rather more like Chaucer's Troilus than like Shakespeare's: with a level of disdain for women and joy only in the idea of honor through battle.[10] The Troilus of Chaucer's Romance, Henryson's moral poem, and even Shakespeare's play shows a similar detachment, though he also has behind me a good deal of combat experience at the time we take up his story. Bertram asserts that what he wants — to leave his home to seek adventure — comprises the King's command, and he shows no patience with his mother's concerns. Perhaps he sees them as false or disingenuous, or perhaps he simply doesn't care: Bertram doesn't show himself as a person of compassionate feelings. He begs the King not to tie him to Helena, but failing in his suit, flees to Florence to fight, again preferring his own choice to the duty he claims as his rationale in I.1.5. For a brief time he gains, Troilus-like, success in war, but not for any significant purpose: he wants a *place* to fight to show that he has courage and fortitude, not a *cause* for which to fight — he doesn't care about that. Troilus, of course, fights to defend his city and people from destruction at the hands of fierce and committed invaders. Bertram suggests a lesser Troilus, one whose motivations derive from a floating, Romantic sense of personal accomplishment rather than any public need. Shakespeare's Troilus then becomes a lesser Bertram: once he loses Cressid, he fights only in a mad frenzy of vengeance; at least Bertram nominally and publicly comes at last to express (reluctantly) some regret for his actions and appreciation for Helena's sacrifices, and unlike Troilus he will have a chance to make up for any mistakes or to grow past lust for battle into more of a complete, mature being — if only we could believe his claim that he will "love her dearly, ever, ever dearly" (5.3.316). Like Troilus, Bertram, in his attempt to seduce Diana, pursues an unattached girl, but clandestinely, and he tries to bed her out of wedlock; where Troilus succeeds, Bertram does not, meeting in his dark rendezvous his wife instead. Bertram ends up with a loving — but obsessed — wife, while Troilus ends up on the way to death in battle; there the narrative changes, but with little hint that Bertram believes he will find more happiness than Troilus does: Helena has won him by the infamous "bed trick," so how can he feel content with that? Again he has lost the freedom he had barely won, a battle he has fought desperately. Has his brief war experience satisfied his youthful desire for honor and glory, or after the events of the play will he simply leave Helena again to pursue his own concept of honor? Some readers may think it useless to guess what will happen after the confines of the play, but I think Shakespeare in nearly every play urges us to ask that very question. It proves essential to an understanding of *A Midsummer Night's Dream*, *Twelfth Night*, *Much Ado About Nothing*, *The Merchant of Venice*, and *The Tempest*, just to name a few, and in *Henry V* he makes explicit what happens after so that we may have that information at hand to help us contemplate the actions and results of the play: all that Henry has won, the next generation will lose, and civil war will result.

Bertram's struggle for and ultimate loss of freedom parallels him also to Cressida. Because her father has left Troy, in one sense understandably for self-preservation, though in another as a betrayer of his city, Cressida hasn't the freedom she might want either to live as she chooses in Troy (because of the taint on her family) or to leave to join him (because of the dangers of war and the Greek camp). Bertram chooses to leave home probably to avoid the overprotectiveness of his mother, but he finds another aggressively demanding figure in the King, whose rule he must also flee. He has given up his freedom of reason to a terrible adviser, Parolles, who leads him into both deadly and damnable trouble in Florence, from which his courage in battle (and the merciful brevity of the war, which seems not to have had too serious a cause) and his good luck in general (including Helena's obsessive ministrations) finally deliver him. His good luck rather than Cressid's bad leads him to the potential for a happier ending, which at the end of the play he has the option of accepting or rejecting once again. Helena's attentions to Bertram should prove safer than Diomed's to Cressid, but they may still not lead to happiness, since he is married to a woman he has admitted hating.[11] Will her successful plot now make him love her, any more than Cressid, who in a kind of necessity for protection accepts a Diomed who intends nothing but to exploit her, will continue to love Diomed?

Helena appears not as this play's Cressid, other than as another version of the soon-to-be-scorned woman: she has much more courage, character, and wit to act. Rather, she appears here as a second Troilus: having fixed on her love, she goes through whatever she must to get him, and she beds him against his will. Chaucer, who treats both Cressid and Troylus more sympathetically than does Shakespeare, shows their first sexual encounter in images of rape: Troylus leaps on Criseyde like a hawk grasping a lark to devour it, with palpable violence. Helena gets her man through tenacious pursuit, cagey dissembling that puts another woman, Diana, in potentially dangerous and degrading circumstances, and by winning a rash promise from the monarch who commands him.[12] Helena expects, then, afterward, faithfulness from

3. All's Well That Ends Well

Bertram — but, again, have we sufficient reason to believe he will fulfill her wish? She has Troylus' fixed sense of purpose: "my intents are fix'd, and will not leave me" (1.1.229). But that doesn't mean Bertram will share her fixity (or fixation): he has shown himself youthfully irrational, mutable, and exploitative, and he may well have gone to Paris believing Parolles' notion of the "thousand loves" to which a noble and attractive young man may find access.[13] Like Troylus, Helena may well have chosen to see Bertram as tartish; like Troylus she chooses fidelity anyway; unlike Troylus she spares no ends to stick to her beloved and believe her love will produce in him a commitment to fidelity. Like Bertram and Troylus Helena shows courage — she shows perhaps more than they do, as she puts her life at stake without even a sword in hand for self-defense — but she shows a commitment to what she wants that borders on Ahabian monomania.

While Chaucer (unlike Shakespeare) creates a grown-up couple who make choices with some worldly knowledge — Criseyde is a widow and Troylus already a veteran soldier — *All's Well*'s couple still dwell fully in the romantic notions of youth. Troylus and Criseyde may follow the urging of Pandarus, but they act on their own desires having considered the implications of their choices: they come to bad ends that seemed to them from the beginning of their relationship as stark possibilities. Bertram gives no evidence of having considered the ramifications of his actions, and Helena tells us she has pushed them off and will not consider them: she commits to her fixation. Helena and Bertram both represent a youthful Troilus: driven, selfish, emotional, brave, romantic (though for different ends, love and honor, respectively), insistent, immature, precipitous — and suffering from a typical youthful lack of scope. We can read the play as Shakespeare's commentary on exactly that sort of character. Here, by good fortune and the fact that no army of heroes is relentlessly besieging their city, they reach a point where happiness *may* lie ahead for them. As passionate and talented young persons, they may make a good couple, but only if they can learn to change radically: Helena must become less obsessive and fixated, and Bertram must become less selfish and must find a way to love a young woman he has despised. While he may admire her tenacity and find ego gratification in the fact that she will do anything to win him, the reasons for his dismissing her remain. Her background and social class haven't changed. He will still find himself stripped of the freedom to seek adventure that he sought; can he really love a woman who has enforced confinement on him? And will Helena, once she has got him, love the real Bertram, not her romantic idealization of him, after she gains the day-to-day experience of life in his company and perhaps under *his* control? She, too, will have lost the freedom of movement and choice that she has had. Shakespeare, as we so often find, deals despite romantic settings with the issues of real life. Do these characters have the traits, experiences, or even desire to live happily with the spouse they are poised to acquire?

The Pandarus in this play leads the young couple not to sexual consummation, but away from it. Parolles urges Bertram not to accept Helena or even the King's command, but to steal away to the wars — in this case, to a war in which none among our characters has anything serious invested. Those interested in war may go, the King says, for the sake of experience, to avoid getting stale, and may fight on either side they want! The King himself will help neither side in the conflict, though he has allies involved. Parolles draws Bertram into war rather than the bedroom, but he conducts no less of a seduction than his parallel in *Troilus and Cressida*. In II.3 "What's the matter, sweet heart?" Parolles ask Bertram. "O, my Parolles, they have married me!" Bertram replies in disgust. Parolles follows him there, "France is a dog-hole, and it no more merits/ The tread of a man's foot. To th' wars! ... To th'wars, my boy, to th' wars!" (lines 268–78). As so many Achaeans (Greeks) found themselves drawn into ten long years of war at Troy, Bertram makes the same choice, though in this case for satire rather than epic-sorrow: he fights with no purpose but to fight and would as willingly have fought on either side, as the conflict has no apparent purpose in the play (certainly not for the French mercenaries, who go only for exercise).[14] Having got Bertram that far, Parolles, in an act of phony bravery, gets himself caught and duped by soldiers of his own side who scare him into a false betrayal: he answers his own failure by saying to himself "that's who I am, so I have acted and will continue to act according to my nature": he essentially bequeaths the audience his diseases, as does Pandarus at the end of *Troilus and Cressida*. Parolles gets his forgiveness, gets a place in the household of Lafew, who has scorned and hated him, and suggests to the audience as a character that betraying your fellows doesn't come out all that badly if you get lucky and admit your failings — an idea that Shakespeare repeatedly either condemns or satirizes through the course of his work. In that sense, Parolles emerges as an even more dangerous character than the equally willing Pandarus, who betrays fewer friends and, at least to begin with, perhaps has rather better motivations.

The play includes several other significant references to the Troy story. In I.3, when the Countess calls for Helen, Lavatch sings, recalling the line from Marlowe's *Doctor Faustus*, "'Was this fair face the cause,' quoth she,/ "Why the Grecians sacked Troy?/ Fond done, done fond,/ Was this King Priam's joy?'" (lines 71–73). By *fond* he means, of course, *foolish*: from a distance we can see the cause of the Trojan War as silly, too, but we can even more readily see the foolishness in Helena's following a Bertram who doesn't love her to Paris, in the King's agreement with Helena, and in Bertram's mad dash to war to flee her. Later in I.3 the Steward's speech to the Countess about

Helena's sorrowful expression of love for Bertram contains a possible allusion to Henryson's Cresseid, who cursed the gods for her misfortunes:

> Fortune, she said, was no goddess, that had put such difference betwixt their two estates; Love no god, that would not extend his might only where qualities were level; [Diana no] queen of virgins, that would suffer her poor knight surpris'd without rescue ... [lines 111–15].

Helena's echo of the leprous Cresseid implies that she too has a kind of wasting disease: perhaps Shakespeare's point about a love unlikely to find requital and the emotional extent to which youths push themselves in pursuit of what, without much reason beyond the good looks of another, they believe they must have or die. The Countess's suggesting Helena think of her as a mother recalls the astonishing and appalling scene in Book 24 of the *Iliad* where Priam appears suddenly before Achilles in his tent in the Greek camp to try to claim Hector's body to conduct proper funeral rights. Homer's scene, both moving and horrifyingly sad, has Achilles see his own father in Troy's king; he learns thereby a sense of compassion, but the idea also repels him partly as demeaning but partly because he wants to maintain his hatred of the Trojans so he may bring down their city both for his glory and for revenge. The Countess shows extraordinary generosity and love towards Helena, which Helena finds both moving and appalling: she must appreciate it, but she doesn't want to think of Bertram, the man she wants, as her brother: she draws away much as does Homer's hero. In II.1 Lafew calls himself "Cressid's uncle" who "dare leave two together" (lines 97–98): he refers to bringing Helena, whom he has praised, to treat the King's illness. The allusion bears two meanings: Lafew seems to intend the good will result from their meeting, but the allusion rather hints that as the go-between he is causing more harm than good — the line might better have applied to his leaving Bertram and Parolles together, except that in this case it establishes Lafew as not an entirely trustworthy character, either. He discerns the failings and dangers of Parolles' company, but he has his own self-serving goals as well: he isn't trustworthy as a touchstone of wisdom in the poem. Diana serves the play as a better touchstone, almost as a Cassandra, a prophet for the world of this story. No one wants to believer her at court until Helen appears to release her from trouble, but reflecting on Bertram earlier she makes one of the most important points of the play: "'tis a most gallant fellow./ I would he lov'd his wife. If her were honester/ He were much goodlier" (3.5.78–80).

In Act IV, scene three, one of the ubiquitous lords makes a similar point that would apply as well to *Troilus and Cressida* as to this play (and to many other Shakespeare plays and the *Iliad* as well), but extends its implications: "The web of our life is of a mingled yarn, good and ill together; our virtues would be proud, if our faults whipt them not, and our crimes would despair, if they were not cherish'd by our virtues" (lines 71–74). We meet good and bad, we do good and bad; we could feel proud of our virtues if sins didn't taint them, but fall into despair over our sins if our virtues didn't appear to rescue us. If he had only added the fear of punishment and the astonishing joy of unexpected mercy, he'd have spoken the play in little. It ends, pointing a finger toward *Measure for Measure*, with the King of France repeating a mistake he has already made and that the Duke of Vienna makes at the end of *Measure*: arranging more marriages at his own whim without the consent of the parties involved. Given what we've seen, how can anyone feel confident that kind of action, any more than war, can lead to happiness?

Courtly, Private and Personal Language: Who's Fooling Whom?

From the very beginning of the play Shakespeare uses some odd and even occasionally irritating language. The Countess of Rossillion begins the play, as Bertram is taking his leave from her court, with thoroughly formal words: "In delivering my son from me, I bury a second husband." The conjunction of birth and death metaphors rings grandiloquent and even a trifle cold. His leaving means for her a second birthing, but also his death to her by means of his departure and subsequent absence, two sources of terrible pain and sacrifice — not the sort of parting words that will make leaving easier for Bertram, either. Bertram doesn't seem any the better for that, as he replies, "And I in going, madam, weep o'er my father's death anew; but I must attend his Majesty's command, to whom I am now in ward, evermore in subjection." Either her point has given him additional pain as well, so that he must choke down thoughts of his father's death, or he is simply following what formal public dialogue requires of him, a statement of filial love. Regardless of his "real" feelings he is merely leaving one sort of subjection for another: the King will stand both as his liege and as a substitute father, allowing Bertram no more freedom that he suggests he has had in his mother's court. Lord Lafew then adds, "You shall find of the King a husband, madam; you, sir, a father." He means that the King will treat her son as if her were the lad's father, not that the King will act toward the Countess as a husband would toward a wife — quite an improper notion and rather inexactly if tersely spoken. And to expect the King to go so far as to treat Bertram as a son also stretches both likelihood and all reasonable hope for generosity: to treat him well, yes, but to treat him as a son, and thus an heir, preposterous. Fortunately for them, though not really for Bertram, the King agrees to do so.

To send Bertram to the King at all sounds inappropriate given the King's state of health: his illness, whatever Shakespeare was implying by a "fistula," must be threatening his life[15]: Lafew explains, "He hath abandon'd his physicians, madam, under whose practices he hath persecuted time with hope, and finds no other advantage in the process but only the losing of hope by time" (lines 13–16), an elaborate (and apparently in this world courtly) way of saying no one has helped him and he has given up hope of recovery.

Before Bertram departs he asks for the Countess's "holy wishes" (59); Lafew doesn't understand what he means, and Bertram probably doesn't mean what he says: he wants her permission without too many hindrances on his intentions. His mother gives him instead a litany of formal directives reminiscent of Polonius's advice to Laertes in *Hamlet*—in fact the her words and even her cadence follow the same, typical "fatherly advice" pattern, though more briefly. She advises,

> ... [S]ucceed thy father
> In manners as in shape. Thy blood and virtue
> Contend for empire in thee, and thy goodness
> Share with thy birthright! Love all, trust a few,
> Do wrong to none. Be able for thine enemy
> Rather in power than use, and keep they friend
> Under thy own life's key. Be check'd for silence,
> But never tax'd for speech. What heaven more will,
> That thee may furnish, and my prayers pluck down,
> Fall on thy head! [1.1.61–70].

She concludes by asking Lord Lafew, apparently a court favorite and her trusted advisor, not Parolles, Bertram's friend whom Helena tells us no one else trusts, to offer more, but he declines, apparently satisfied with what the Countess has already said. He can offer no love where she cannot, and he can offer no more traditional wisdom than she has already done, because he knows no more about Bertram's motivations or about Helena's intentions toward Bertram. Really good advice proves hard to come by. The hint of familial coldness rings distant, sad, and true.

Polonius's famous speech details advice both true and useful and also cliché: Shakespeare's audience had heard it all before—a collection of old saws, in fact—but that doesn't make it any the less true or worth repeating. The language of the Countess's speech, though terse and pithy, doesn't parse easily, and it has ambiguities typical of this play. She says, here in paraphrase,

> Gee, you look like your dad. May your noble heritage and youthful energy balance with the virtue [that we've taught you and you'd better remember!]. Let people know you're good as well as nobly born. Love everyone [as a Christian, you must], but don't trust much of anyone, and wrong no one [the best way to stay out of

trouble]. Keep up your strength and skill in case you need to fight, but stay out of any fight you can. Value your friends, and keep them close by treating them so well they won't want to betray you. If anyone censures you, let it be for talking too little rather than too much [don't be like Parolles!]. Do what God would want you to do, but don't be dangerously generous! And may my prayers bring you good fortune!

Be good, be frugal, be like your father, and be safe: that advice might come from any parent. It lacks, though, a bit of feeling: nothing of "I'll miss you! Give me a hug!" Like her words that begin the play, they deal more with her than with her son: an obligation to say something solemn and parental, even sovereign, rather stodgier even than Polonius's (and that takes some doing). He seems either to know or to feel that, and he ignores the lot. Does the Countess speak for Bertram's sake, for her court's, or for her own?

That opening scene creates a tone that remains to some extent throughout the play, one of stiff and cold formality and lack of concern for the needs and wants of others, even those whom one loves or advises or from whom one asks considerable favors. It applies the formal language of court aptly, but shows little genuine human connection or affection — a good dose of logic, but little of any expression of emotion that can move the reader or suggest the participants feel moved themselves. The sense of a lack of honest and deep emotion changes when the others exit and Helena remains on stage alone: her soliloquy, as Shakespeare's characters' often do, rings truer, if nearly as cold and even more overtly selfish — honest and perhaps deep, but lacking compassion.

While the Countess believes Helena feels sad because she mourns her dead father, she tells us otherwise:

> I think not on my father....
> What was he like?
> I have forgot him. My imagination
> Carries no favor in't but Bertram's.
> I am undone, there is no living, none,
> If Bertram be away. 'Twere all one
> That I should love a bright particular star
> And think to wed it, he is so above me....
> Th'ambition in my love this plagues itself:
> The hind that would be mated by the lion
> Must die for love. 'Twas pretty, though a plague,
> To see him every hour ... and my idolatrous fancy
> Must sanctify his reliques [1.1. 79–98].

She says quite plainly that she doesn't care at all about her father's death, only about her love for Bertram, a love she knows she has no right to expect to come to fruition, because he stands above her socially. Yet obviously she is thinking of marrying him anyway. He apparently has given her no encouragement, shown no interest, thinks of her as well below him — he has inherited the title Count, and though the Countess does refer to Helena as "daughter" and herself with respect to Helena as mother, Helena by class is at best her "gentlewoman" (line 17), in this case trusted member of her retinue, but still technically a servant. Helena makes an assertion fairly typical of a young lover: I'll die without him.[16] Her own love, like the King's fistula, eats her alive; or, as the lion would eat a deer, Bertram would kill her if he she made her attentions clear to him. He has even become a kind of idol to her: everything he leaves behind becomes has a blasphemous, fetishized power over her. In our youth we may, in our own thoughts, turn the beloved into what we want him or her to be, paying no attention to the real person who may or may not deserve our admiration.

Therein lie the problems of this speech: she fails in her love for the father she knew and believes she loves a young man she barely knows, other than by his looks and courtly manners — a bit the way Portia (who should be much smarter and more worldly) loves Bassanio. Unless we pay attention, we may tend to agree with Helena as we often do with Jessica in *The Merchant of Venice*, out of sympathy for the constrained youth we want to see happy. Helena, lost in her romanticism, will still attempt to reach a "star" and cure a "plague" when she wagers her life to cure the King. Ironically, she neither makes nor understands the medicine. She relies for it on what her father has left her, and she willfully dismisses her memory of her him in that conundrum: I think not on my father. To get what she wants, she must dismiss both what he must have taught her and religious precepts against trying to control another person. She must fool herself into abandoning ideas of decorum, free will, and spirituality to reach a nebulous goal: what will marriage with Bertram be like if she forces him into it? But she will fool herself, the King, and Bertram to get him regardless.

We may see here a parallel to Antonio, who says to others that he can't explain his sadness — perhaps he simply won't explain it to them or doesn't want even to clarify it for himself. Helena will mislead others about her grief, but in private she at least unveils the truth to herself. The problem for the audience lies, then, in how we will process that truth against what she does. Do we accept and respect self-honesty even when it results in improper behavior? Experience tells us that often love comes of its own accord: we may have little control over with whom we fall in love. But Christian tradition, philosophical tradition, and Shakespeare's use of both suggest we have control over — or at least responsibility for — how we act in response to that love. Do we accept, in *All's Well*, any means to reach the goal that don't rely on free will and responsible moral choice?

We may also note that Helena and the King make a bond reminiscent of that of Antonio and Shylock: kill me horribly and painfully if I fail to deliver, Helena says, and, I think oddly, the King agrees to the bond. He has nothing to lose, so why not simply let her try? He has apparently reached a point of frustration and despair with his illness that will not allow another failed cure. Why, though, allow a young person with great potential to risk her life for him? The move adds drama, but lacks compassion — another common turn of character and narrative in *All's Well*.

Following Helena's soliloquy comes the dialogue on virginity between Helena and Parolles. She knows him for a "notorious liar ... fool ... a coward" (100–101), but she will love him for Bertram's sake, because Bertram does. There, where she has just shown truth to herself, she tries to fool herself: no one could get herself to love someone after what she has just said of him; she will try, but she will fear for Bertram in the company of such a man. Parolles addresses her as "fair queen" and she him as "monarch": they must have had playful dialogues, matching wits, before to move so quickly into repartee. "Are you meditating on virginity?" he asks, an odd and intrusive question indeed, unless they have joked similarly before, he knows or suspects something about her obsession with Bertram, or he intends to try to seduce her.

Helena then shifts the metaphor: "You have some strain of soldier in you.... Man is enemy to virginity; how may we barricado against him?" (111–13). Parolles asserts that women have no defense: "Man, setting down before you, will undermine you and blow you up" (118–19). In the midst of a number of bawdy puns, he argues for the uselessness of virginity: "Loss of virginity is rational increase, and there was never virgin [got] till virginity was first lost" (127–29); "To speak on the part of virginity is to accuse your mothers, which is most infallible disobedience" (136–38); "virginity murthers itself, and should be buried in highways out of all sanctified limit, as a desperate offendress[17] against nature" (138–40); "virginity is peevish, proud, idle, made of self-love, which is the most inhibited sin in the canon" (144–45). Helena then replies as if she has accepted his argument, but tries to retain some free choice: "How might one do, sir, to lose it to her own liking?" (150). Parolles sidesteps the question by suggesting what sounds like either prostitution or gold-digging: "'Tis a commodity will lose the gloss with lying: the longer kept, the less worth. Off with't while 'tis vendible; answer the time of request" (153–55). He suggests that she not choose for herself, but sell her virginity to the first man who makes an offer, so that she doesn't get so old that no one will take an interest.

After a series of images of withered fruit, he asks Helena, "Will you any thing with it?" (163–64), meaning her virginity: he must be asking either for Bertram or for himself. When she says no, he tries to rouse her jealousy or

3. All's Well That Ends Well

her despair: at the King's court Bertram will learn about the world and have "a thousand loves," and he follows with a long, strange list of them:

> A mother, and a mistress, and a friend,
> A phoenix, captain, and an enemy,
> A guide, a goddess, and a sovereign,
> A counselor, a traitress, and a dear;
> His humble ambition, proud humility;
> His jarring concord, and his discord dulcet;
> His faith, his sweet disaster; with a world
> Of pretty, fond, adoptious christendoms
> That blinking Cupid gossips [166–74].

Bertram's loves will include, Parolles lists, a woman who will treat him in a motherly way, a sex object, a confidant, someone he will find (or at least say he finds) unique among women, someone who will guide him, someone who will rule him, someone who will advise him, someone who will betray him (but whom he'll "love" anyway, out of the youthful fashion for painful romantic love), someone who will treat him kindly and to whom he'll feel emotionally close. Parolles then gives two lines of oxymorons, each line structured as a chiasmus. He may mean that Bertram will love, as if they were women, his sense of his own ambition and humility, as well as instances when things look difficult but turn out well, or when their difficulty brings a sense of romantic sweetness. He may mean that Bertram will love women who flatter his ambition and his humility and those who give him a difficult time, regardless of how the love affair goes, as long as he finds them appealing. This relatively accurate if equally silly retinue of youthful romantic dreams hardly deters Helena; it merely reminds her of the fact that she comes from a lower class and of her desire not only to wish him well, but to be physically near him so she might do well by him.

Helena then briefly appears to be flattering Parolles for his warlike courage, but she quickly turns to quips so she can insult him for running away rather than fighting, probably to get even for his rousing her jealousy over Bertram. Hearing that insult, which Parolles knows but doesn't want to admit as true, he excuses himself, asking for her prayers and suggesting she get a good husband. After those insults he knows immediately he will gain from Helena neither something to prop his ego nor any hope of a successful seduction. Lost entirely in himself, he can gain nothing, so he will try to do nothing for her.

By herself, Helena concludes the first scene with another soliloquy, structured as a sonnet of couplets, about her own circumstance and how she will respond to it. I will excerpt from it here to call attention to what Shakespeare reveals of Helena's thought processes:

> Our remedies oft in ourselves do lie,
> Which we ascribe to heaven. The fated sky
> Gives us free scope, only doth backward pull
> Our slow designs when we ourselves are dull....
> Impossible be strange attempts to those
> That weigh their pains in sense, and do suppose
> What hath been cannot be. Who ever strove
> To show her merit, that did miss her love?

Helena recognizes and asserts a belief in free will: we may effect our own ends, if we commit to them, and we can't depend on God to give us what we want — life doesn't work that way. Heaven allows us a range of action, and we must exploit that range: if we fall short of it, we must take the blame, because we lack the will to reach our goals. If we see the suffering our attempts may produce, we may see our goals as unreachable, but then we fail to remember that others in the past have striven and won the ends they sought. Those who make an unrestrained effort will find the love they seek, but the one who fails in love may fail also to have the strength to show her merits thereafter: there she concludes, with a dubious assertion indeed.

While we know that in life we may only reach our goals by working for them, even forcing ourselves to the far reaches of our abilities to get them, striving alone doesn't achieve them: we must also have luck, health, and opportunity. What we often tell young people, and what Helena tells herself here, however noble the sentiment, that we can get whatever we want if we want it badly enough and try hard enough, simply isn't always true. More often than not we fall short of the goal, though we achieve more than we would had we not made the commitment to work at all. Helena suffers from the same youthful delusion as Bertram: I can get what I want (honor, love) if I pursue it with all energy regardless of circumstance or what others tell me. The truth that Shakespeare knew is that we may get it or we may not, and once we get it, it may prove worthwhile or it may not: often the end won't live up to expectations. The end doesn't matter nearly so much as the means and the process of getting there. We don't know if, at the end of the play, Helena and Bertram have learned anything about that lesson. We do know that in whatever action happens after the narrative of the play, they will have to deal with the consequences of the choice they've made, and those consequences may lead to some happiness, or they may not. All isn't well that ends well because, while we live, we don't reach an end: we reach the next point from which we must make choices and take new action. We can hope that the experiences that come from our choices will produce pleasure and betterment for ourselves and those others affected by them.

The other message at the end of Helena's speech suggests something even more problematic: all of one's success and happiness depends on winning the beloved. If that were true, anyone who ever fails in a love affair will never do anything worthwhile thereafter: an adolescent romantic sentiment, not the sort of truth we would expect from a more practical Beatrice or Rosalind. Sometimes we believe our first "love," especially once it has ended badly, will be our only love—a dangerous notion that can lead to terrible choices and terrible waste.

Those themes, plus the fact that *All's Well* shows us some good in its characters, makes it a somewhat brighter play than either *The Merchant of Venice* or *Troilus and Cressida*. It remains a problem play because it resists genre classification and leaves us with several difficult-to-solve problems. The King has found his cure and has shown generosity toward Helena, and generosity tends to lead toward happiness, and Helena has cured the king and so won her husband of choice, drawing it close to comedy. But Bertram has ditched her before and has lied to the King, and he has still not clarified, only hinted, that he feels ready to accept a bride of low birth, regardless of what honors the King may bestow upon her. Shakespeare's young men tend to fail in their promises. So we have yet to find a reason to trust that Bertram will become a good husband: he may still prefer glory in battle and sneak off at the first opportunity to win the martial honor he has shown us he values most. Helena still has a husband she can't trust and an obsession she can't shake, so her happiness still hangs on the thread of his willingness to remain with her—and what might his death in battle do to her, since, regardless of his youthful courage, he can't have acquired sufficient skill to protect himself in combat, where chance as well as a superior foe can bring swift and implacable disaster? In her willingness to accept Helena as a daughter, the Countess, like the King, has grown toward a sense of human value and equality unusual among the elite. Though the King still makes rash choices, allowing Helena the husband of her choice takes away all choice from the man she picks—a point Bertram makes clear with which the audience may—improperly—fail to sympathize. Both Countess and King have shown willingness to raise the state of a poor but good person and to recognize the failings of either high- or low-born who act badly—and chastise them for it (part of what makes a good sovereign in Shakespeare's world). But Helena and Bertram, not the Countess and the King, remain the central figures of the play, and they fail to learn the lessons that their more worthy elders might teach them. Without that wisdom, they depart the narrative of the play poised for disaster and unhappiness—not a formula for comedy.

The play diverges from comedy and tragedy, but it does have some of the central traits of Romance, parallel in some ways to *Cymbeline*, *Pericles*, and *The Winter's Tale*. It has adventure (Helena's and Bertram's quests), love (at least on one side), and something akin to magic (Helena's father's prescription which seems to have the virtue to cure any illness). But it lacks the magnitude and moral weight of good Romance. Romance employs something of the grandeur of epic, and we see little action here: that occurs offstage. We hear language about action and language about love, but we depart the play with the great question of free will unanswered: while the superior person may make demands on an inferior, what demands may he or she reasonably make? While the inferior may win a chance to direct a superior, does he or she ever do well to take advantage of it? While Shakespeare struggled with nascent notions of personal and social freedom, his plays suggest that he believed still in degree: we owe a debt of respect and reverence to rank and office, however painful that idea may prove in practice.[18] In Shakespeare's world breaking degree — breaking the Great Chain of Being — can lead, if we don't take care, to tragedy; taking away another's freedom, particularly if that person has yet done nothing wrong, nearly always leads, in the absence of divine or powerful sovereign intervention, to suffering, disaster, and revenge.[19] Though the idea of mercy sits at the center of many Shakespeare plays, forgiveness often proves hard to get, hard to give, and weak in its own defense.

Shakespeare packed Act I not with beautiful poetry, but with difficult and troubling poetry. Pride, commoditization, hidden motives, obsessions, dubious affections and advice, and even lies: the stuff of Act I could as readily lead to tragedy as comedy, if we had sufficiently noble protagonists. Act II moves us in the direction of courage and honor, motifs that can save the world if they work or damn it if they fail. Act III shows us Bertram gaining military success, but already plotting to use that honor to seduce Diana, to the loss of her honor. In II.2, the Countess asks a lord to forward to her son the message that "his sword can never win/ The honor that he loses" though immoral behavior (lines 92–93), one of the main themes of the play. We find Helena plotting, dissembling, and lying. We see more of Lavatch's silly clowning and Parolles' parallel blustering: the nominal clown with the false hero. Act IV gives a lengthy account of Parolles' betrayal of his fellows paralleled with Bertram's betrayal of Helena in the attempt to bed Diana. In one of the truly troubling speeches of the play — more so than those of Parolles, from whom we expect bad behavior — Bertram gives a chilling list of his evening's activities:

> I have to-night dispatch'd sixteen businesses, a month's length a-piece, by an abstract of success: I have congied with the Duke, done my adieu with his nearest; buried a wife, mourn'd for her, writ to my lady mother I am returning, entertain'd my convoy, and between these main parcels of dispatch [effected] many nicer deeds. The last was the greatest, but that I have not ended yet [4.3.85–92].

3. All's Well That Ends Well

If he mourned Helena at all, he didn't give her much effort, and he certainly didn't bury her. And the business he considers "greatest" must refer to the seduction of a girl he intends to use and leave — sad behavior indeed and little human feeling to accompany it. Act IV concludes with Lafew's begging the Countess to marry Bertram to his daughter: he should have learned better by now and shows himself little better than the other schemers who inhabit the world of the play. Act V includes Parolles' reduction to "clown" by pairing him directly with Lavatch, but also the Countess's court forgiving him even after his dreadful display in Florence. We also see Bertram's return to his doubly and perhaps too willingly forgiving mother, the exposure of Bertram's seduction plot and the rise of Diana's fortunes, and the return of Helena to get what she has wanted throughout. The nearest we see to comedy in the play comes in that last act, and it comes in the form of forgiveness: the Countess and the King grant a general clemency, and everyone gets another chance, more in each case than he or she has deserved. But that's the nature of *mercy*, to which Shakespeare repeatedly returns as a central motif. Mercy comes from grace granted by an outside source, not earned by human action, which too often fails at need: an essential idea of Christian thought, though in this case cast in the secular sphere.

But little happens in the way of justice. Of all the play's characters we may most sympathize with Diana. She has risked quite a lot to gain the promise of a husband and a dowry, though Helena shouldn't have asked her to take that risk (Helena returns barely in time to save her from the King's wrath), and the King makes with her the same mistake he made with Helena: giving her the choice of her husband without any input from the man she may choose. The Countess stands out as potentially the wisest and kindest of the characters, but her acceptance of her returning son's behavior smacks of moral weakness: we forgive our children because they are our children, and they may get away with anything if they simply come back to us, since maybe if we treat them kindly, they will love us better than they did before — a common but dubious turn. The King, too, readily forgives Bertram: his immoral and disloyal choices go unpunished — in fact, rewarded. Parolles simply accepts who he is and what he has done, and he plans to do as he has always done, except more slothfully:

> Simply the thing I am
> Shall make me live....
> Rust, sword, cool, blushes, and, Parolles, live
> Safest in shame! Being fooled, by fool'ry thrive!
> There's place and means for every man alive [5.3.330–339].

No one in the play has learned or given any evidence of having changed for the better. If we watch plays to see how characters face adversity, learn, and improve, we must depart *All's Well* disappointed: the play suggests, as a whole, along with Parolles, that we are who we are, and anyone who expects us to change — except for the worse — must face the disappointment that we probably won't.

Though we may not find justice in *All's Well*, we do find at least attempts at generosity. In I.2 the King, who knew and honored Bertram's father for courage, directness, and his desire not to live past the waning of his prowess, and he welcomes Bertram as though he were his own: "My son's no dearer" (line 76). The King echoes the Countess's acceptance of Helena as though she were her own daughter, but his welcome creates an unstated problem: why would he consider a stranger, even the son of a great friend, as dear as his own son, the heir to the throne? The statement bears a kind of rashness in judgment of which the King proves occasionally guilty, notably again in Act V when he is willing to throw Diana into prison for not clarifying the ring riddle by which Helena finally wins Bertram. He reacts emotionally rather than intellectually, a dangerous trait for a king — and conceivably for his heir. But like Bertram's father, who always treated those ranked below him as if they had higher standing, with humility toward all (a trait Bertram, ironically, needs to learn),[20] the King will eagerly raise the degree of a worthy person (e.g., Helena and, finally, Diana), appreciate the good he finds in others and, after his anger abates, forgive their faults, and do his best to set right even situations that have gone wrong.

Lavatch, who fills the position often taken in Shakespeare's plays by a "wise" fool and who terms himself a *prophet* (1.3.59), doesn't even offer in wisdom's stead any significant humor.[21] Instead, he descends quickly into the kind of quibbles that so annoyed Samuel Johnson and a series of bawdy jokes inappropriate to the courtly milieu, annoying to listeners, and as self-absorbed as everything and everyone else (including all the major characters) in the play. He expresses pride in his own lechery and condemns women generally, despite the fact that he serves competent and generous if rather cold lady. In II.2 Lavatch explains to the Countess that when he wants favor from another person, he simply prefaces everything he says with "O Lord, sir," and he gets what he wants: others respond to that as deferential, earnest, and pious. Actually it constitutes a kind of blasphemy, taking the Lord's name in vain, but apparently no one notices — though Shakespeare and his audience probably would have. In III.2 he fails stupendously at offering comfort to the Countess about her son's activities: "Your son will not be kill'd so soon as I thought he would ... if he run away, as I hear he does" (lines 36–40). Of course the clown doesn't have correct information: Bertram has run away from the King to the war, not from the war to safety, and he all but calls Bertram a coward, thus demeaning the one virtue Bertram actually shows in the play — no Learean Fool, this fellow.

The one person in the play who can speak powerfully, clearly and effectively, Helena, clearly and bravely proclaims her love for Bertram to the Countess in I.3:

> ... Then I confess
> Here on my knee, before high heaven and you ...
> I love your son.
> My friends were poor, but honest, so's my love.
> Be not offended, for it hurts not him
> That he is lov'd of me; I follow him not
> By any token of presumptuous suit,
> Nor would I have him till I do deserve him....
> I know I love in vain, strive against hope....
> Thus Indian-like
> Religious in mine error, I adore
> The sun, that looks upon his worshipper
> But knows of him no more. My dearest madam,
> Let not your hate encounter with my love
> For loving where you do; but if yourself,
> Whose aged honor cites a virtuous youth,
> Did ever in so true a flame of liking
> Wish chastely, and love dearly, that your Dian
> Was both herself and Love, O then give pity
> To her whose state is such that cannot choose
> But lend and give where she is sure to lose ... [lines 192–215].

While the speech can hardly fail to move an audience, as it certainly moves the Countess, it contains both lie and equivocation as well as impertinent pleading. She doesn't claim that she won't pursue Bertram, only that she will try to do something to deserve him, yet the problem for Bertram lies not in her virtuous actions, but in her class — even the King's willingness to ennoble her will not help Bertram's perception of that, because he knows and despises her origins. She doesn't know that she loves in vain, because she intends to do everything she can to win him whether he wishes or not: she suggests he is dangerously beyond her ("the sun"), but she acts otherwise. And Helena both calls the Countess old and suggests ("if") the noblewoman probably hasn't loved as chastely and passionately as she has! Yet the Countess admirably forgives all that and gives Helena her "leave and love" (line 251) to try to cure the King and win her son. Helena, for all our wish to see her as admirable, makes a number of troubling rhetorical if youthful errors.

In II.5, after Bertram lies that he will obey the King's will with respect to Helena, Helena also claims she will do as her lord, Bertram, likes: she will not. He puts her off with the silly trick — when you have my ring and bear my child — but she immediately refigures her plans to find a new means to win him by fulfilling his conditions, conditions that once again have nothing to do with love and everything to do with contempt. Having returned then to Rossillion, Helena claims she will undertake a pilgrimage to Santiago de Compostella, since "and though I kill him not, I am the cause/ His death was so effected" (3.2.115–16): she believes, she says, he will die in battle fleeing her love. But she has lied again: she makes no such pilgrimage, but goes in disguise to Florence to trick Bertram so she can bed him and get the ring. And her placing Diana in danger to help her win Bertram worsens the lie, because it shows he little she values another young women with similar poverty, however she may claim to provide her a dowry and a means to a husband of her own. She returns in Act V just in time to save Diana from prison[22]: too great a risk of too great a friend and benefactor. She has even sent letters that lie about her death on the pilgrimage to make her victory more likely. In the culminating scene, V.3, Bertram lies again about what he believes was his seduction of Diana, and, having spent the plot in a supposed search for honor, he treats her terribly dishonorably. He becomes another Parolles, trying to save himself after having acted poorly. Diana, too, lies, about the King's ring: "this was it I gave him, being a-bed," and, doubly, "I have spoke the truth" (lines 228 and 230); she did not give him the ring in bed, because Helena did.[23] She participates in Helena's lie to regain her beloved. Helena, upon her "miraculous" re-appearance, at first claims herself a ghost to add drama to the situation and gain additional sympathy from her audience. Lafew claims that he will weep — presumably because of happiness at Helena's return, not the dissolution of the intended wedding between his daughter and Bertram. The King's final words, while poetic, ring untrue: "All yet seems well, and it end so meet,/ The bitter past, more welcome is the sweet." I would trust them more if the Countess were to speak them, but she remains silent, even after Helena addresses her directly. We don't know if sweetness will come; we do know that we have a number of persons with problems who find themselves forced into resolution, who find themselves allotted kindness rather than some firm instruction on how to behave, which they desperately need.

Beginning with I.2, in the King's welcome speech to Bertram, the word *honor* appears often and significantly nearly throughout the play. The repetition doesn't signal honorable behavior, but does recall our attention to the idea of honor in the world of the play — and to the few instances in which we see someone practice it. When the Countess learns of Bertram's bad behavior, she laments, "tell him that his sword can never win/ The honor that he loses" (3.1.93–94). One of the main themes in the play comes in Shakespeare's getting us to question what we say about honor, what we mean when we say it, and what the actual practice of honor involves. The play teaches by bad example how little honor has to do with rank, battle, boldness, or even love.

3. All's Well That Ends Well

A nominal "good ending" doesn't signify that those benefiting have acted honorably; we must leave the play considering the significance of the word and its complex resonances in our own thoughts and actions.

Shakespeare also filled the play with maxims: for example, "I see things may serve long, but not serve ever" (Lavatch in II.2. 59), and "From lowest place [when] virtuous things proceed,/ The place is dignified by th' doer's deed" (the King in II.3.125–26). When Bertram dismisses Helena in II.3 to her "single sorrow," he proclaims, "War is no strife/ To the dark house and the [detested] wife" (291-92)—a maxim, if a particularly cruel one. Diana perhaps best expresses the philosophy of the play when she says in Act IV, scene 2, lines 21–22, "'Tis not the many oaths that makes the truth,' But the plain single vow that is vow'd true." Whether we go to war, to marriage, or just to the day's activities, we must rely not only on the truth of the vow, Shakespeare seems to say in *All's Well*, but also that we make the vow nobly, with virtuous and compassionate intent, and hope to keep it nobly.

As the play ends we might return, first and foremost, to why Helena still wants Bertram after all he has done—except that she has behaved rather badly herself. She hopes that he will get better, and we may hope that they both will.

At least we may answer such a doubt that, unlike in *Merchant of Venice* and *Troilus and Cressida*, *All's Well* ends with that ray of hope—hope, though, laden with a very difficult problem.

4

Straining the Quality of Mercy
Measure for Measure

"Few of Shakespeare's plays," Wright and LaMar begin their introduction to the play in *The Folger Guide to Shakespeare*, "have aroused more diverse and contradictory interpretations" (274). Anne Barton wrote that the play exhibits "a sense of dissatisfaction with its own dramatic mode" and a "predominant harshness of tone, a savagery even in its clowning."[1] Marjorie Garber notes, with artful understatement, "On the hatefulness/delightfulness scale articulated by Coleridge it is surely 'dark' rather than 'festive'" (563), while W. W. Lawrence begins his analysis by suggesting, "What Shakespeare failed to do in *All's Well* he achieved in *Measure for Measure*, a play surcharged with emotion and suffused with sympathy for the frailties of mankind" (978). Lawrence adds that the theme of *Measure* grows out of (and perhaps improves upon) *All's Well*: "It presents one of those dreadful alternatives between conflicting demands of honor and affection which have in them the very essence of tragic drama" (79), even as it hinges very late in the play on the Duke's conclusion that "mercy should temper justice, and that the strict letter of the law should not be enforced" (121). As we have seen, Shakespeare had particularly exploited these tensions in *All's Well*, the play that probably directly preceded *Measure*, but there he suggests that romance and honor need not conflict: in fact, if they do, we must be behaving badly, since we should act honorably in love as in all endeavors. *Measure for Measure* goes further to question whether we can ever find honorable behavior in the world and if we did, whether we could recognize it and come, with any consistency, to practice it.

The marriage problem that appears in *All's Well* returns in *Measure for Measure:* Shakespeare might have subtitled the play, borrowing further from the gospel of Matthew (7:2), Judge Not, Lest Ye Get Badly Married. Marriage again becomes a fulcrum on which the genre and problems of the play balance dynamically and dangerously: if the marriages the Duke imposes at the end of the play can (by miraculous good fortune) turn out well, the play in retro-

4. Straining the Quality of Mercy

spect becomes something close to comedy; if they turn out poorly (as the dubious coupling suggests they will), the play becomes not a tragedy, but a tortured farce — or the kind of problem play Shakespeare apparently loved to create to lead his audience past simple entertainment into deep and serious consideration of human choices.

Certainly the play deals also with the responsibility of authority, since the "deployment of what the play calls 'power divine' ... devolves upon the good ruler," who must stand for "reason and ethical judgment" (Garber 564). No wonder, then, as Goddard observes, "the word 'authority' occurs more often than in any other" of Shakespeare's plays (50) — curious, then, that *Measure* "continually suggests the resemblance of the main world, not so much to a prison — though it is that too — as to a house of ill fame, where men and women sell their honors in a dozen senses" (62).[2]

The greater conflict may occur here not between love and honor, but between authority and honor. Does the Duke grant a kind of general amnesty out of mercy, for the playwright an allegorical or religious method of showing kindness, or does the Duke's judgment simply allow him to err in much the ways other characters have already done? At the end of the play he makes the same mistake that the King of France makes twice in *All's Well*: he commits others to marriages they don't really want. But in *All's Well*, at least the King doesn't participate in an enforced marriage, as the Duke intends to do in *Measure*: he essentially forgives himself for the error he is about to commit by forgiving those who have already sinned and those who are about to err according to his command — dubious leadership and dubious theology with which Shakespeare, I think, wants his audience to feel uncomfortable.[3]

While the Duke imposes a nominal fix on the problems of the world of the play, once again we have no reason to believe that the characters of the persons involved have changed. Public awareness of their bad behaviors may drive them to better behavior in the future, or it may lead them to act more secretively in the future or even to thoughts of vengeance — as an audience we can only speculate, though Shakespeare's endings always urge us to do so. And bad behaviors tend to thrive in the absence of authority: in the beginning of the play the Duke absents himself to test the quality of his subjects and deputies, particularly Angelo,[4] but in doing so he abandons his duty — a problem that Shakespeare presents most forcefully in *King Lear*. Vincentio doesn't want his people to dislike him for clamping down on their behavior after they have become accustomed to his leniency: they won't like him if they perceive him turning harsh where before they saw him as kind. So he passes along the duty of his office to another man who he believes can handle that responsibility technically and emotionally, but Angelo proves unprepared for the task.[5] The Duke explains to Friar Thomas,

> We have strict statutes and most biting laws
> (The needful bits and curbs to headstrong weeds),
> Which for fourteen years we have let slip....
> Now, as fond fathers,
> Having bound up the threat'ning twigs of birch ...
> [I]n time the rod
> [Becomes] more mock'd than fear'd ...
> And liberty plucks justice by the nose....
> Sith 'twas my fault to give the people scope,
> 'Twould be my tyranny to strike and gall them
> For what I bid them do....
> I have on Angelo impos'd the office,
> Who may, in th'ambush of my name, strike home,
> And yet my nature never in the fight
> To do in slander [1.3.19–43].

Though the Friar counsels him against it, the Duke insists on his plot — his dissembling — more than anything else for his own comfort: he doesn't want his folk to see him as equivocal and tyrannical. The state has strict laws the execution of which "we" have let slip, though "'twas my fault," he admits — a kindness of allowing freedom that becomes a fault because the people abuse that freedom. Even though the people have lost respect for authority — not for the Duke as a Duke, but for the law as law — he feels as though he can't enforce where he has dealt with laxity, so someone else must do so in his stead. He believes Angelo can and will wield authority strictly; in a sense he is suggesting that Angelo would make a better Duke than he does — interesting, though, that he can't hold back from counseling Angelo to remember mercy as well as justice, the turn that has got him into the awkward situation in which he finds himself as duke, as governor of a people. The choice of the word *impos'd* has great force here because he gives Angelo no latitude to refuse or limit the responsibility that the Duke should have accepted as his own, not delegate. Mainly he believes that Angelo as judge will not slander the Duke as a man or as a leader, and Angelo's enacting of justice will free the Duke from the bad opinion of his people: they will continue to seem him as consistently kind. Imposed authority creates as many problems as imposed marriage, but for even more people: not merely for the couple involved, but for anyone who steps into the way of judgment.

That idea fails miserably, of course, as it must: in a sinful world, Shakespeare's play suggests, we must temper mercy with justice even more than justice with mercy. The Duke returns to his position of authority in time to prevent executions of failed justice, but not in time to prevent Angelo's fall. Angelo doesn't lose his position, but he does lose his reputation and his freedom of choice: he must marry a woman he had chosen not to marry. The

4. Straining the Quality of Mercy

"justness" of that marriage choice, that Angelo had chosen not to marry based on the woman's lack of dowry, doesn't mitigate the removal of free will from one of the parties. In moral terms Angelo should keep his promise, but the fact that the Duke now forces the marriage also creates a punishment on Mariana, whether or not she recognizes it as such. Though she may love Angelo despite his bad treatment of her, no one can make him love her in return. They begin with little hope of a happy marriage, even if they are both bound to a politically solid one. And Angelo must continue in his old office knowing, as the public know, that given the chance to lead, he has failed. Private knowledge of our failings can lead to humility; public knowledge leads to embarrassment and the kind of ineffectuality the Duke feared for himself when he placed Angelo in his stead. He has imposed his failing and his bond on another man.

While Angelo plays the part of an exposed "everyman," the Duke serves as a "dark comedy's" version of "tragedy's" King Lear and "Romance's" Prospero. Lear also abdicates, but he gives authority to persons much worse than Angelo: at least Angelo begins with good intent. Plus Vincentio still has the youth, energy, and wits not to give up that authority entirely, but to stay close, observe, and re-assert his authority when his world would fail without him. Lucky for him that he is dealing with Angelo, as bad is he is, and not Goneril and Regan, who are far worse: Angelo is a fallen, but redeemable, angel, but Goneril and Regan have already become monsters, ready to devour as soon as opportunity permits. The break in the Great Chain of Being that Lear creates has created a chasm beyond healing; the Duke breaks the Chain, too, but he remains present and strong enough to heal the brief rift he makes.

That healing doesn't place him above culpability. The foreboding darkness of the play, the problems created by and for other characters, and the play's troublesome ending come from his errors. The Duke fails to fix the problem that lead to his plot to begin with: he forgives everyone, and he has not learned to pass the kind of judgments that will lead to better behavior among his citizens. He acts kindly, with considerable generosity, but neither justly nor wisely, so the world of the play undergoes no improvement and will probably still suffer from the same problems it has (if not more, given all the forced weddings). The Duke has perhaps overstrained the quality of mercy.

While the Duke absents himself from office, Prospero's brother has removed him from office and set him, with his daughter, asea, likely to their deaths. They survive, and good fortune and careful watchfulness allow Prospero to return to his dukedom and to place his daughter in a promising marriage. But once again those who have deposed Prospero promise far worse behavior than those who, unwillingly, have replaced Vincentio and who must experience a great deal of relief at his return to office. In *The Tempest* Antonio and his comrade Sebastian want power they shouldn't have, and they have no scruples about plotting and murdering to get it. The danger of the movement of power that we see in the Romance (others will kill for it) doesn't exist in *Measure for Measure,* the nominal problem-comedy — though it could have. Vincentio in his very fist speech in the play identifies Escalus as in many ways more fit to rule than he is: if we believe that Vincentio is telling the truth rather than testing Escalus as he tests Angelo, the old lord has better knowledge of government, "as pregnant in [the] art and practice" as the Duke himself. He believes, too, that Angelo will not only rise to the occasion of authority with solemn good judgment, but that the experience will also improve him as a person: "Spirits are not finely touch'd/ But to fine issues" (1.1.35–36). Vincentio commands, "In our remove be thou at full ourself./ Morality and mercy in Vienna/ Live in they tongue and heart" (43–45). They won't, of course; though Angelo will try, he will fail. Nothing in his experience has prepared him for true authority, and he knows it. Sadly, that knowledge doesn't inhibit his rapid descent into utter failure in both morality and mercy. Shakespeare's choice of the seemingly unshakable Angelo (angel-o!) for this fall raises the question of whether any of us in such a circumstance would do any better. We may not like Angelo for his cold heart, but as the play begins we have no reason to question his desire to execute his duties faithfully.

But at least we have in this play the hopefulness that comes from knowing Escalus and Angelo are good enough not to have plotted to kill Vincentio before he could return to the seat of power, unlike their parallels in *The Tempest.* The world of *Measure for Measure* has not yet gone that far wrong. We do end the play, though, with a sense of foreboding that comes from the public imminence (and eminence) of failings: everyone in the play has failed in duty and kindness to a greater of lesser degree. That dark tone prohibits a sense of comic catharsis, leading instead to a meditation on our mutual limitations and the dangers of power.

The problems of mood and tone that Barton and Garber address, the problems of social metaphor that Barton and Goddard raise, and the problems of humility and authority that move the plot direct our attention to how to understand the form and genre of *Measure for Measure.* Its thematic problems come in three areas: problems of leadership, problems of character, and problematic weddings. I will treat them in that order through the course of this chapter and use them to help develop a reading of the form and function of the play as a whole. Shakespeare aimed, I will assert again, to raise the problems for meditation, not to oversimplify them. If he makes a judgment at last, he does so not to attack specific persons or characters, but aims to show

how easily we humans can slip into (or be led into) the abdication or abuse of authority, solipsistic or selfish pride, and inappropriate relationships for which we haven't properly prepared.[6] A great deal of the tension in this play comes from the clash of active and passive principles, and the genre problem comes from characters' nearly complete failures in leadership and character, with worse yet to come from bad alliances.

More on Problems of Leadership in Measure for Measure

Many commentators aptly suggest a reading of the Duke as Shakespeare himself, as a playwright more generally (a good one or a bad one), as King James, or even as God (or, more exactly, God-like). Such allegorical readings do help produce a reasonable understanding of the play, and that kind of thinking would have had a much less odious effect on audiences of Shakespeare's time than it does on readers of ours — allegory remained pervasive and popular into the eighteenth century. The Duke creates a "plot" (or play, which he directs and in which he acts) that unfolds to show truths about human experience and to suggest ways of understanding and dealing with human behavior. Garber notes with what energy King James, "an absolutist ruler who believed strongly in the divine right of kings" kept an elaborate network of spying amidst a government "equally watchful but more entrepreneurial" than that of Elizabeth (564). The Duke, like James, watches closely, if from a distance, and casts strict an exact judgment when he finally desires to do so: he moves from observer to plotter to judge of the action. The way the Duke loves his people sufficiently to forgive them for nearly anything, desires their love in return, watches them and sets up tests of their mettle to improve them even more than to judge them falls into line with popular notions of God's relationship with his creatures. We know and must admit when we've done wrong, but with confession, penitence, and new humility we may hope for mercy and for a return to active life — we may think of this play as Shakespeare's most Catholic work.

But allegory alone doesn't account for the real philosophical problems of the play; heavenly governance doesn't remove free will and demand specific marriage partners, and good earthly governance requires more than too willing forgiveness of dangerous sins. A good leader shouldn't absent himself to the danger and near destruction of law-abiding citizens. Not only do the people get into trouble without the figure of true authority before them, but the possibility of war looms ahead, and the Duke shows no evidence of preparing his people for it. In the beginning of I.2 Lucio and a Gentleman discuss the situation, which then fades into the background as the plot progresses:

> LUCIO: If the Duke and the other dukes come not to composition with the King of Hungary, why then all the dukes fall upon the King.
> 1ST GENTLEMAN: Heaven grant us its peace, but not the King of Hungary's!

They fear not only war, but also having a stricter, foreign government imposed on them. What will the Duke do about it? Looming war is hardly the matter of comedy or a situation for laxity in vigilance. But instead of adhering to his responsibilities, he indulges not only his curious desire to test Angelo, but also his own distaste for court: "I have ever lov'd the life removed,/ And held in elde price to haunt assemblies/ Where youth, and cost, witless bravery keeps" (1.3.8–10). We may easily appreciate the desire for a quieter, more spiritual, less foppish life, but for an age that believed in the divine right of kings and leaders more generally, the Duke doesn't have that option if he wants Vienna to dwell in peace and prosperity and if he wants to follow what Shakespeare's time saw as God's will.

The Duke's soliloquy that concludes Act III neatly encapsulates the problems of leadership — and of poetry — in *Measure*.[7] One important though hardly esoteric theme comes through quite clearly in the first two lines: "He who the sword of heaven will bear/ Should be as holy as severe": pretty clearly, the person who passes judgment on others must prove worthy of that duty by living as nearly as possible a spotless life, must balance mercy and justice. Then he adds, "Shame to him whose cruel striking/ Kills for faults of his own liking": shame to persons who don't practice what they preach, who punish others for their own sins. "O, what may man within him hide,/ Though angel on the outward side": we may think evil that we don't show publicly, but we may also go so far as to indulge that sin in private. The greater problem comes, though, not in that obvious truth, but in the notion of Angelo as in any way angelic: he acts pompously, passes judgment coldly, and ignores his own hypocrisy — nothing angelic there. "Angelic" should imply loving, helping, forgiving, not rendering death for common offenses. The Duke concludes that he must apply "craft" against such "vice," and he iterates the plot to bring Mariana to Angelo in the dark: "So disguise shall by th'disguised/ Pay with falsehood false exacting,/ And perform an old contracting." Do we ever choose well when we dissemble, when we willingly mislead, when we get others to act the way we want them to by tricking them rather than teaching them? Shouldn't someone like the Duke aim to improve their intellectual and emotional abilities to make good choices? That unsettling passage may have good, if cliché, points, but it aims at their achievement by deception: better as a means to a joke than as a means to lead a peaceful and virtuous city.

That laxity of leadership responsibility comes not only from the Duke,

4. Straining the Quality of Mercy   97

but pervades the play. Shakespeare devoted Act II, scene 1, to showing a series of problematic deputations. Angelo begins the scene by claiming, "We must not make a scarecrow of the law," but Escalus responds, "Let us be keen and rather cut a little,/ Than fall and bruise to death." He adds that if Angelo had been in Claudio's position, he might well have made the same error, getting a young woman pregnant before marriage. Notably, Claudio and Juliet had, in fact, lawfully pledged their marriage publicly, just not yet gone through the religious ceremony. Angelo responds, "'Tis one thing to be tempted, Escalus,/ Another thing to fall" (lines 16–170) — yes, indeed. He admits, too, that others may have greater guilt than Claudio, but the law can only seize upon what it finds, not on what it doesn't know. Then he uses an odd metaphor, in fact a bad analogy: "The jewel that we find, we stoop and take't,/ Because we see it; but what we do not see/ We tread upon, and never think of it" (lines 24–26). He hasn't found a jewel, but a crime, and one that several in the play readily admit happens all the time. Lucio, for instance, has fathered a child on Kate Keepdown, but no one has brought him to prison for it (see 3.2.199–203). Angelo intends to use Claudio's case as an example so that others will not behave badly, but as the Provost of the prison will say in II.2, "All sects, all ages smack of this vice, and he [Claudio] to die for't!" (5–6). Angelo sees the crime as the province of young males; for the woman involved, Juliet, the "fornicatress," as Angelo calls her, he commands she be "removed," taken from town, and "let her have needful but not lavish means" (2.2.23–24): he will execute the man and hide the woman so she may have her child out of the public eye. Perhaps she gets leniency because of her pregnancy, but she has committed the same "crime" with mutual responsibility, as she readily admits: when the Duke asks if she loves the man who "wrong'd" her, Juliet replies, "Yes, as I love the woman that wronged him" (2.3.25) — she may be pregnant, but Claudio must face a death sentence. We don't have justice when the same "crime" brings different punishments.

When in IV.4 Angelo explains in soliloquy his reason for having Claudio executed (as he believes, by then, he has), he admits to himself that he has done it not for law and order, but to avoid vengeance for his sin against Isabella: "He should have liv'd,/ Save that his riotous youth with dangerous sense/ Might in the times to come have ta'en revenge,/ By so receiving a dishonor'd life/ With ransom of such shame" (28–32). In the Duke's absence he governs first by merciless coldness, second by selfish desire, and last by fear. "This deed [both the supposed rape of Isabella and the execution of Claudio, which he doesn't know he hasn't done] unshapes me quite," he says, "makes me unpregnant/ And dull to all proceedings" (20–21): this time the recurrent pregnancy image appears as a negation, since Angelo has lost his power to conceive goodness and to bear kindness. Authority has ruined him. When he sends in IV.2 to demand the immediate execution of Claudio, he requires that the Provost, far too gentle a man for such a duty, send him Claudio's severed head "[f]or my better satisfaction," and if he does not, "you will answer it at your peril" (122, 126). His failure is turning him to serial violence, first against law and goodness, then against Isabella, then against Claudio, and then against the Provost — Shakespeare shows that sin and deception lead only to more sin and deception.

When the Provost brings Elbow, Froth, and Pompey to court before Angelo and Escalus in II.1, Elbow makes a complaint that the tapster and his friend have treated his wife badly. When Angelo can make no sense of what any of them has to say, he leaves the case to Escalus to judge, "Hoping you'll find good cause to whip them all" (line 137). Escalus, also unable to make any sense of their malapropism-filled banter, simply dismisses the case. He has a ready enough if dubious excuse: "Truly, officer, because he [Froth] hath some offenses in him that thou wouldst discover if thou couldst, let him continue in his courses till thou know'st what they are" (lines 185–87). Elbow turns Froth loose almost urging him to criminal activity: "Thou art to continue now, thou varlet, thou art to continue" (191–92), so that the law may catch him later for something worse. All the clowns will undoubtedly continue in the same activities in which they have already indulged, whatever they are: they never fully come exactly to light, though as part of the regular running of a brothel, they must have greater legal import than Claudio's getting his civil-law spouse pregnant.[8]

Escalus also finds, though, that Elbow, the constable, is not really the Duke's appointee, but a deputy of others who have received charge to do the job but don't want the bother of it: we gave a whole string of shirking and no result for any of it. Elbow, he learns, has kept his office (badly) for seven and half years and, Escalus suggests he might give it up to someone else more "sufficient to serve it" (267). But Elbow replies, "Faith, sir, few of any wit in such matters. As they are chosen, they are glad to choose me for them. I do it for some piece of money, and go through with all" (268–70). Elbow does for a little money what others more able and who have received appointment to the office fail to do, probably because of sloth. Escalus requests that Elbow give him the names of "some six or seven, the most sufficient of your parish" (272–73), but he probably won't, since if he does, he'll lose his living, and because if the others actually deserved the office or could manage it, they would already have had it and wouldn't have given it up. The world of the play suffers from series of shirkers and shirkings, and when we see anyone attempting to live up to duties or responsibilities, he or she largely fails.

With the possible exception of the Provost,[9] Escalus makes the greatest effort of any of the characters to remain true to his sense of duty, but he hasn't

4. Straining the Quality of Mercy

the power or energy to effect any change, and he, too, can turn cruel in judgment. He can release from prosecution employees of a brothel, but whatever he were to do with them, the brothel would continue as usual: they neither create the citizens' sexual desires nor can they end them. For Escalus mercy contributes to justice; it need not imply shirking. But mercy with no public action will not change any of the bad behaviors that the Duke believes he must change for the good of Vienna. The fact that the Duke most trusts Escalus but places power in the hands of Angelo to test him raises the question of the legitimacy of authority: who has it, why, and what will he or she do with it? Escalus, an older man, hasn't the problem of sexual desire that will afflict Angelo and the Duke as well. He can perform his duty without concern over that temptation, but not to the extent that Vienna will be better off for his service. He does, though, give in to a temptation of his own: to chastise Angelo for his failure to avoid sexual temptation, one that Escalus should realize troubles Angelo more than it troubles him. We must always struggle, Shakespeare suggests, with compassion, but leaders particularly so, since when their compassion fails, they can do great damage. In *Measure for Measure* Angelo's compassion fails quickly, if he ever had it. Escalus's fails later, with Isabella and Angelo,[10] and the Duke's fails entirely at the end of the play, as the same desire that has moved others to "crimes" moves him as well. Having shown at least some sense of concern for all the persons on whom he passes judgment to that point, he commits Isabella to marry him with no worry whatsoever for her own feelings: he doesn't bother to ask, assuming that because he considers the match good, so will she. He makes in that thoughtless choice a failure of leadership and a failure in character, and his choice has little chance of leading to a happy marriage for Isabella, and thus it will fall short of his wishes, too.

Early in the play Isabella has the greatest desire to create duties that she can and wishes to fulfill, but she loses agency. We also may wonder if Shakespeare sympathized with her desires: she aims to take herself out of the world of action and human experience and place herself entirely under the strict enforcement of religious code. That choice replaces social responsibility with absolute commitment to rigid ascetic exercise of prayer and contemplation; as such it further distances her from the big questions that are troubling the world around her. Her choice echoes the medieval world rather than the concerns of Shakespeare's England. Having chosen the *via contemplativa*, she finds herself yanked back into the *via activa*, so the integrity we expect she would have shown in her life choice has no chance of coming to fruition. She must suffer the consequences of new responsibilities she hasn't chosen. A question remains for the audience at the end of the play: though she says nothing to the Duke's proposal in the play, will she later simply accept his proposal, or will she assert her free will to make a choice of her own. She gives no reason in the play for us to believe she wants to marry; she has the emotional strength — or perhaps the coldness — to deny her brother compassion when she finds his fear of death overwhelming, but will she have the strength to reject the Duke's proposal? It tears her from the life she has willingly chosen, that of ascetic spirituality rather than worldly attachment, and throws her directly into a life even more problematic than the one she has already rejected.

Lucio, too, briefly takes over the role of Duke in III.2, when, in the presence of the Duke disguised as friar, he directs Elbow to imprison the inveterate bawd Pompey. While he has deputed himself, the Duke watches passively, though he does then engage Lucio in an ironic dialogue, Lucio telling the "friar" how well he knows the Duke, knows him as merciful and kind but also lascivious, immoderate with drink, not very wise, and a "superficial, ignorant, unweighing fellow" (line 140). The Duke takes exception, of course, referring to himself as a "scholar, statesman, and soldier" — we don't know if he speaks correctly or not, though later in the scene Escalus will report him instead as temperate and rejoicing in others' happiness — and after Lucio leaves, he will observe to himself that "no might nor greatness in mortality/ Can censure scape; back-wounding calumny/ The whitest virtue strikes" (185–87): someone will slander even the best of persons, regardless of his or her virtue. There, too, we see a problem of leadership: the people must allow their leader to lead them well and must pursue their own virtue; as Henry V says, "Every subject's duty's the King's, but every subject's soul's his own" (*Henry V*, 4.1.176–77). In IV.4 Lucio will admit not only his guilt in "getting a wench with child," but also that he lied about in court to avoid the sentence of having to marry her — one, unlike Bernardine's, that he can't avoid at last. In V.1 Lucio will continually interrupt the proceedings with unwanted jokes, jabs, and opinions; both the Duke and Escalus will repeatedly and unsuccessfully attempt to silence him. But when the Duke reappears onstage in his disguise as friar, they accept Lucio's accusations that the friar has slandered the Duke — Angelo specifically asks his opinion and will call on Lucio to help the Provost arrest the friar. Authority devolves too easily upon those who have no right or ability to manage it.

Bernardine, another proven rascal and a drunkard who has already spent nine years in prison, will also usurp the Duke's privilege. In one of the funniest scenes in the play, when the Duke comes to call him to execution, Bernardine, having claimed he is drunk, sleepy, and not fit to die, simply refuses to go: "I swear I will not die to-day for any man's persuasion.... Not a word. If you have any thing to say to me, come to my ward [cell]; for thence will I not to-day" (4.3.59–62). The Duke can only reply with flummoxed consternation, "A creature unprepar'd, unmeet for death;/ And to transport him in the mind he is/ Were damnable" (lines 67–69). The Duke will not force to execution a man unready and unwilling to go, and in the final scene of the play will pardon him entirely; what makes good humor, though, hardly makes fair judgment, and the Duke again opts for mercy rather than justice.

The problematic ending—the enforcement of dubious marriages—creates a genre problem as well as a leadership problem: what comic catharsis can come from a situation nearer to horror than happy resolution? Measure for measure: as you mete out, so will God measure you—we find in the play both inappropriate mercy and errant justice, so neither good measuring nor good meting. No one in the play, from Duke to clowns, has earned either reasonable justice or kind mercy. The Duke has proceeded passively in all those years he should have acted, and he uses bad judgment at the end when mercy could improve the world. More selfish action condemns his people to more suffering. And he fails still to deal with the other Dukes and the King of Hungary: what rough beast lurks in the future to disturb the unstable peace that the Duke, in whose responsibility such action lies, has failed to stabilize?

Problems of Character

So much of Shakespeare's work with character hinges on a principle essential to Christian thought: free will. In this play we see a range of problems that come from the exhibition of free will without the concomitant necessities of reason, faith, and self-control and from too great a willingness to impose on others' free will. Free will, too, doesn't imply *laissez-faire*: whether for rulers or subjects, it comes with the responsibility of self-control and the necessity to practice the virtues one preaches. In Act II, scene 2, we see the notion of an ideal sternness of character already beginning its fall. Angelo expresses impatience that Claudio hasn't yet been executed, and Escalus urges him to avoid rash action, a central motif in Shakespeare's tragedies. Yet having passed rash judgment, Angelo rapidly loses his own self-control in the presence of Isabel, who's stony virtue appeals to him even more than her beauty.

Isabella, who like the Duke wishes to retreat from public life to a life of strict and spartan spirituality, feels bound to plead for her brother's life. She doesn't go to Angelo willingly. In I.4, as she begins to receive instruction toward taking holy vows, she asks her instructor about privileges only to explain that "I speak not as desiring more,/ But rather wishing a more strict restraint" (lines 3–4). When Lucio comes to explain her brother's plight and to beg her help, she expresses doubt that she can effect any change in Angelo. But then, wooed to the task by Lucio, she says that soon "I'll send him [Claudio] certain word of my success" (89), an uncharacteristic assurance and an odd change of mind. Why does she suddenly believe in the certainty of success?

Just before Isabella meets Angelo, he has passed his fairly merciful judgment on Juliet, which the Provost has approved with "Save your honor!" (2.2.25). The line makes a telling pun, as it suggests both "God save your Honor as thanks for your mercy to the young woman" and a preparatory "May God save your honor from the evil you'll attempt to do to the other young woman who is just coming to plead with you for mercy for another." Meeting Angelo, Isabella twice refers to him as "your honor," but again in phrasing that suggests two meanings: "I am a woeful suitor to your honor,/ Please but your honor hear me" (27–28). She asks mercy not only of him but of *his honor*, and she asks that his *honor* hear her: sadly, he does not treat her request with honor, and his honor does not hear her. Instead, he finds himself swayed to the lust he claims beneath his stoic dignity. Isabella pleads at first tepidly, and gives in easily to Angelo's insistence that Claudio will die: "O just but severe law!/ I had a brother then. Heaven keep your honor" (42–43). With one try she would give up and go away, but Lucio, who has accompanied her, keeps urging her to try again: "Give't no o'er so," "Your are too cold," "to him, to him, wench" (lines 43, 56, and 123). Isabella does suffer from coldness, but at Lucio's urging she increases the intensity of her pleas: condemn the fault, not the person; neither God nor person grieves at mercy; mercy becomes the powerful person more than does any ceremonial act; since all souls fail at some point, one should give mercy so as in turn to receive it; if you can't show mercy, show pity, or better yet, compassion, since, while a person may have power, he does ill to use it proudly or tyrannously; authority may err, and so it should not move too quickly to punish; check your own heart to make sure the same sin has not grown there. The last finally strikes home, as Angelo finds himself falling for Isabella regardless of his belief in his own untouchable heart. "Heaven keep your honor safe," she says before she leaves, but his honor is already failing, as Angelo says, aside, "For I am that way going to temptation,/ Where prayers cross" (157–58): he finds himself wanting to pray both to resist sexual temptation and to have the opportunity to give in to it. Perhaps the most potent argument comes in a pun that Isabella speaks, but that both she and Angelo miss: she argues by asking if anyone else, having been arrested for fornication, has suffered death for it: "Who is it that hath died for this offense?" (line 88). The line obviously includes a reference to Christ's dying for humanity's sins; that point if any should have swayed Angelo, but neither the holy deputy nor the holy postulant gets the obvious if unintended allusion.

Isabella argues with increasing passion seemingly for the sake of arguing, because Lucio keeps pushing her, rather than because her ardor to save her brother increases — she has already declared his punishment severe but just. When she leaves, Angelo identifies her not as virtuous, but as satanic: "Is this [his sexual arousal] her fault, or mine?/ The tempter, or the tempted, who sins most, ha?" (162–63). He blames her modesty rather than his own weakness, and he gives in to the extent that he commands her to come the next day to plead again: he leaves her with the possibility that she may yet succeed in her suit, having no interest in mercy — so much for the "demands" of law.

The most interesting problems in the scene come in how it, also, strains the quality of mercy and in what it says about character. Mercy doesn't come from reason or kindness, and it will even, in the heat of the moment, ignore (or fail to remember) the source of all mercy. The potential for mercy in this world comes from sexual arousal, in this case strained out of Angelo by Isabella's cold and eloquent beauty and at the end of the play wrought similarly from the Duke. We find, too, that even good character only waits for the instance that will exploit its particular weakness. Angelo's failure becomes obvious to him, but he subdues the full recognition of it so he may pursue action on his temptation. Sadly, Isabella doesn't perceive her failure, or she misperceives it, as the audience may readily do as well. She pleads not because she believes her brother deserves mercy and she wants him to live, but because Lucio imposes on her a misplaced responsibility to argue for mercy when she would rather not: she should argue out of love, and not because an uncertain sense of duty drives her. A curious tension appears in this case where we do finally see someone, Isabella, act for the benefit of another out of a sense of duty and responsibility. Her commitment to them comes, though, not out of the sense of doing right or acting for love; she acts nominally, from the wrong motivations, not from the heart. There we find a philosophical and aesthetic crux. Isabella may be easy for the other characters to admire and love, and audiences will certainly sympathize with her plight, but if we see her plainly, she's difficult to like. Self-righteousness dominates her judgments.[11]

The problem of the quality of mercy and its effects on character intensifies in Act III, scene 1, when Isabella must confront her brother with Angelo's proposition. She doesn't want to tell him, probably partly out of embarrassment and partly out of fear that he'll beg her to capitulate. When Isabella arrives at the prison, the Duke in his guise as friar is counseling Claudio to prepare for death; he makes a traditional but eloquent argument, full of *contemptus mundi* and irony: "If thou art rich, thou'rt poor/ For like an ass, whose back with ingots bows,/ Thou bear'st they heavy riches but a journey,/ And death unloads thee" (lines 25–28) — one wonders how a wealthy Duke can make such an argument other than as part of a plot that tests not only Angelo, but everyone his disguise allows him to fool. The homily seemingly works, as Claudio penitently resolves, "I find I seek to die,/ And seeking death, find life" (42–43). That resolve quickly wavers and then capitulates entirely. Isabella quips that Angelo has "affairs to heaven,/ Intends you for his swift ambassador" (line 56–57, again with an almost stunning chill), and Claudio responds, "Is there no remedy?"

Isabella hints of a "devilish mercy," but Claudio must press her for it. Then she comes right out and says she doesn't want to tell him, "lest thou a feverous life shouldst entertain,/ And six or seven winters more respect/ Than a perpetual honor" (74–76). She doesn't grant him much of a life expectancy, six or seven years more, little for a young man even in Shakespeare's time, and she doesn't mention that she refers to her honor rather than his.[12] Claudio asks why Isabella is trying to shame him: he has prepared to meet death as a "bride" he will embrace. She praises him, comparing him to their father — always an emotionally powerful move, whether positive or negative, for a man — and finally gets to Angelo's proposition. Claudio immediately responds, "O heavens, it cannot be" (98) and "Thou shalt not do't" (102). If she need only lay down her life, and not her body, she would, Isabella assures him, but Claudio is already reconsidering: it wouldn't be a sin, at least not a deadly one, if she were to give in under such compulsion, and "O Isabel ... Death is a fearful thing" (114–15), followed by Dantesque images of "fiery floods," "thick-ribbed ice," and "viewless winds" in "restless violence," Infernal punishments for the wrathful, the betrayers of benefactors, and the lecherous. He fears not only death, but hell, even after his time with the "friar." When he begs, "Sweet sister, let me live," she responds with a violent attack of her own — "O you beast," "dishonest wretch" — and she accuses him of a kind of "incest," to "take life/ From thine own sister's shame"; she offers instead of understanding "defiance": "Die, perish! ... I'll pray a thousand prayers for thy death,/ No word to save thee" (135–46). He must die by the law, and now she's almost hideously glad of it.

Anyone paying attention at that point must take a deep breath. One can appreciate both Claudio's lack of resolve and Isabella's horror, but Claudio's change of heart happens nearly instantly, and Isabella's change of attitude goes from praise to damnation: both characters, faced with their own horrors, fail understandably but monumentally and miserably. The bitterness of the scene comes in the emotional poles of the dialogue: it would produce laughter if did not produce revulsion.

The Duke, having listened in secret to the whole exchange, catches Isabella as she leaves and proposes, by the old ruse of the bed trick, which we have seen in *All's Well*, to save Claudio's life, Isabella's honor, and Marianna's wedding, but this new act of dissembling hardly removes the effects of the painfully self-absorbed quarrel — it merely mitigates the results. We have no way to repair the character damage that the brother and sister have done — another of the great lingering problems of *Measure for Measure*.

Regardless of the fact that the Duke uses his plot to help Isabella and Marianna, he not only neglects duties of state, but he lies repeatedly and to nearly everyone he meets. We could perhaps forgive the lies if they accomplished something, but about all he gains is firmer knowledge that he can't trust Angelo to govern in his stead: he guessed that already, but had no reason to prove it. If he had simply kept his place, not much about the situation at the end of the play would have changed: he still could have pardoned those he pardoned and arranged the marriages he arranged. He could have saved Isabella quite a good deal of pain, and may not even have met her, so leaving her to her chosen contemplative life — better for her, probably, and maybe in the long run better for him. Will she make him the wife he now believes he wants?

The level of anger (and perhaps love?) that returns to Isabella's speech in IV.3, when she believes Claudio has died, hardly redeems her: she could have shown some passionate kindness to Claudio more fruitfully. "O, I will too him, and pluck out his [Angelo's] eyes!" she says, Regan-like, and adds in summary, "Unhappy[13] Claudio! Wretched Isabel! Injurious world! Most damned Angelo!" (119, 121–22). Vincentio calms her and assures her that "you shall have your bosom on this wretch, Grace of the Duke, revenges to your heart,/ And general honor" (134–36), but he has lied to her again, and cruelly, probably to test her patience in the way he has tested Angelo's judgment and chastity. Neither character comes away from the exchange looking very good, and they both maintain a kind of vengeful selfishness that clouds the action throughout.

The major thematic thrust of the play reappears in the continuation of Angelo's soliloquy at the end of II.2:

> ... what art thou, Angelo?
> Dost thou desire her foully for those things
> That make her good? O, let her brother live!
> Thieves for their robbery have authority
> When judges steal themselves. What, do I love her,
> That I desire to hear her speak again? ...
> O cunning enemy, that to catch a saint,
> With saints dost bait thy hook! ...
> ... Never could strumpet ...
> Once stir my temper; but this virtuous maid
> Subdues me quite. Ever till now,
> When men were fond, I smil'd and wond'red how [172–86].

What are you, Angelo? He has seen himself as a saint, as he admits in line 179, almost an angel, as seeking only the good (174) and remaining above the desires of other men, as he admits in line 186.[14] His sudden and powerful passion hasn't bereft him of reason: he realizes we can hardly expect criminals to behave well when authorities behave badly. We can sympathize with errant feelings, but he fails to place any blame on himself for the directions his actions will take; he blames instead, ironically, Isabella's goodness, even virtue itself, and, perhaps somewhat aptly, the devil, though he fails to pursue that suggestion. The "cunning enemy" uses one saint to catch another: if Angelo were only to think through what he has said to himself, rather than burying it away, he would have a means to check his actions, if not his passions. He permits "the devil" to drive him on and readily forgoes his own free will, which might, if he were the saint he claims to be, lead him to accept the passion and deny the action. The excesses draw particular attention: after only one brief meeting, he wants to spare her brother and believes that he loves her; he calls a thoroughly natural passion "foul" (the foulness comes not in the desire, but how he must be already, unconsciously planning to satiate it). He lacks a sense of humanity, his own or others'.

Angelo iterates those thoughts, but with deeper commitment to them, soon after, in II.4:

> When I would pray and think, I think and pray
> To several subjects. Heaven hath my empty words,
> Whilst my invention, hearing not my tongue,
> Anchors on Isabel; heaven in my mouth,
> As if I did but only chew his name,
> And in my heart the strong and swelling evil
> Of my conception....
>   ... [M]y gravity,
> Wherein (let no man hear me) I take pride,
> Could I, with boot, change for an idle plume....
>   ... O place, O form,
> How often doest thou with thy case, thy habit,
> Wrench awe from fools, and tie the wiser souls
> To thy false seeming! Blood, thou art blood.
> Let's write "good angel" on the devil's horn ... [1–16].

Angelo's inability to pray recalls Claudius in Act III, scene 3 of *Hamlet*: "My words fly up, my thoughts remain below:/ Words without thoughts never to heaven go" (97–98). He wants to pray to rid him of wants, but what he really wants he can't pray for: he doesn't really *mean* the prayer he makes. Instead, he chews on the name of heaven, unable to swallow and digest his own words and thoughts.[15] He feels and understands the evil of his thoughts, but refuses to take responsibility for them. The pregnancy image appears often in *Measure*, here to clarify Angelo's connection to the lawbreakers he persecutes. He takes pride in his stoic behavior and demeanor, but will do nothing about the dangers pride creates; he blames instead his office, which the Duke has given him, which allows him to act on baser desires that he otherwise wouldn't have had the opportunity to exploit; he blames his blood, which he must recognize as human after all. The reference to "habit," the outer trappings that fool others into believing one has wisdom and deserves power, reflects not only the notion of sin as common experience, but the disguise that the Duke takes to test his charge. Sadly, the person in the habit should aid confession and contrition, not provide the means to propagate evil. "Blood, thou art blood": in recognizing his mutual humanity, Angelo can't get himself to spare Claudio his life and Isabella her honor, but instead excuses his own abuses of office — and so he, the self-proclaimed good angel, must accept the devil's horn. He does his evil willingly, in full possession of the knowledge it is evil, the point Milton will make in *Paradise Lost* about Satan — and Adam and Eve as well.[16]

Angelo also acts more devilish than angelic when the Duke returns to pass judgment on him. Escalus observes, "I am sorry, one so learned and so wise/ As you, Lord Angelo, have still appear'd/ Should slip so grossly, both in the heat of blood/ And lack of temper'd judgment afterward" (5.1. 470–73). Hearing that, Angelo doesn't even wait for the Duke's judgment; he repents in part: "I am sorry that such sorrow I procure,/ And so deep sticks it in my penitent heart/ That I crave death more willingly than mercy:/ 'Tis my deserving, and I do entreat it" (474–77). Like Marlowe's Faustus — or, later, Milton's Satan — Angelo either sees his fault as too great for forgiveness, or he would feel too embarrassed to accept forgiveness and go on amidst the public's knowledge of his failure. In either case, what he calls penitence we may equally consider a form of pride, a dangerous form that we must also recognize and defeat. Accepting forgiveness can prove even more difficult than accepting blame, if one then realizes the accompanying responsibility to do better thereafter. He must see himself as no better or worse than other mortals, equally subject to judgment, equally subject to failure, inferior in power, status, and perhaps quality to the judge.

In Angelo's actual proposition to Isabella, he shows a character that has not only fallen, but that continues to fall even further. Rather than ask her directly, he gives evasive hints of what he wants, attempting to lure her to proposition him instead, so that he need not take the blame for doing so. When he does pose the question, he presents it first as a hypothetical: would you rather that the law take your brother's life, or that you were to "[g]ive up your body to such sweet uncleanness/ As she that he hath stain'd?" (2.4.54–55). He adds, "I talk not of your soul; our compelled sins/ Stand more for number than for accompt." The uncleanness that might seem sweet to him wouldn't necessarily seem so to her, though, and his assertion that what she does under compulsion doesn't count as sin — though it will remain illegal, which he doesn't specify — won't apply if she *does* choose so to save her brother's life. Isabella either doesn't or refuses to understand, so again he states a hypothetical: consider "that either/ You must lay down the treasures of your body/ To this supposed, or else to let him suffer — what would you do?" (2.4.95–98). The Duke, still disguised as a friar, will later suggest to Isabella that Angelo was merely testing her, and were Isabella to complain of Angelo at this point, he could assert that he didn't mean it as she took it. But Isabella still resists Angelo's hints and replies with her own hypothetical: "Better it were a brother died at once,/ Than that a sister, by redeeming him,/ Should die for ever" (106–108). Angelo passes on her a direct and harsh religious judgment, "Were you not then as cruel as the sentence/ That you have slander'd so?" but even that doesn't sway her. Then he moves to another sort of insult, this time with a directive: "Be that you are,/ That is a woman; if you be more, you're none;/ If you be one ... show it now,/ By putting on the destin'd livery" (134–38). Angelo attempts to take away her freedom to choose in a particularly troubling way, especially to audiences of our time: be a real woman and submit to a man when he commands you, he says. Again Isabella claims not to feel revulsion, but not to understand. Finally Angelo makes his purpose so direct that Isabella can't ignore it: he claims, by his "honor," he loves her, and Claudio will not face execution if she loves him in return.

He doesn't love her, of course, but wants her body, and finally she reacts with revulsion: "Ha? little honor.... And most pernicious purpose! Seeming, seeming!/ I will proclaim thee, Angelo, look for't!" He gives the age-old answer: no one will believe you, because everyone knows me for austerity, and you will besmirch yourself instead. If that answer weren't bad enough, he then threatens not only to press on with the execution, but to torture Claudio first. Angelo has become the devil he already unconsciously knew himself to be. The Duke's exercise in dissembling has achieved its most horrid and horrifying result: power has not only corrupted Angelo, but wrought his utter fall, and that fall leaves the audience with the play's great problem, questioning whom, if anyone, we can trust. How at he end of the play can we feel happy about Marianna's marriage to such a man?

What can we do with Marianna as character? When we meet her at the beginning of Act IV, scene 1, she is listening, apparently with pleasure, to a boy sing a sad song about spurned love: she is still enjoying wallowing in her grief. When the Duke/friar arrives — apparently he has counseled her often, and she trusts him — she apologizes for experiencing any pleasure: "Let me excuse me, and believe me so,/ My mirth it much displeased, but pleased my woe" (lines 12–13). Why should a woman who suffered a kind of desertion through no fault of her own feel guilty about pleasure, and why should she take pleasure in recapitulating her woe? She does; Shakespeare, the great poet of human nature, knew that we indulge in that sort of silly self-torture and that it makes us feel better about ourselves. Offstage the Duke then acquaints her with his plot, to which she willingly submits: she still either believes she loves Angelo, asserts she loves him so that she looks faithful rather than frivolous, or really does love him even after what he has done to her and what he proposes to do to Isabella. Again we find a response partly surprising, but, maddeningly, humanly true. What we may call extreme fidelity in Marianna's case we may also call obsessive and blindly self-destructive — much like what we see in Helena in *All's Well*. Marianna lacks the strength of character to assert herself as a human being worthy of respect, honor, and love: marriage alone will be enough for her. We may too easily attribute that sort of reaction simply to Shakespeare's time, but Shakespeare has many female characters who assert themselves and seek what they want with courage, energy, and good spirits: Rosalind, Viola, Beatrice, Portia. We may wonder why they want what they want, but they have at least elements of admirable character, something of which we see little in *Measure for Measure*.

Problematic Weddings, and the Typical Lack of Closure

Act V restores the Duke to his public position of power and nominally resolves the relationships of the play with mercy, marriage, or both. But closure doesn't come more easily in *Measure for Measure* than it does in most Shakespeare plays.

Act IV, scene 4, prepares for the Duke's public return: "Every letter he hath write hath disvouch'd other," notes Escalus, and Angelo suggests, "His actions show much like to madness, pray heaven his wisdom be not tainted! And why meet him at the gates.... [W]hy should we proclaim it in an hour before his ent'ring, that if any crave redress of injustice, they should exhibit their petitions in the street?" (lines 1–9). Here we see the work of the Duke as "bad" playwright. Fortunately for him Angelo and Escalus intend him no harm: many of Shakespeare's characters would have killed in such an instance to keep they power they had received. And the Duke's actions, in fact, do seem mad, the whole elaborate plot built on a series of lies to uncover the inner failings of a man who to that point, while he has not been loving and kind, has at least acted lawfully. The orchestration of the ending gets everyone some degree of mercy for past actions, but some degree of trouble for the future.

Once again Shakespeare ends a play with complex circumstances surrounding marriages. One takes place offstage, with the promise of marriage—three more of them, in fact, to come, not one of them entirely appealing and hopeful. The potential marriages come from leadership problems, and the potential marital problems in each case come down to character problems. The problem-play problem comes from the fact that these bad weddings will fix nothing: if anything, they will make the situation of the world worse, and nothing has happened, through these matches or otherwise, to relieve the problems that have plagued the world or those pending problems that can turn it from merely topsy-turvy to disastrous.

Vincentio has prepared Isabella to make her case in public at the city gate, and he has warned her it may not go easily at first, but it will end well: she must exhibit courage and patience. That's a lot to ask of someone who has faced so much already and who experiences considerable vicissitudes of emotion. He has also prepared Angelo to believe he may get away with what he has done: "[W]e hear/ Such goodness of your justice, that our soul/ Cannot but yield you forth to public thanks,/ Forerunning more requital" (5.1.5–8). Angelo replies, "You make my bonds still greater." Both lines have the obvious and secondary meanings: the Duke must indeed requite Angelo for what he has done, and Angelo, hearing the Duke's praise, is more fully bound to him, but also suffers more from the bonds of sin that he has imposed on himself.

Isabella then comes forward on cue calling for justice. The Duke, as if he didn't know the problem, turns her appeal over to Angelo, asking her, again in a kind of pun, to "reveal yourself to him." She realizes he will accuse her of lying, but she states her case anyway; Angelo holds his bluff, but Isabella doesn't tell the truth, either: she claims that Angelo has deflowered her, not Mariana, as the Duke has instructed her. In the course of ten lines of exchange among Isabella, Angelo, and the Duke, we hear the word *strange* eight times and the word *truth* (or some close variant of it) six times: indeed the scene reveals strange truth, both unexpected and only partly true, the warning that Shakespeare delivers with sufficient force to make sure that the audience gets it. Truths usually come in pieces, mixed with untruths and outright lies, and getting a sense of resolution relies on happenstance or brave persistence, if we can reach it at all. Isabella accuses Angelo of lying, murder, adultery, and sexual violation, all partly true, and he in turn accuses her of madness. The Duke allows all that and orders Isabella carried off to prison, and Escalus, who has seemed rather cooler of mind and warmer of heart, offers, "Give me leave to question, you shall see how I'll handle her" (271–72): cruelty, again, comes too easily. When Mariana appears to confront the "cruel" Angelo, he asserts that he did indeed break their engagement, both because she didn't deliver her dowry and because he learned that "her reputation was disvalued/ In levity" (221–22): she wasn't rich enough or solemn enough for him. He even dares to express indignation and asks the Duke for "the scope of justice,/ My patience here is touched" (234–35): he suggests both Isabella and Mariana are part of a plot to ruin him, and there he is partly right, as the Duke has plotted to uncover his weaknesses. Lucio, for all his intrusive mouthiness, will utter one of the major points of the play in a Latin maxim: *Cucullus non facit monachum*, "the hood doesn't make the monk" (line 262): that point applies not only to Angelo, but to the Duke and to Isabella as well.

The Duke badly manages — and almost disastrously mismanages — his "return" to Vienna, nearly getting himself arrested in the process. Once again in charge, he immediately decrees that Angelo must pay for the death of Claudio — which of course hasn't happened — with his life, continuing to pursue his test. Instead, Angelo will end up "paying" by living married to Mariana, an odd "punishment" for his having on one hand followed the Duke's orders and on the other hand having committed what he believes to be a rape justifiable by his lustful compulsion.[17] Isabella still doesn't seem to feel too sad about her brother's death, nor can she feel too happy at his return: he has shown he doesn't regard her honor with as great esteem as she does.[18] The Duke pardons Lucio, an inveterate rascal (who has repeatedly insulted him), if occasionally a charming one,[19] and orders that he marry a prostitute: his punishment, and a legally appropriate if ethically disturbing one. While that punishment may fit the pattern of the other marriages, in that Lucio is now bound to the woman he has impregnated, as she to him, it has the secondary effect of creating another union that neither partner is likely to find appealing. Will Lucio treat his new wife lovingly?[20]

Vincentio then produces Claudio, who will now officially marry Juliet, pardon's him probably to gain Isabella's approval — not exactly a good reason — and essentially orders Isabella, regardless of her own wishes for her future — to marry him: "Give me your hand, and say you will be mine, he is my brother too" (5.1.492–93). She doesn't reply, apparently dumbfounded at the turn of events. His sexual temptation overcomes his own probably spurious claims to asceticism and ignores her probably genuine desire for it. He marries outside his class, and she acquires responsibilities to which she has not aspired and for which she has no preparation. Claudio and Juliet get the official marriage they want, but for a bad reason; they bring to the ending of the play the one reasonable hope of a happy match. But how will Claudio deal with his sister's powerful sense of his dishonor, and how will the Duke and Claudio deal with each other as brothers-in-law? No one has time to think through these rag-tag relationships, but everyone must deal with them: what should have involved active choice has become passive acceptance for everyone but the Duke, and the fact that he has arranged the end through deception doesn't place it in a more appealing light.

The Duke concludes the play (in an echo of Henry V's speech to Princess Katherine of France), "Whereto if you'll a willing ear incline,/ What's mine is yours, and what is yours is mine" (536–37). That would seem a generous offer if we had any reason to believe Isabella so inclined. The lines and their offer, though, typify *Measure for Measure*, as do those where the Duke speaks the title of the play: "An Angelo for Claudio, death for death! ... Like doth quit like, and *Measure* still for *Measure*" (5.1.409–11). Measure doesn't always follow measure: sometimes it does, sometimes it depends on whim and the anger, selfishness, or foolishness of the person who measures, and sometimes mercy wipes it away quite. That's the problem that leaves the play short of comedy or Romance and a step kinder than tragedy, with a hint of hope but with the lingering worry of more suffering lurking close by.

5

Comedic Problem Plays

    Like Shakespeare's other plays even those that we normally (and pretty comfortably) call comedies don't resolve so easily into generic category. Unlike those plays that steadfastly resist generic qualifications, *The Merchant of Venice*, *Troilus and Cressida*, *All's Well That Ends Well*, and *Measure for Measure*, the plays in this chapter use humor that does more than satirize painfully awful behavior or apply sarcasm to seemingly intractable human problems: they are actually at times funny with at least a brief touch of something joyful and affirming. They do, though, resist "happy endings": they conclude with problems either for the audience to try to solve or with which the world of the text must still deal. One leaves these plays, as usual with Shakespeare's work, feeling troubled, still without a strong sense of comic catharsis. I'll treat them—*Much Ado About Nothing*, *A Midsummer Night's Dream*, and *Twelfth Night*—in order from the funniest to the least funny, which also turns out to mean from the most problematic ending to the least problematic ending (though it still causes plenty of problems). Like the plays we have studied so far, the plays here highlight the problems they address first and last, so they remain more problem plays than comedies. They provide actors and directors more opportunity for light-hearted moments, but they either resist easy resolution, put it off, or undermine it entirely. *Much Ado* calls our attention both to how we often make something (and something awful) out of nothing and how we must also take care in *noting*: the two words would have sounded similar in Shakespeare's time and dialect. If we note carefully, Shakespeare suggests, we may take the positive step to make less ado over nothing; the problem often remains, though, because we so seldom pay careful attention to one another, blinded and deafened by our own thoughts and desires. *A Midsummer Night's Dream* warns us of rash action and even the rash expression of emotions; we must tread particularly carefully when we impose our feelings on others' romantic preferences, because those intrusions, though they may seem small or well intended, can lead to disaster. We must remain open and generous and avoid solipsism. *Twelfth Night* warns us about both of the above problems, but it adds particularly that we should appreciate the dangers and stupidity of practical jokes: the jokesters will inevitably make light of them — just a joke, right? — but the subjects of the jokes will not find the means to take them so lightly. If we think carefully and compassionately, we must agree with them that the joke can do more harm than good, whether we like them or not. We also learn, if we note carefully, to be true to our feelings as well as our thoughts: lying to oneself never helps. Each of these plays focuses on warnings and wariness rather than happiness and light-heartedness. The characters have found uncertainty rather than assurance: their choices and the results of those choices foreground problems rather than solutions and bring the plays to conclusion in doubt rather than joy.

Much Ado: *Dissembling and Delayed Salvation*

Readers and adapters of *Much Ado* have shown a tendency to want to re-name it "Benedick and Beatrice," based on the pleasure they have found in the witty exchanges between two funny characters that had such influence on the English stage in later times: banter became the dramatic centerpiece of comedy in many subsequent generations of plays from Restoration Comedy to Wilde and Bernard Shaw. I suspect our interest in Beatrice and Benedick also comes from our desire not to focus too much on the other half of the "romantic" plot, the wooing, almost killing, and almost wedding of Hero by Claudio: it comes closer to a horror story than a love story, and even the characters we like reach an unsettling conclusion. Beatrice becomes the center of wit and wisdom in the play, hers the voice the world of the play needs to hear and heed. But even in the final scene, when we may believe (or wish to believe) that love has won, she still rails at Benedick — and still probably reasonably so — until he quiets her with a kiss: "I yield upon great persuasion, and partly to save your life, for I was told you were in a consumption" (5.4.95–96), she says, giving in at last to the idea of marriage that she has resisted; "Peace," says Benedick, "I will stop your mouth." And he does, with a kiss. But in Shakespeare's idiom to stop one's mouth can mean to kiss or to kill, and in a sense Benedick kills Beatrice with that kiss: she speaks no more for the remainder of the play, and we must greatly fear the loss of her voice in this world that needs strength of character and resistance to tyranny and convention and prosaic idiocies so desperately.

Marjorie Garber calls *Much Ado* "Shakespeare's great play about gossip" (375), and that point more accurately but incompletely identifies the problem: we must add what people do with gossip once they hear it and when they fail to speak despite our need to listen. David Bevington finds Shakespeare "thinking his way through to a less paternalistic and less male-dominated idea about men and women" (*Ideas*, 31); much as does *A Midsummer Night's Dream*, the play condemns overzealous patriarchal control, and it shows the danger of silencing female voices or any voices that may express knowledge or wisdom that the world of the play definitely needs. The men in *Much Ado* do act paternalistically, and they act mostly badly: Leonato willingly believes what Don Pedro and Claudio say about his daughter though he has no evidence that she has ever acted other than perfectly morally: he doesn't even bother to ask her the truth! The plot hinges on rumors or assertions that are not only wrong, but also lies: Antonio has heard wrongly that Don Pedro woos Hero for himself; Don John lies that Don Pedro has wooed Hero for himself; Don John deceives Claudio and Don Pedro about Hero, who has never had a romantic (let alone sexual) assignation. But even the "good" characters practice deception, using gossip or rumor and positions of power to produce ends that they want to see, whether good or not.

Most of all, I think, the play addresses the problems of *dissembling*, or misleading others, even if an act nominally aims at someone else's good. We have addressed this problem in other plays, but in *Much Ado* it takes center stage in the movement of the plot and the foregrounding of the problems — which, once again, the end of the play leaves lingering. When Leonato finally gathers his sense and courage after what Claudio has done to his daughter, he accuses him, "Marry, thou dost wrong me, thou dissembler, thou" (5.1.52–53). Leonato gets the point wrong — Claudio has wronged Hero, not him, other than by association — but he gets the word right: *dissembling*, Claudio's and that of others, provides the means by which the problems in *Much Ado* cause their harm. Dogberry, for all his hilarious malapropisms — and after Beatrice he provides most of the enjoyable and useful comedy in the play — gets the statement of the problem right when for the examination of Borachio and Conrade in V.2.1 he asks, "Is our whole dissembly appear'd?" He means *assembly*, and of course the whole *dissembly* hasn't appeared — that would take the whole cast — but the play gives us an assembly of dissemblers. Not much of anyone represents himself or herself truly. Shakespeare uses that point thematically and narratively to drive character and plot so we may see how epidemic dissembling unfolds.

The most obvious act of dissembling occurs when Don John sets up his "play within the play," when his man Borachio meets Margaret at Hero's window. Don John aims to break up the marriage for no other reason than it will please him to hurt Claudio, who has received praise and preferment from his brother the Prince. Borachio knows that he is creating "poison," and he will later call Don John "the devil my master" (3.3.155): Don John begins the course of evil action in the play, but he doesn't bear responsibility for all of it: like the Devil in Christian tradition, he takes away no one's free will, but misleads us so that we will choose poorly: cruelly and self-indulgently. "Only to despite them [the lovers], I will endeavor any thing" (2.2.31–32), Don John scowls. Like Milton's Satan two generations after Shakespeare's play, he knowingly commits evil to cause pain, sets himself against good as a continuing act of despite.[1] He dissembles for evil purpose with no equivocation, so in his case we can readily call the dissembling "bad." Beatrice sees through him, but no one pays attention: "I never can see him but I am heart-burn'd an hour after" (2.1.3–4). The odd eating image that appears repeatedly in the play makes the metaphor difficult to parse, but probably more important here is the "burning" part of the image: bad actions or a bad person will burn one's heart, and heart pain doesn't heal so easily — it makes a hell of its own.

But the "good" characters dissemble with equal energy and nonchalance. The masked ball of II.1 encourages everyone to dissemble, to hide identity, and everyone does. Don Pedro does it for good intention in the wooing of Hero for Claudio, though the result nearly turns bad, but he also uses the occasion, once he has unmasked, in what may or may not be an attempt to woo (or seduce?) Beatrice. He threatens to find her a husband and suddenly asks, "Will you have me, lady?" She brushes him off with a half-taunt, "No, my lord, unless I might have another for working-days. Your Grace is too costly to wear every day." (lines 326–29). She knows he must marry someone of higher status, but rather than accuse him of simply trying to seduce her, she hints that because of his status he would take her lightly and she, in return, would have to cuckold him. He takes her taunt playfully ("to be merry most becomes you"), probably as fearful of her jokes as Benedick but too princely to admit it. Beatrice, too, uses the dance to taunt Benedick again; he pretends not to recognize her to try to find out what she really thinks of him, and she pretends equally, calling him "the Prince's jester, a very dull fool" (137–38). Though we must call her "good" for her morality, her wit and wisdom, and her defense of her friend and truth, Beatrice doesn't rise above the temptation to use her wit cruelly: it defends her, and she doesn't spare her opponents.

The deceptions that lead to Beatrice and Benedick's expressing their feelings to each other we may also want to consider benign, but they, too, lead others to say what they don't feel willing or ready to say. Do even friends have the right to deceive for what they consider good? Shakespeare doesn't answer that question in *Much Ado*, but he certainly raises it: can we call a method of interaction good if characters (and persons) can use it for evil as well as good ends? Doesn't it simply amount to deception either way, when honesty and directness might work better or at least be more ethical? And how do we process the problem that even Hero, an otherwise nearly salvific character, also willingly participates in the dissembling?

5. Comedic Problem Plays

The scene that reunites Hero and Claudio (V.4) also involves dissembling, though for the ostensible purpose of a holy rite: by means of the Friar's plan Claudio comes to take "another Hero" for his wife, still believing the first dead. "Hymen now with luckier issue speed's/ Than this for whom we rend'red up this woe," he has said at the end of scene 3: now he refuses to accept responsibility for what he has already done to Hero, claiming it bad luck rather than his childish, cruel, and shameful choice to abuse her publicly. Having learned of Don John's dissembling directly from Borachio, he exclaims, "Sweet Hero, now thy image doth appear in the rare semblance that I lov'd it first" (5.1.251–52), but he admits only that he loved an image, a semblance, not the young woman herself. A gentleman, even finding dependable evidence of Hero's infidelity, wouldn't have found any need to cause harm: "where I would wed her, there will I shame her" (3.2.125). In V.4 he asks, "Which is the lady I must seize upon?" The image suggests not only emotional disengagement but brutality: he will seize the lady, not try to love her and honor her. Often the only positive we can gain from our bad actions is that we have learned better; Claudio has learned nothing. Hero will marry him, but with no reason yet to believe he has become any better person than the Claudio who leaped to a rash and nearly destructive judgment without troubling to note the truth of the circumstance. The Friar's dissembling may renew a marriage commitment, but it has little chance of working for the happiness of the couple involved. He can't help a man who doesn't know what love means and doesn't appear to want to know.

Not surprisingly the characters in this world find love *strange*. In IV.1 Benedick tells Beatrice, "I do love nothing in the world so well as you — is not that strange?" and she replies, "As strange as the thing I know not. It were as possible for me to say I lov'd nothing so well as you, but believe me not; and yet I lie not: I confess nothing, nor I deny nothing" (267–73). Benedick finally declares his love, but also declares it strange, and Beatrice finds it too strange to declares at all. She equivocates and changes the subject: "I am sorry for my cousin." In II.1 Beatrice warns Hero that "wooing, wedding, and repenting, is as a Scotch jig, a measure, and a cinquepace; the first suit is hot and hasty ... the wedding, mannerly-modest ... and then comes repentance, and with his bad legs falls into the cinquepace faster and faster, till he sink into his grave" (73–80). The order comes out wrong for a happy marriage: one should first repent of any sins, then woo, then wed. The person who repents afterward has married poorly: exactly the warning Beatrice intends, suggesting Hero move slowly toward wedding so that she doesn't end up in a bad marriage merely waiting (and hoping) to die. A few lines below when Don Pedro asks Hero if she will "walk about with your friend" — he wants to tell her something in private that he intends in a friendly manner — apt to

Beatrice's warning she replies, "So you walk softly, and look sweetly, and say nothing, I am yours for the walk, and especially when I walk away" (87–90). She expects, and perhaps fears, from what her uncle has heard and her father has told her, that Don Pedro will woo her for himself, and she essentially asks him to do no such thing: say *nothing*. He woos for Claudio rather than himself, and by the end of the dance she has accepted Claudio through Don John's proposal. She has by then either forgotten Beatrice's warning or ignored it, or she has felt too intimidated to joke further with Don Pedro or too ready to love Claudio, so that she has given in to him. As Hero and Don Pedro speak offstage, Beatrice and Benedick are dancing onstage. Perhaps too intent on their conversation, they must miss a step and fall behind the other dancers, since Beatrice recalls his attention to their movement: "We must follow the leaders" (150–51). "In every good thing," Benedick answers, and Beatrice adds, "Nay, if they lead to any ill, I will leave them at the next turning." Indeed, they should follow their leaders only in their good choices, not their bad ones, and they must feel willing to plot their own course should the leaders act badly. Beatrice apparently has always done so, and Benedick understands the need to do so as well. They bear the responsibility of fee will and must choose wisely, or they too will end up failing and repenting—they, unlike the other characters, at least recognize that wisdom.

Circumspection allows for wisdom, and wisdom allows for fidelity, avoiding false steps. Fidelity can lead to salvation at last. The other characters, rash in their judgments and too quick to bad judgments, must wait and hope for mercy. Eventually Beatrice and Benedick may grant mercy to each other and enjoy their mutual love. Hero grants mercy to Claudio and forgives him for judging and shaming her cruelly and hastily. Will Claudio grant Hero real love and prove to her his fidelity? Whether he can find salvation in love we don't know—the play ends before he can prove it—but what we have seen of his character gives us no reason yet to believe that he will. We may hope for it, but not expect it: there we find the great problem of the ending.

MY LADY TONGUE: ARE YOU YET LIVING?

We know from their very first actions that Beatrice and Benedick are, if not in love, at least attracted to each other. At the beginning of the play, when Don Pedro's soldiers enter Messina after a victorious military campaign,[2] Beatrice's first words concern Benedick: "I pray you, is Signior Mountanto[3] return'd from the wars or no?" Beatrice then says a number of insulting things about Benedick: she hints at cowardice, for she has "promis'd to eat all of his killing," meaning that she told him before he left that he wouldn't actually have enough courage to face and kill an enemy in battle — ironic, since she will ask him to kill Claudio, the apparent "hero" of the war, after he has shamed Hero in Act IV, scene 1. She will suggest that though Benedick might do good service to a lady (i.e., show courtly affection), he could never have sufficient courage to serve a lord in battle and that he eats with more energy than he fights, that he is a "stuff'd man," someone who tries to appear gallant but who has no heart for real fighting. She calls their exchanges of wit "conflict," and Leonato refers to them as "skirmishes," continuing the motif of war with which the play begins — not a hopeful volley of love.

When Benedick appears shortly after, also in scene 1, Beatrice insults him directly, saying that he need not speak, since no one listens to him anyway. He addresses her as "my Lady Disdain" and asks, "Are you yet living?" Oddly he asks the same question she does, though unlike Beatrice he already knows the answer. Benedick's question both insults Beatrice in return — it paraphrases something like "oh, you: we'd be better off if you were dead" — and serves the audience as a *memento mori*: while he could have died in battle, she could have died of illness. In Shakespeare's time the average life-span hovered around thirty-five or forty years. They immediately begin an insult match, which Beatrice would probably win; Benedick tries to get in the last word and make a hasty exit, but he fails, and fortunately for him the others present break in to redirect conversation. Claudio addresses Benedick aside, proclaiming his love for Hero, and Benedick tries through jokes and evasions to dissuade him. Claudio explains his love synaesthetically, "In mine eye, she is the sweetest lady that ever I looked on" (lines 187–88): she looks such that if I could taste her, she would taste sweet. The mixing of metaphors suggests Claudio's confusion, and we see that confusion come out later in how he treats Hero. That confusion also troubles Beatrice and Benedick: when they meet, they fight; Beatrice wouldn't ask about him if she didn't care about him, and Benedick admires and fears her wit, or he wouldn't both engage it and then flee from it.

We soon see, however, how far their feelings stray from disdain. In II.3 Don Pedro and Claudio dissemble: that is, they play a trick on Benedick to get him to fall for Beatrice. "[M]an is a fool when he dedicates his behaviors to love," (lines 8–9), Benedick says, but as soon as he hears from his friends that Beatrice is suffering for love of him, he immediately converts: "I must not seem proud; happy are they that hear their detractions, and can put them to mending" (228–30),[4] and he adds as a more practical consideration "the world must be peopled" (242). He talks himself into doing what Don Pedro and Claudio needn't have talked him into doing, because he wants to do it: he needs only a reason and an opportunity to proclaim his affection for Beatrice. He must have loved her all along. Hero and Ursula play the same joke on Beatrice in III.1. Knowing Beatrice is listening, they claim that Benedick loves her, but that she has too great a pride in her wit and will only sport with him, however much he may love her. Beatrice, too, would not have her friends condemn her "for pride and scorn," so she will eagerly requite him (108–111). When they must publicly proclaim their mutual love in Act V, they both try to get out of it, and only written documents that state their love and that their friends produce for public view direct them to accept their feelings — which, even then, they refuse to admit and accept fully. "Do you not love me?" Benedick asks, and Beatrice replies, "No more than reason," and he answers her like question in kind (5.4.73–78). They both claim to love reason, though they probably love wisdom, which is only part reason, more, and they resist giving in to love even when they can hardly deny it any longer. They take the opposite course of Claudio and Hero's: those two leap in regardless of the problems that haunt their match. Benedick will even overrule the Prince and put off the wedding one last time, calling for a dance instead. The dance creates a festive ending for stage performance, but it suspends ritual and commitment — a final warning against rashness but also a closing expression of diffidence toward committed love.

And we must wonder whether the use of dissembling to get someone to proclaim love, though it seem good, actually does good. Do we have the right to intrude on others' private thoughts and feelings to try to make them act?

So what keeps them apart? René Girard suggests they "are really afraid of each other" (80). That makes sense: if either were to make the first move, the other may ridicule him or her mercilessly. The one who dares to show affection may then become the object of public scorn as well as personal embarrassment. The problem then carries over to Hero and Claudio. Claudio fears telling Hero that he has fallen in love with her, so he allows Don Pedro to woo her for him. Don Pedro agrees and succeeds, but Don John leads him to believe that Don Pedro has wooed for himself, not for Claudio. Don Pedro immediately dispels that error, and Claudio wins his bride. Leonato, hearing a rumor that the Prince will woo his daughter, instructs her that she should accept him. But Hero willingly accepts not Don Pedro's suit, but Claudio's without question. Why doesn't she show the fear that Beatrice and Benedick — though they must at least suspect each other's interest — show and that Claudio shows? She acts, unlike Hermia in *A Midsummer Night's Dream*, as the perfect submissive and agreeable daughter. But she has made a terrible error in accepting Claudio: he is youthful and rash, and the easy path by which he goes from claiming to love her to his willingness to shame her at their wedding mass should astonish an audience. If he loved her, he might back away from marrying her, but he certainly wouldn't subject her to public shame: he would try to learn more about what happened expecting to find not that Hero had done wrong, but that someone had tried to ruin her. Why would he believe what he doesn't see, but what someone tells him he sees *in the dark*— and that someone is Don John, though the Prince's brother, hardly a person to trust. Hero and Claudio will need to do what perhaps Beatrice and Benedick have learned to do: mend the breach between them.[5]

We must learn to *note*, to make choices, and to choose wisely enough to come to trust our judgment. In V.2 Benedick will reflect to Beatrice that the world is full of suffering, "therefore is it most expedient for the wise, if Don Worm (his conscience) find no impediment to the contrary, to be the trumpet of his own virtues" (83–86): he must take some initiative to tell and show Beatrice he loves her. She, however, is reflecting on her sorrow for Hero, not on Benedick or herself. Attentive, *noting*, he asks how Hero is doing: "Very ill," she answers. "And how do you?" he asks; "Very ill too." "Serve God, love me, and mend" (93), Benedick suggests, both to Beatrice and in a broader sense to the audience. People will do evil things; we will make mistakes ourselves; we may choose to serve God, love each other and one another, and try to heal from what we have done and what others have done to us: Shakespeare's answer to the problems that come from dissembling and that constitute the general human plight.

The Good and Bad in Being an Ass

When Dogberry and the other watchmen catch Conrade and Borachio talking about what they have done to Hero, Don John's henchmen insult them repeatedly. In IV.2, having arrested Borachio and Conrade in a street after hearing their overzealous conversation about what they have done to Hero, the Watch have brought them to prison for questioning. Dogberry asks them, "Masters, do you serve God?" (16). "Yea, sir, we hope," but Borachio has already said that he serves "the devil my master," Don John, and they have in fact served the Devil through the evil they have done. Dogberry makes a terrible mess of the questioning, both in protocol and in language. He accuses them of burglary, which they didn't do, and proclaims they shall be "condemned into everlasting redemption for this" (56–57). He means of course *perdition*, but the malapropism makes a point of its own: Hero as Christ-figure will forgive Claudio, and these men, too, can find forgiveness if they wish it. With the evidence and their admission of what they've done in III.3, plus the fact of Don John's flight from Messina, Dogberry insists "let them be opinion'd" (67): he means *pinioned*, bound, but the error calls attention to the importance of the tension between *opinion* and *noting* in the play: characters often make statements or take action without really *knowing* what they're doing — they act in response to rumors or lies or their own desires rather than whatever truth they might potentially find. "Coxcomb," Conrade calls Verges, and "Away, you are an ass, you are an ass," he exclaims at Dogberry. The miffed constable responds with consternation, "Dost thou not suspect my place? Dost thou not suspect my years? ... But, masters, remember that I am an ass; though it be not written down, yet forget not that I am an ass.... Bring him away. O that I had been writ down an ass!" (74–87). He means that they show no *respect* for his position and his age, and he wants them punished for calling him an ass. They don't respect him because he speaks and carries out his office so poorly, but Shakespeare wants to make sure that the audience sees Dogberry specifically as ass, partly in the modern sense of a stupid person, but partly in the use more typical of Shakespeare's time as beast of burden. Dogberry in fact carries the burden of the play that no one else wants to carry. He may not want to do his job, but he does it when others fail in theirs, and because he does it the world finds what redemption it can: by catching Don John's henchmen, he has uncovered the plot against Hero, and that information will allow for Claudio's potential redemption. Hero may forgive him. He will get another chance that he doesn't deserve, but that he receives through mercy. Dogberry, like Hero, serves God, ass though he be.

When we meet Dogberry in III.3, he is questioning the watchmen, and he and his assistant Verges are already full of malapropisms. "Are they good men and true?" Dogberry asks. "Yea, or else it were pity but they should suffer salvation [he means *damnation*], body and soul," Verges answers. Dogberry asks him who he believes the most "desartless" man (he means *deserving*) for constable. He errs again with *senseless* for *sensible* and *comprehend* for *apprehend*. The errors provide humor, in that they words say the opposite of what the speaker means, but that verbal trope tells us what Shakespeare is doing in the play: we often don't say what we mean, and the intentions we express to others seldom indicate our true motivations. Dogberry tells his watchmen, essentially, not to do their job: if they run into troublesome persons, let them go, because troublesome persons make trouble, and one should leave that sort alone and not meddle with them, the better to keep one's own honesty. He does, though, appropriately and by good hap assign them to watch Leonato's door because of the upcoming wedding, and they immediately meet Borachio and Conrade, with Borachio bragging about their successful plot against Hero. They are also discussing, oddly, fashion, apparently as a part of normal conversation because they have no qualms whatever about the trouble they have caused. "[W]hat a deformed thief this fashion is" (3.3.130–31), Borachio says, and one of the Watch will insist that they catch this fellow "Deformed," too, who has participated in the plot. One suspects that Borachio and Conrade could have escaped such incompetent watchmen had they wished, but, as the scene ends, they practically lead the way to jail themselves: "Come, we'll obey you." Don John's men know they have done wrong, and they have served someone "deformed," not of body, but of character. We know Don John is a bastard, and Shakespeare's time thought bastardy likely to produce bad character, but Don John has free will, as do the other characters, and he chooses to use it specifically to do ill. Sadly enough, the dialogue suggests, deformity of character is the "fashion" rather than the exception. Don John may act badly, but so do many of the other characters. His men having caught the plotters, Dogberry asks Leonato to examine the miscreants, but Leonato brushes off his duty and asks Dogberry, whom he recognizes as someone of limited ability and intelligence, to do it himself. Leonato fails there as governor, and he also fails as father: he assumes Hero guilty when he should know better. Leonato has also fallen into the fashion of "deformed" character: he avoids his duty. Similarly Don Pedro should know better than to believe his brother and accept what Don John tells him to see from a distance in the shadows, and he should stop Claudio from trying to shame Hero in public: a good leader would leave private matters private. The Prince also fails in his duty, falling into the fashion of the time.

For Hero, too, we must have great admiration: she show incredible, even in-human kindness not only in forgiving Claudio, but in forgiving her father for not believing in her innocence. She "dies" metaphorically for the good of the world, and she rises from the dead to show everyone the value of self-sacrificing love. Hero as *hero* of the play also bears a kind of burden, but one too great for most humans: few of us can go through mortification and resurrection without a trace of spite or vengeful will. Benedick also accepts a burden against his will that, fortunately for all involved, Hero's forgiveness of Claudio relieves him of carrying out. But all that heroic thought and action depends on the most common and least verbally adept of characters, one for whom wit and nobility of blood have no tangible reality. Duty comes from action, not from pedigree or repartee.

We may not admire Dogberry, but as the "ass" in the play he carries the burden others will not carry: he does their duties and helps produce what justice and mercy the world of the play will allow. Shakespeare takes particular pains, in fact, to make sure we understand that Dogberry, despite even Leonato's disrespect for him, carries that burden. The noble folk may speak of love and duty, but they often fail to carry it out; Dogberry speaks to the watch of avoiding their duty, but when necessity comes, he and they carry it out and do not fail. Dogberry alerts Leonato to what has occurred with Hero and saves Hero's reputation and in a sense her life. He does what the other characters should have done, but don't. Beatrice would fight for her cousin, but her society won't permit her; Benedick will fight at Beatrice's behest, but even were he to avenge Hero, he would serve honor and properly chastise Claudio, but he could not bring back to life a dead Hero. Were he to kill Claudio, he would deprive the Prince of a good young soldier: Benedick's choice, though honorable, will not in any way make the world better. Benedick for his desire to do well and Beatrice for all her brilliant wit can't carry the burden of justice and mercy; Dogberry must lead the noble folk to justice so Hero can offer the mercy they don't deserve, but that they desperately need.

LOVE AND MARRIAGE — AND SALVATION IN ALLEGORY

We expect a Shakespeare comedy to end with a marriage, but *Much Ado* does not: in ends with the promise of two marriages, the progress toward which is interrupted by the resistance of one or more of the participants, by devilish dissembling, and finally by Benedick's insistence that they have a dance first.

Even from the beginning of the "marriage plot," we may reasonably ask about motivation. Claudio responds to Hero's beauty: he knows little about her character. When he asks for information, he doesn't seek further knowledge of her as a person, but instead requests of Don Pedro, "Hath Leonato any son, my lord?" (I.1.293). Don Pedro answers, "No child but Hero, she's his only heir." Why does Claudio ask that question? Don Pedro's answer seems to suggest the reason, which Claudio doesn't correct: Claudio wonders what he will inherit if he marries Hero. He wants her not just for herself and for love of her, but partly for what he can get from her: quite a bit, since Leonato is governor of Messina and well off. The text gives us no sense that Claudio has any particular wealth of his own, though he does have a title, *Count*. We may consider him practical in quickly latching onto a beautiful, wealthy, and socially well-placed wife, but that reading undermines the notion of Claudio as a *naïf* who hasn't quite the grown-up gumption to woo for himself. Shakespeare, I think, intended it too, because he wanted us not to like Claudio too completely and too easily. Audiences may readily sympathize with young persons in love: we want that person to find his or her love and happiness. Especially once we learn of Claudio's heroism, we want him to win his Hero: he is young, handsome, and eager. But, like the other characters in *Much Ado*, he schemes, and what we find beneath his surface looks not nearly so appealing as we had hoped.

In many ways *Much Ado About Nothing*, as much fun as we find in it, dwells more, if we read it as a piece of realism, in the realm of melancholy than of comedy. We may admire the wit of Beatrice and Benedick and the mercy and forgiveness that Hero shows Claudio and our belief in the strength of young, romantic love so much that we forget what has actually happened. Don John is a storm-cloud waiting to drown any happiness he can find, and even Beatrice, for all her wit and beauty and love for her friend, eagerly consigns the man she loves to a dual that will throw his life — or the life of his battle-companion — into the hazard. But we must recognize the danger in a world where such a figurative devil as Don John can so easily ruin a marriage out of simple mean-spiritedness. We must remain wary, even when we want escape.

Normally in a Shakespeare play the person in power gets the last word. Here Don Pedro does not; Benedick does. A messenger has arrived to proclaim to the Prince that "your brother John is ta'en in flight,/ And brought with armed men back to Messina" (125–26). Benedick takes over Don Pedro's role, commanding, "Think not on him till to-morrow. I'll devise thee brave punishments for him. Strike up, pipers." A dangerous and cagey man, Don John may well escape his captors, but whether he does or not, Benedick shouldn't be working out his punishments: he should be enjoying his marriage to Beatrice. He puts off both his own wedding (and Claudio and Hero's) and public justice (on Don John) for a dance, another turn from practical resolution to frivolity. Again the nobles have failed in their duty, and they have even failed in their own pleasure, which apparently places even torturous punishments above marriage. Dogberry's lesson has failed: the nobility still have not learned how to direct their attention. But perhaps Hero's lesson may yet work.

The only means to save the play from what looks like a horrific pending marriage and the persistent disease of bad judgment is to read it allegorically. Hero serves not as a real girl waiting for a real marriage, but as a Christ figure, someone willing to forgive and love unconditionally the person who will accept that love. At the same time she creates a human hero who has learned the Christian lesson of forgiveness, one that Shakespeare's often violent and retributive audience had hardly assimilated.

I have my doubts: the silence of Beatrice creates another sense of trouble as the play ends. We need her voice, that of wisdom in wit, more than we ever have, and we must depart hoping that pending marriage hasn't silenced it. Leonato, in mourning for what has happened to his daughter as Act V begins, responds to Antonio's attempts to ease his grief with "I pray thee peace. I will be flesh and blood,/ For there was never yet philosopher/ That could endure the toothache patiently" (34–36). The folk of *Much Ado* haven't done well with their toothaches, and they seem to have trouble distinguishing small pains from big ones. Like Benedick's challenging Claudio, their wit (Beatrice's discernment even more than Benedick's discoveries) has left them, and they had better hope to get it back. Wit alone doesn't suffice, but a world without wit has little hope of understanding much beyond peopling and punishment. We just need to learn to heed and use it better. But Beatrice and Benedick have not married yet; nor have Hero and Claudio. Perhaps they won't. And maybe that's good.

A Midsummer Night's Dream *and a Table for Eight*

Harold Goddard calls *A Midsummer Night's Dream* "one of the lightest and in many respects the most playful of Shakespeare's plays," but he adds that it also announces the "conviction that underlies every one of his supreme Tragedies: that the world of sense ... is but the surface of a vaster unseen world by which the actions of men are affected or overruled" (Vol. 1, 74). The Faeries in this world do have some control over humans: they can cast spells to change feelings, tastes, or the shapes of the humans they meet. They appear to bear no ill-will towards humans, and they may even try to do some good, but they haven't the skill or power to bless people or help us avoid bad decisions or tragic errors, and their attempts to help may do more harm than good. Regardless of otherworldly intervention, we humans will make our mistakes anyway and suffer the consequences: this play points directly to that truth. We still bear the responsibility to do our duty, behave well — in or out of love — and take care of one another. Metamorphoses, our periodic transitions from human to beast, can teach us that lesson, but they can't make us practice better discipline and greater kindness. We must learn and push ourselves to do so even when duty and love don't seem in our own best interest. This dramatic whirlwind begins in dangerous if spirited disobedience and ends with a warning against rashness even in love and a blessing that won't work. It begins and ends with problems.

STARTING WITH AN ENDING

Because the study of Classical myth has less importance and less educational influence in our time than it did in Shakespeare's, audiences now miss one of the major points of the play as a whole. The blessings that Oberon's faeries bestow on the court of Theseus and Hippolyta and on their marriage will fail: Theseus and Hippolyta do not have a "happy ending." Their story appeared in Plutarch's *Lives* but also in many other sources, for instance in Seneca's *Phaedra* and Euripides *Hippolytus*.[6] Theseus does not remain happily married to Hippolyta, but puts her aside and marries the younger Phaedra, who falls in love with her stepson (Hippolyta's son) Hippolytus. When the boy spurns her, she accuses him of attempting to rape her, and Theseus call's down the wrath of Neptune/Poseidon upon him: Hippolytus is killed by a rushing wave, but the truth comes out, Phaedra hangs herself, and Theseus is left alone to ponder his rash and destructive judgments and the great sorrows of mortality and betrayal.

That "ending" comes well after the conclusion of *A Midsummer Night's Dream*, but, once we recall it, it colors how we perceive the whole. The play becomes not a nostalgic screwball comedy of youthful love and adventure, but a prelude that offered hope for something good and lasting that we know did not come to pass: it turns, in a sense, elegiac, to lament, where the comedy of the couples and the rustics fails even to lighten the pain. We would wish that a world with that potential for humor and giving could produce people with compassion and fidelity. Our best hope for that understanding lies not with the nobles, but with the this play's version of the Shakespearean *ass*: in this case Bottom, who in his few moments on stage carries the play both as entertainment and as a conveyor of its most important ideas. He looks for poetry and art in his soul, he enjoys the moment when it allows, and he thinks both of himself and of others: regardless of abilities, he tries to do well and to do good, to understand where he can, and to allow for a touch of mystery.

We have at the end of the play at least one happy and lasting marriage, one of the few in all of Shakespeare's plays: that of Oberon and Titania. Despite what Oberon does to Titania, their marriage goes on, as it must already have for time out of mind. We don't see kindness in it, nor generosity, nor equality, but we do see forgiveness and something that looks like the true love of a long-married couple. It isn't always pretty, but it lasts, and both of them want to keep it. Where it lacks equality, it has mutuality. One gets the sense that they must over time regularly have quarreled and played tricks on each other. They get over it. They stay in love. Not easy, but they try...

Their subplot, essentially the "middle" of the play, paralleling or accompanying the time the two young couples-to-be dash about the woods, points back to the hint of problem at the beginning of the play and the hint of hope at the end. Happiness in this world is possible, if we work on it, but unless one happens to be immortal, it may well remain fleeting. Despite the nastiness of Oberon's joke, the Faery King and Queen look like one of Shakespeare's happiest married couples, a sobering notion indeed.

A Second Ass, and the Rustics

Perhaps the most loved character in the play, Bottom, changes shape: Oberon gives him the head of an ass as a further step in the joke he plays on

Titania — bad enough simply using the love potion to make her fall for a mortal. But like Dogberry in *Much Ado,* Bottom does serve as the "ass" in the play, the beast of burden who carries the most important idea. He explains the meaning of *Pyramus and Thisby,* whether correctly or not, and he shows concern for the play's audience: he wants to please and not offend them, much like what we find in Shakespeare's occasional epilogues. He wants to do not only his duty, but everyone else's: he would eagerly take every part in the play if Quince would let him, even parts not in the play: "I could play Ercles rarely, or a part to tear a cat in" (1.2.29–30) — he presents an excessive and comic but eager and in many ways admirable energy.[7] He will willingly and cheerfully attempt whatever burdens come his way, a lesson many of Shakespeare's characters should learn.

When Puck intervenes in the rustics' play practice to work mischief and to enact Bottom's metamorphosis, they run away in fear. Snout, entering late and coming on Bottom transformed": "O Bottom, thou art chang'd! What do I see on thee?" "You see an ass-head of your own, do you?" Bottom replies (3.1.114–117) Bottom is calling Snout an ass because he can't see his own transformation, into which he settles quite comfortably. Quince returns to help, but can do nothing for his friend, who feels mostly just perplexed when Titania awakes, dosed with the love potion by Oberon as a joke, and falls in love with him: "Methinks, mistress, you should have little reason for that. And yet, to say the truth, reason and love keep little company together now-a-days" (142–44). There we find the great problem of the play: how to make sense of love relationships (both in and outside the play) when we seldom have good reasons for why we feel as we do (or as we proclaim we do). Bottom accepts the circumstance readily enough and settles comfortably into it, even his imprisonment by Titania: "Thou shalt remain here, whether thou wilt or no" (153), a command that also refers to the state of love in the play. Bottom gets content enough with a good head-scratch, a little honey, oats, and hay, and a nap: "I am such a tender ass" (4.1.25), he says, and Titania doesn't object.

"Jealous Oberon" (2.1.24)[8] has got Titania — and Bottom — into this embarrassment, but he acts no differently, no better, than the other "noble" characters: Titania won't give him what he wants, so he gets his revenge. Before the story of the play began Demetrius claimed to love Helena, but at Egeus's urging he shifts his affections to Hermia — we never quite learn why. Hermia rejects him for Lysander — again, hard to know why, as the two young men seem mostly interchangeable — she at least tries to remain true. Lysander at least shows a little wisdom: "The course of true love never did run smooth" (1.1.134),[9] he observes to Hermia. But he errs as she does, also escaping to the woods with Hermia without parental consent and against the Duke's wish. Hippolyta will marry Theseus not because she loves him, but because he has kidnapped her and insists on it: she has no choice. Repeated attempts to take away the free will of another move the plot and establish one source of the problems in the play; the other comes simply from characters' making their own bad decisions. Whether by Puck's mischief, Oberon's jealousy, Egeus's parental bullying, or Theseus' version of *droit de seigneur*, too many characters impose their will, creating likely but chaotic and dangerous results.[10]

Bottom, awakening at the end of IV.1, has come to himself again, ready to play Pyramus, but first he must reflect on his dream, that "most rare vision":

> Man is but an ass, if he go about [t']expound this dream.... Methought I was, and methought I had — but man is but [a patch'd] fool, if he will offer to say what methought I had. The eye of man hath not heard, the ear of man hath not seen, man's hand is not able to taste, his tongue to conceive, nor his heart to report.... I will get Peter Quince to write a ballet of this dream. It shall be call'd "Bottom's Dream," because it hath no bottom, and I will sing it in the latter end of the play, before the Duke. Peradventure, to make it more gracious, I shall sing it at her death [204–19].

His synaesthetic mixed metaphors express both the clouded state of his mind and impossibility that any mortal can understand what Bottom has undergone. His desire to sing his dream at Thisby's death shows both the elegiac sentiment he associates with his experience — the sadness of its loss as well as the horror of shape-change — and his inability to reign himself, to stop with the appropriate and avoid the excess: he wants the play to tell everything, and he wants to play all the parts so he can tell everything himself. That self-obsession affects all the other characters, but most of them lack any of Bottom's generosity. He does it to share; they do it to control. Bottom as ass carries the burden of showing us not the good, but the better way. He, too, needs balance and judgment, but at least he has kindness. That trait distinguishes the rustics generally and accounts for their importance in the play as a whole: they serve as "lower" but better versions of their social superiors.

PARENTAL LAW, MORE DISSEMBLING, AND A PLAY WARNS ALL

A Midsummer Night's Dream begins with a serious problem: Egeus insists that his daughter marry the man he chooses for her, or, according to the parental power Athens allows, she must die.[11] Theseus as symbolic father to Athens adds the possibility that, if she chooses neither, she must enter a convent and "abjure/ For ever the society of men" (1.1.65–66).[12] Egeus's demands strike a modern audience as hasty and cruel — probably some of Shakespeare's audience would have felt the same, though parents still had similar power in his time — and for Shakespeare's Protestant audience Theseus' option wouldn't have amounted to much better. A modern audience will also sympathize with Hermia's flight from her father, her King, and Athens — symbols of patriarchal authority — more than would Shakespeare's: they might appreciate what she will do for love, but they would not feel comfortable with such a breach of authority, and flight to the forest in Renaissance (and medieval) literature more often than not meant trouble. The woods may look lovely, dark and deep, but they house bandits, monsters, and evil of all sorts: darkness covers sin from view, but also from prevention or retribution. When the other youths flee after Hermia, they compound the problem: they flout authority and create more opportunity for disaster. While we see only the faeries, who in this case create trouble but not deep trouble because of their benign intent, Renaissance audiences would have imagined monsters, dragons, outlaws, all bearing the potential for spiritual as well as physical harm to anyone who dares enter their lair.

The rustics, too, enter heedlessly to practice their play: while the young noble folk may not have learned better from their romp in the darkness — they conclude it with a gentle sleep and a return to a world now willing to accept their choices of mates — the rustics have had a scare that may inspire Bottom's poetry, but that may keep them from entering the woods again for a long time. Their play reinforces that warning, the dangers of rushing from civilization and safety into the perilous — and deadly — freedom of the world beyond.

Shakespeare always loved and used his Ovid, and the *Pyramus and Thisby* that the rustics perform at the end of *MSND* tells a great deal about how to read the play as a whole and how to avoid the problems that mistakes in judgment cause throughout. Shakespeare uses the play-within-the-play as microcosm to macrocosm. It clarifies points we need if we want to understand the whole play: to avoid the rash, the excessive, the domineering.

The Prologue, which Quince presents, comprises a tour de force of malapropish syntax caused by faulty punctuation; the funny sentences, though, tell us truths not only about the rustics who perform *Pyramus*, but about all the characters we meet. Quince begins, "If we offend, it is with our good will./ That you should think, we come not to offend,/ But with good will." He means, of course, if we offend, we want you to know that we give our play only intending be nice. But he says, if we offend you, we do that with good will. Sometimes we do offend others by telling our showing them something they need to know; they may take offense though we do so with good intention — regardless of offense or intention, they still need to know, so we are still trying to do something good. Quince continues, "To show our simple skill,/ That is the true beginning of our end"; there he should have begun with the previous clause, as he means that to show their good will they intend to do their best, though they may not do very well — he offers an apology before the fact. As tradesmen, they have what their audience would consider "simple skills," but those skills have enormous importance to their society whether the rich folk pay them any attention or not. Those simple skills constitute their beginnings, but they aim in their play to a different end: to use their minimal acting skills to show something that even their audience will find important: avoid rash judgments and rash actions and take better care of your young people, because in their youthful passions they will make mistakes, and you must do your best to take care of them. Quince again: "Consider then, we come but in despite./ We do not come, as minding to content you,/ Our true intent is. All for your delight/ We are not here. That you should here repent you/ The actors are at hand; and, by their show,/ You shall know all, that you are like to know." They don't come in despite: they come with great respect for their social superiors; they come despite their minimal abilities to do what they can to contribute to the festivities: a worthy goal with little likelihood of success but a great deal of deferential kindness. That we see as they prepare, in their concern for their audiences sympathies, and in Bottom's speech at the end to reassure them: "No, I assure you the wall is down that parted their fathers" (V.1.351–52). Their audience will laugh when the Prologue says the players don't intend to content them, but if they pay attention to their play, it won't content them: it will teach them the errors they've very nearly made and may yet make. *Pyramus* teaches lessons they all very badly need to learn. And yet they may gain some delight if they come to understand what the play teaches, and they may repent of the rash actions that they, as actors, have themselves committed in pursuing their loves rashly. If they attend, they may learn all they are likely to learn from such a play, but they probably won't, and apparently they don't.

The speech that ends the play has, as one reads it, simple and hardly above insipid poetry. But often in the acting of the play, this speech gains the ability to move an audience because of its sadness and the reality of the disaster of the deaths of young persons. Francis Flute, the bellows-mender, plays Thisby thus:

> Asleep, my love?
> What, dead, my dove?
> O Pyramus, arise!
> Speak, speak! Quite dumb? ...
> Tongue, not a word!
> Come, trusty sword,
> Come, blade, my breast imbrue!
> And farewell, friends;
> Thus Thisby ends;
> Adieu....

The simple-minded lines belie the fact that an audience, if it gets through the unprofessional rendering of the story by the rustics, must see the same sadness, the same sorrow, the same tragedy in the Classical and Renaissance sense as one finds in *Romeo and Juliet*. The brief lines echo the brief lives of the lovers, and the same problem should yield the same potential for an emotional response. The young couple escape their parents (also like those in *MSND*) and meet an unexpected terror; one believes the other dead and kills himself, and the other finds her lover dead and kills herself as well — horrifying loss, and all to no purpose! The couples in our play may have come to the same end, but they met Faeries instead of lions, and they may still come to sad or evil ends: Theseus and Hippolyta will. The warning of the *Pyramus and Thisby* will, in that case at least, not work, and if we read the other couples as doubles or parallels for the royals, they may be headed toward sorrow — if not tragedy — alike.

The nobles, though, seem not to have got it: as the play ends they joke that Lion and Wall must bury the dead. But Bottom won't let them off so easily. He makes certain that they get the point of the play: "I assure you, the wall is down that parted their fathers" (5.1.351–52). After making his own fun, the best Theseus can offer them is "very notably discharged"— at least some kind recognition of their efforts — and, and after an intervening dance, he adds, to the wedding party, the observation that "This palpable-gross play hath well beguil'd/ The heavy gait of night. Sweet friends, to bed" (367–68). He hasn't got the idea of the play at all — if he had, he would pause to ponder it — but he expresses his eagerness finally to get his new wife to bed. As in *Much Ado* the characters in charge simply ignore the problems before them. They command readily enough, but without having paid attention to what they could have learned that would have made their commands the more valuable and worth following.

One of the great and helpful problems in the play comes in the repeated mis-identification of *Pyramus and Thisby*, that "*most lamentable comedy*" (1.2.11–12), as Peter Quince calls it. In III.1 Bottom repeats "this comedy of Pyramus and Thisby" (9–10); he argues that it will never please the audience because "the ladies cannot abide" Pyramus' killing himself (he doesn't mention Thisby), and the Lion will frighten them: "there is not a more fearful wildfowl than your lion living" (11–12, 31–32). Errors and incongruities aside, at least he considers his audience. The paper that Theseus reads that lists the possible entertainments for the after-feast celebration includes the rustics' description: "A tedious brief scene of young Pyramus/ And his love Thisby; very tragical mirth" (5.1.56–57). Philostrate, Master of Revels, discourages Theseus from selecting it, as the work of "hard-handed men.... Which never labor'd in their minds till now" (72–73), but Theseus insists on choosing it, and for a good reason: "never any thing can be amiss,/ When simpleness and duty tender it" (82–83). By *simpleness* he doesn't mean stupidity, but sincerely good intentions; that judgment would fit well in many of Shakespeare's plays, and many of his characters would have done better by practicing both. Shakespeare would probably have sympathized with Hermia's dilemma of wanting to marry the one she loves, not the one her father wants to force on her, but he probably wouldn't have approved of her defying and running away from her father.[13] Dogberry and the Watch in *Much Ado* represent the sort, the simple (today we might say "working class") persons who do their duty: regardless of what they may say he'll do, when the necessity arises, they get things done. Henry V makes the same point, though incongruously with respect to himself, in the response to Montjoy's final offer than Henry ransom himself: "We are but warriors for the working day.... But, by the mass, our hearts are in the trim" (*Henry V* 4.3.109, 115). The working people not only keep the society together nearly unnoticed by the rich and powerful, but they also deliver the message that they and we need to know. Dogberry makes this point to Leonato in *Much Ado*, though without meaning to: "I beseech your worship to correct yourself, for the example of others" (5.1.322–23); he probably means "correct (punish) Borachio yourself, so that others will learn by that example not to do ill," but an attentive audience will get the suggestion that Leonato has earlier failed in his duty both as governor and as father.

Theseus understands that point, but doesn't *learn* from it. Shakespeare's audience, though, will hear the repeated discrepancies and ask the question: why are we hearing *Pyramus and Thisby* called a comedy, and what is Shakespeare telling us about romance and duty? The nobles of Athens see this sad, even horrific story not as the lion it is, but as the wild-fowl it appears to be in the hands of amateur actors. To them the tragedy becomes a comedy. But for *MSND* to have its full effect, we must see both the tragedy in *Pyramus*— one of rash choices and love not only lost, but dead—and the tragedy in Shakespeare's play: that Theseus has not learned enough to avoid tragedies of failed love in his own life, and that the young couples, Hermia and Lysander and Helena and Demetrius, may not do so well either. They nominally understand the plot and what happens in it, but they don't apply it to their own lives, exactly what Quince's botched syntax asks them to do and exactly what Shakespeare was asking his audience to do. The play represents a benign kind of dissembling, but, sorrowfully, it won't serve its purpose without the audience internalizing what they see and hear: the failure we fear in the couples as well. All have grown too accustomed to dissembling, Shakespeare suggests, not honestly sharing what they feel and know and not paying attention to truth even when they find it before them. For them to find the courage to understand the point of the play, to reflect on who they are and what they do and to avoid the errors that lead to such horrors as happen to the young lovers in the Pyramus and Thisby story, they must apply both thought and feeling, and they must abandon the pride of class that keeps them from seeing the matter that a group of rustics put clearly, if amateurishly, before them.

The youths' romp in the woods seems to have done them, unlike Pyramus and Thisby, no harm. But they have gone through, in their own transformations, quite a number of insults, threats, and changes of affection. Because of Puck's misplacement of the love potion, Lysander comes not only (if briefly) to leave his love for Hermia, but to "hate" her. His expression of love for Helena leads her to believe that all the others have leagued together to torment her, and it leads Hermia to believe both have betrayed her, thus severing the young ladies' friendship, something they have had far longer than the romantic loves they pursue now. Helena has demeaned herself horribly: when Demetrius expresses for her only despite, she cries that such treatment only makes her love him more: "I am your spaniel; and, Demetrius,/ The more you beat me, I will fawn on you" (2.1.204–205). The fact that at the end of the play he is again willing to express love for her, and that Egeus at Theseus insistence must accept Lysander as son-in-law, and each couple has returned to their pre-play match may not mitigate all that has happened. Will they, like Bottom, brush off the whole experience as a dream, or will they reflect back on it and wonder why they did what they did? They don't know about the love potion: did it cause or just enable? Can they thereafter believe and trust their affections true?

Unlike many of the comedies, this one actually has its marriages. We have survived the woods and the Pyramus-and-Thisby staging, parental disapproval and threats of mutual violence. We have a bad role model ahead in Theseus' behavior with Hippolyta. The lovers, like the audience, must learn fidelity, and for the sake of their world, they must not just claim to love, but learn to love: faithfully, reasonably, kindly.

Twelfth Night, *or What You Will Ill*

In Act IV, scene 1 of *Twelfth Night* Feste, thinking he has found "Cesario" rather than Sebastian, says tartly to the young man "No, I do not know you, nor am I sent to you by my lady ... nor your name is not Master Cesario, nor this is not my nose neither: nothing that is so is so" (lines 5–9). There we find the major problem of this play: we can't trust that anything we think we know will hold true. Sebastian, next finding himself again accosted by someone he doesn't know and this time also struck by him wonders, "Are all the people here mad?" (27). There he goes not far wrong: everyone in the play

5. Comedic Problem Plays

turns either toward madness or dissembling or both. Either way, they try not to be themselves, whether in the service of love or humor or pathos. The plot moves by surprising twists, getting sillier and sillier to match the characters who enact it — the play practically buzzes with satire of humans' energetic efforts to avoid knowing and showing themselves.

"I am not what I am" (3.1.141), Viola warns the enamored Olivia. Nobody is in *Twelfth Night*. The Duke, seeing Viola and Sebastian together in V.1, observes (not very closely, apparently), "One face, one voice, one habit, and two persons,/ A natural perspective, that is and is not!" (216–17). The Duke claims love for Olivia, but finds her proud and cruel. Sir Toby and Sir Andrew act like drunkards and cowards, hardly knights. Olivia claims herself too deep in mourning to love, but falls immediately for Cesario/Viola/Sebastian. She mourns a brother; Viola mourns a brother and Sebastian a sister; the three have lost their parents — but they find no common ground in grief. That comes only in love-longing: Orsino, Olivia, Viola, and Antonio all suffer from it, but no one seems to understand it in anyone else. Malvolio, a staid and trustworthy if self-important steward, gives in immediately to the joke that implies he should woo Olivia — his humility is barely skin-deep. Antonio, for love of Sebastian whom he has saved from drowning, tries to hide among the Illyrian populace, though nearly everyone he meets recognizes him; they claim he is a pirate and a thief, and he claims he is none, having an honest quarrel with Orsino — we never hear the resolution of the quarrel. Maria shows a quicker (if meaner) wit than Feste or anyone else, and for a reward — or punishment — she gets to marry Sir Toby, a drunkard with a title and a niece about to throw him out. Everyone but Malvolio (and perhaps Antonio) falls into an overly simple — and hardly satisfying — ending. The marriages done or to come begin in confusion, with complications of identity, affection, class, and sexuality — who could ask for more?

Louis Wright and Virginia LaMar in *The Folger Guide to Shakespeare* call *Twelfth Night* "his highest achievement in sheer comedy, the comedy of merriment and gaiety without any shadow of unhappiness. Not even Malvolio's discomfiture is anything more than a practical joke on a pompous official who would be the wiser for the lessons of the jokesters" (229). Possibly the *audience* would gain that understanding, or wishes it would do so, but, sadly, Malvolio does not wish to gain wisdom from that elaborate, silly, and to him unhealably painful public joke. A person who once had a tendency to give in to ill-will comes at the end of the play to have embodied it, to have committed to it, to represent it: the world will not find itself better off for Malvolio's metamorphosis. And how can we trust the relationships at the end of the play, based as they are on mistaken identity, personal blindness, and illusion? The potential relationship problems look just as likely if no so egregious as those in *MSND*.

Ann Barton suggests the play "mediat[es] between the early comedies and the last romances" (406)—I would add that the idea applies with the tragedies also—and she points to its "world that is ritually upside down," where "almost anything can happen" (404).[14] I see that latter point as truer of *A Midsummer Night's Dream*, but it directs us to one of the problems of all of Shakespeare's plays: almost anything can happen because the world is alive with possibilities, powers of all sorts in nature's creatures, and the power in humans to choose well or disastrously. And if we worry about Malvolio's effect on the world of the play, shouldn't we worry about Orsino' even more? Barton asserts that "[w]hatever some critics may say, the lovelorn Orsino is not a figure of fun" (405), but, fun or not, he hardly escapes satire; the "sterile and self-induced" as well as sentimental and silly "love-melancholy" (405) makes him look like someone who desperately needs something useful and productive to do. He suffers more from the self-absorption that Shakespeare so often points out than from rejection: he may even feel that annoying pleasure-melancholy of one who, because they must listen, gets the glory of complaining to his companions about the depth of his continuing sorrows. Where Malvolio may enjoy wishing others ill, Orsino apparently enjoys wishing himself ill—as long as he retains the right to shift his affections when he chooses. The main problem of *Twelfth Night* resides in what Barton calls its "basic pessimism" (407); though love may arise to "sweeten" it, the play still ends with the troubling uncertainty of rapidly established love matches built on—again—dissembling and misidentifications. We may end with hope, but hope accompanied by grave concern in a world drained of its humor and still lacking a sober wisdom.

Looking for Love, or Not

The play begins with Duke Orsino (supposedly) suffering from love-longing for the beautiful but indifferent Olivia. He suffers from what Robert Burton in *The Anatomy of Melancholy* calls "heroic melancholy" or the great sadness of unrequited love, a particularly youthful emotion. Does Orsino really *love* Olivia? In II.4 he says that her beauty attracts his soul, but how much does he know about her beauty? Has he seen her without the veil she wears when outsiders call on her? Most persons wouldn't call someone they love "yond same sovereign cruelty" (2.4.80): that kind of comment suggests only sexual infatuation based on one's own imagination, not on any real experience of the person.[15] It also suggests a kind of peevish inattention to others, which the Duke shows in his dialogue with Viola/Cesario: he comments first on the frailty of men's affections ("however we do praise ourselves,/ Our fancies are more giddy and unfirm,/ More longing, wavering, sooner lost and worn,/

Than women's are," 2.4.32–35); then he contradicts himself as soon as his new friend tries to ease his pain ("no woman's sides/ Can bide the beating of so strong a passion ... no woman's heart/ So big, to hold so much; they lack retention./ Alas, their love may be call'd appetite/ No motion of the liver, but the palate,/ That suffer surfeit, cloyment, and revolt," lines 93–99). He completely misses her hints of who she is, her hints of her love for him, and her gender, and he insists that she must succeed in pleading with Olivia for him where he has failed and long after Olivia has repeated that she "cannot love him."

Orsino cares more for his melancholy than he does for his companions. In II.4 he asks Feste to repeat for him a sad, old song that seemed to "relieve my passion much" (4), but he expresses not so much passion as insistence on continuing to pursue the reasons for his sadness. As Act I, scene 1, begins, he asks similarly for more music, if it "be the food of love," so that "surfeiting,/ The appetite may sicken, and so die." He asks even for the repetition of a strain that "had a dying fall," because it "came o'er my ear like the sweet sound/ That breathes upon a bank of violets,/ Stealing and giving odor." What does he mean by that? He claims to want his appetite for love to reach surfeit and sicken, and he hopes music will do that. The music may well produce sadness, and if it can lead him to a catharsis, it may relieve that sadness, but it should have nothing to do with his love, and that love has any reality for him: either surfeit should come from Olivia's repeatedly rejecting him, or he must come to live with it and move on. At the end of the play, when the opportunity comes to transfer his love to Viola, he does so readily; so easy a shift suggests the love for Olivia, if it existed at all, burnt not so very deeply. For Orsino how much of love comes from imagination, how much from the desire to desire, and how much from the desire to behold and possess? Shakespeare creates that problem at the onset, and he doesn't solve it at the end: we must still ask after the play concludes what love — and what kind of love — the Duke can express toward Viola. She becomes his new "instrument" upon which the music lover can try to play at love, but will she find her own passions requited?

At least we have good reason to call Viola's passion real. Shipwrecked in a foreign country, she forms a reasonable plan for her safety: to seek help from the highest ranking local nobleman. She goes intending to disguise herself as a eunuch: that notion quickly fades, and she goes instead simply as a boy. But once she has reached the safety of the Duke's residence, why not uncover her identity? What good does the continued dissembling accomplish for her or anyone else? She no longer need maintain it for safety's sake, but perhaps she enjoys the disguise. It has also given her a safe means to remain in the Duke's company without the fear of having him dismiss her as an uninteresting female, since he has directed his obsession at Olivia alone. They can talk, and she can get to know him, but once she reveals herself, she must deal with the effects of her dissembling and having won his confidence by false means.

Orsino's opening speech creates a contrast between "fresh" and "surfeit" that lasts throughout the play. By the end of the play Olivia's freshness has grown stale to him, and he easily replaces her with Viola. Olivia's mourning has grown stale, and she has fallen for Cesario/Sebastian. The fresh joke on Malvolio quickly grows stale even for the jokesters, and everyone yet may feel the result of it: "I'll be revenged on the whole pack of you" (5.1.378), he says, departing. Not far into it even Sir Toby, in no way and an honorable or admirable fellow, has grown tired of it.[16] The "dying fall" that Orsino so admires in the music he hears suggests a kind of decay in the world of Illyria. Many of the characters have had a brush with death or mortality — theirs or others — and the dialogue repeatedly returns to the use of *mad, devil, fiend, fool*, or variations of those words. Malvolio spends a time locked in "hideous darkness" and accused not only of madness but as a "dishonest Sathan" (4.2.29–31), the whole confirmed by Fabian as "sportful malice" (5.1.365). Viola and Sebastian nearly died before the play began. So much of the characters' perceptions depend on clothing, from Olivia's veil to Malvolio's cross-garters to Viola's cross-dressing: no one will quite yet believe her female until she offers to confirm it by finding the "maiden weeds" that she has left with the sea captain who helped save her. Just to be sure, Orsino agrees: "let me see thee in they maiden weeds" (5.1.273). Asea in seeming, the whole crew of characters fail to pay attention, to *note*, to gain any perspective on what they do or think. Their inattentiveness nearly leads them all to disaster, Shakespeare's warning that this festival comedy leads us in a direction other than festive.

Several characters bear the epithet *ass* or *fool* at one time or another in the play: Feste, Sir Andrew,[17] Sir Toby, Malvolio, perhaps Sebastian or Viola, depending on to whom Sir Toby refers in V.1.206–207,[18] and even Olivia.[19] "Foolery, sir," Feste says, does walk about the orb like the sun, it shines every where" (3.1.38–39). Yet no one serves quite the same function of the Fool in *King Lear* or Dogberry in *Much Ado*. Feste comes close, in that he communicates several of themes of the play, but self-interest most moves him. Antonio comes close: whatever the sort of love he has for Sebastian, he risks his own life to help him. If we consider the main theme of the play our movement from other phases and problems of life toward significant, committed love, Viola bears the greatest burden and has the most profound effect. She moves Olivia from her mourning toward love and prepares her for Sebastian's arrival; she moves the Duke from his obsession with Olivia, who will never love him, to the possibility of a real love, at least one that she will thoroughly requite.

Far from the typical Shakespearean *ass* in that she comes from gentle parents, treats people with kindness and affection (though she gives Olivia an honest dose of reality), and shows pluck and commitment, Viola takes the world in a direction it needs to go, though we must fear her love for Orsino misplaced. In the play he does nothing worthy of a Duke and little of anything at all; he shows a propensity for anger, insult, vengeance, and self-indulgence. He must have physical attractions for Viola, or one would wonder why any woman would want to marry him despite his status. He still looms as a considerable problem at the end of the play, for the world of the play and for Viola.

The name Viola is nearly an anagram for Olivia. Viola begins the play mourning for a dead brother, just as Olivia does. Her mourning doesn't last as long, though, quickly replaced by love for Orsino. Why doesn't Olivia mourn her father as well, when we learn that he too died barely a year before the time in which the action of the play takes place? Why does her mourning disperse entirely with the arrival of Viola/Sebastian? The great problem of the play comes in the rapid and Ovidian transformation of feelings: whose can we trust, and how deep do any of them run? Melancholy and ill-will potentially taint them all, so how can we trust they'll last? And what will become of poor Antonio, uncovered and sentenced to death? He has lost his safety, unless the Duke decides to pardon him, and he has perhaps lost his love as well: what do we make of his affections for Sebastian? Not everyone finds happiness in *Twelfth Night*: "hey, ho, the wind and the rain."

MAL-VOLIO AND CESARIO: SHADOWS AND LIGHT

The terrible joke on Malvolio implies more than good fun. Most audience members relate more to the jokesters than to Malvolio — none of us wants to think ourselves like him. He has reasonable claims against Sir Toby, Sir Andrew, and even Maria: the first two waste Olivia's stores and abuse her hospitality, and Maria encourages them. But given the hint that Olivia loves him, Malvolio immediately becomes even more pompous than before, and his pride comes out in all its colors. But if we imagine ourselves locked in darkness and told we are mad — when we know better — and in Shakespeare's time, when madness meant imprisonment in horrible conditions, not medical treatments and visits from friends and family, we move from the realm of comedy to that of horror, a point we too easily miss. Malvolio, we might argue, deserves some sort of recompense, if not vengeance, but he leaves their society angry and promising harm. "Ill-will" lurks, then, on the periphery of everything they will do, and that doesn't bode well for their future. Shakespeare shows us repeatedly in his plays the importance of forgiveness and kindness; ill-will brings no one good, and it tends to remain until it can create something especially evil and troublesome. In Shakespeare's most obvious examples, Iago and Richard III, it grows into paranoia and murder; in *King Lear* it grows in both Goneril and Regan and Edmund toward patricide; in *Timon of Athens* it establishes the main trait of the protagonist and brings about nothing but suffering. But it afflicts characters in many of the plays if to lesser magnitude, to the point of causing dangerous trouble and irresolution. The humor in the play comes not in the torture of Malvolio, but in Feste's wit. "O, you are sick of self-love, Malvolio, and taste with a distemper'd appetite," Olivia warns: "To be generous, guiltless, and of free disposition, is to take those things for bird-bolts that you deem cannon-bullets" (1.5.91–93) — true enough, but none the easier for him to do. "Dost thou think because thou art virtuous there shall be no more cakes and ale?" Toby asks, but he is guilty of both faulty premises and a *non sequitur*: we see no virtue, and cakes and ale have nothing to do with it. Malvolio neither gains nor shares wisdom, but becomes a source, one of several in the play, for that typical Shakespearean trope: dissembling.

Once again dissembling has a prominent place in moving the action, and once again Shakespeare shows what difficulties it creates even if one uses it out of necessity or with good intention. Realizing that Olivia has fallen for her, Viola laments, "Disguise, I see thou art a wickedness/ Wherein the pregnant enemy does much" (2.2.27–28). She has made herself a "poor monster," a grotesque, stuck between genders and amidst two love relationships. When Viola/Cesario proves diffident, Olivia complains, "A fiend like thee might bear my soul to hell" (3.4.217), a horrible admission and an awful burden for Viola to carry. Time must untangle it, Viola says, since she can't; Shakespeare knew that sometimes it will, and sometimes it won't.

Sir Toby and Fabian dissemble with Viola and Sir Andrew, urging them both to a duel that neither wants; even they would feel embarrassment if they knew Viola a woman. To assist their revenge against Malvolio, Maria will have Feste dress as a curate to visit his prison (unnecessarily, since Malvolio can't see him — method acting?): "I will dissemble myself in't, and I would I were the first that ever dissembled in such a gown" (4.2.4–6). The joke contributes little to the Malvolio subplot, but it does allow an opportunity for anti-clerical satire. Feste's reference to Gorboduc (line 14) helps clarify the scene: *Gorboduc*, 1561, a well-known and successful play preceding Shakespeare's time, dealt with violence, revenge, and the tragedy of civil war — always a concern of Shakespeare's — and here it suggests an unexpected similarity with the lighter events of *Twelfth Night*. We find in Illyria a world in conflict with itself, characters in conflict with themselves: they think themselves in love, but they usually aren't; they think they want violence and revenge, but they don't — only harm and embarrassment come from it. The dissembling in the long run creates similar problems that could have got worse: fortune worked in the characters' favor to turn up the right persons in the right place to avert violence and horror — fortune doesn't often work that way. In V.1 the Duke accuses Viola/Cesario, "O thou dissembling cub!" believing that his friend and servant has wooed Olivia for himself instead. "Kill what I love?" (119) and "sacrifice the lamb that I do love" (130) show how willingly Orsino will turn his hand to violence. And Viola says she will go, suffering death gladly for him: dissembling has led them both to the brink of horror. The nominally happy ending does not wash those words from the play, and one wonders how long they will live in memory.

Viola's self-transformation into Cesario exploits Shakespeare's trope of cross-dressing and dissembling to some extent successfully — she wins her love in the end — but again typically Shakespeare shows that dissembling/deceit has unforeseen and troubling consequences. The play doesn't show the future of the love matches, but it does point to them and hint that they may not resolve so easily: if the characters are paying attention, more of them than Malvolio alone will feel lasting embarrassment from the events that have occurred, and they may not find that problem easy to forget. Olivia has fallen for a girl dressed as a boy and is now matched with a boy barely (if yet) a man — and not even exactly the person she thought he was. She didn't even observe closely enough to tell brother and sister apart. Orsino has shown his "true" love nothing more than a passing fancy over which he mooned annoyingly, and now he claims love for a girl he thought a boy. These mixed-up couples are moving awfully quickly, with Olivia and Sebastian already married and Orsino and Viola soon to follow. There we find one of several difficulties that undermine comedy in *Twelfth Night*: the characters have not learned to avoid rashness any more than they have learned to avoid selfishness (or self-obsession) or to recognize the difference between healthy humor and destructive practical jokes.

While Viola and Sebastian come from a wealthy family, nothing indicates their degree precisely. Viola falls easily into servitude, though her brother has the attitude of someone rather more accustomed to others treating him with respect. Will they make proper matches for a Duke and a Countess in an age that retained fairly strong notions of class distinction? That problem raises only one of the many concerns that continue to trouble the world of this play. Perhaps "some are [born] great, some [achieve] greatness, and some have greatness thrust upon 'em" (2.5.144–46); neither serving nor marrying greatness makes happiness more likely. "This is very midsummer madness," Olivia says of Malvolio's response to Maria's letter; she might have said it of everyone in Illyria.

* * *

While comedy as genre depends most on a nominally "happy ending," comedy as mode or in performance relies most on humor for its entertainment value. Each of the comedic problem plays I have pursued in this chapter has its own interesting and telling use of humor. *Much Ado* contrasts the "upper-class" humor of wit and repartee, which characters admire (and fear) and which those who use it intend, with the "lower-class" humor of malapropism and false dignity, which the characters who use it don't intend and which others find irritating or worthy of lampoon. The humor reinforces the themes of the weakness of wit for its own sake — without a worthy cause that turns it to wisdom, wit will fall in its own tracks — and that, we may say, dutiful is as duty does: the people who do the work, not those who nominally rule, keep the society together, regardless of how their social betters think of them. They may look silly at times, but they set things right, and the nobles look in the long run sillier, unable for all their rank and pride to understand what has gone wrong and fix it. The "lowers" provide the matter for laughter, but the "uppers" provide that matter for satire.

MSND makes a similar kind of class distinction in its humor. It keeps the use of malapropisms by the rustics and adds comic fun in their maladroit efforts as actors — though it contrasts their faulty delivery with the power and significance of their play's message. Upper-class humor comprises sarcastic or satirical responses to the rustics' efforts at a play or practical jokes (e.g., such as Oberon plays on Titania) as well as the playwright's satirical use of the young lovers' excesses during their mad night in the woods. Both in their actions and their proclamations about love they draw laughter and allow the playwright to direct attention to the common silliness of youthful passions. The humor shows that the silliness — to anyone who isn't directly involved in it — of the excesses of youthful love may go unnoticed and unchecked. The sad truth of the play comes in that those who have a short while before acted pretty ridiculously themselves can easily and quickly enough turn to making fun of others. The rustics are at least doing their best to serve others rather than obsessing over themselves.

Twelfth Night uses two parallel practical jokes: the one Maria, Toby, and Andrew play on Malvolio and the one Toby plays on Andrew and Viola (dressed as Cesario). I admit (I hope not in Malvolian fashion) to finding neither particularly funny: both come more from cruelty than from honest, good-natured jest, and they aim to humiliate someone rather than to share the absurdities of life.[20] In a sense these jokes make fun of practical jokes, showing their cruelly and how little effect that can have for anything good. Feste provides the best (if not only) real humor in the play, more in his wordplay than in his fairly benign insults. The wordplay has cleverness and adeptness, but in this play it doesn't lead much of anywhere: unlike the fools in some of

Shakespeare's other plays, it doesn't uncover necessary themes of concerns, but rather shows the fool going about his business as fool with an aim to entertain as a means to make his living. Even his wordplay has a kind of coldness that renders his humor distant and, other than to win some small but steady remuneration, ineffectual.

Feste delivers his quips with an air of superiority rather than a sense of mutual humanity; he adds little to the play in the way of levity, wisdom, or festivity. His dissembling as Sir Thopas the priest in IV.2 recalls Chaucer's truncated and self-deprecating — and truly awful — Romance, and it shows that jokes can impinge on serious and important social ceremonies that we both want and need to keep us together as a society. Perhaps Shakespeare used Feste him not so much to lampoon others as a way to satirize clowns, even professional ones: for some fools humor turns to foolery rather than to understanding. Sebastian finds Feste more foolish than wise, but even he gives the clown money: all reward his wit, though it never amounts to anything useful to them. His last lines remind everyone that "the whirligig of time brings in his revenges" (5.1.376–77), but neither the rapid passing of time nor Fortune's Wheel makes any difference to these characters: they have lost themselves in their own obsessions. Feste finally persists too far in his quest for rewards. In V.1 he shows Orsino how his foes help him more than his friends: friends "praise me, and make an ass of me. Now my foes tell me plainly I am an ass; so that by my foes, sir, I profit in the knowledge of myself" (17–20). The Duke gives him money for the witticism, and so he asks for more: "But that it would be double-dealing, sir, I would you could make it another" (29–30). Orsino does, making himself, in Feste's words at least, a double-dealer: he shows himself so when he so readily abandons his love for Olivia, threatens Viola/Cesario when he believes she has stolen his love from him, then immediately transfers his love to her once he finds she is a young woman. Feste begs Orsino for a third coin, but finally he must work for it, though very little: he need only fetch his mistress, enough in his mind to free him from covetousness. While his wit has brought him money but no self-discovery, his song as the play concludes turns from humor to sadness and the transience of life: we learn as we get older that not every ploy thrives, and everything comes to an end, for "the rain it raineth every day." That message turns toward the audience — "we'll strive to please you every day" — rather than to the characters, who need so badly to know that pain will come, so we do best not to inflict more of it ourselves. "[P]leasure will be paid, one time or another" (2.4.70–71), Feste warns Orsino, but "thought is free" (1.3.69), Maria remarks. They will not find those themes in their jokes. They must find them in fidelity to one another, and they have given us as yet no reason to believe they will — a problem common to so many Shakespeare plays.

6

Tragic Problem Plays

As the last chapter considered the problem of how some of the plays we traditionally label *comedies* don't fit easily within traditional notions of comedy, this chapter will deal with the difficulty of understanding Shakespeare's "tragedies" as examples of tragedy. With respect to genre, Shakespeare was an equal-opportunity transgressor. He played with methods to vary audience sympathy for protagonists, to bring about their fall, to create or suspend catharsis, to toggle between feelings of sadness and happiness or relief as his plays conclude. As always he exploits the idea of the Great Chain of Being as a determiner of one's place and duties in the world, and he experiments with the level of recognition characters achieve of their own or others' culpability. As always he foregrounds the idea of free will and moral choice: despite degree and duty, amidst which we find ourselves irrespective of choice, how we chose to act in response to our position in the world makes a big difference in the course of our lives and those of others.

In our time we use the word *tragedy* gratuitously, employing it for effect whenever something bad or sad happens. For Aristotle and his audience the term referred to a specific literary dramatic form with exact components, and Aristotle's idea (though mostly in translation) prevailed yet in Shakespeare's time. Shakespeare didn't follow Aristotle exclusively, but Aristotle was for the most part not providing instruction on how to make a tragedy. He was explaining what his contemporaries did and what seemed to him to make it work best. Shakespeare played with the components of drama to build plays he believed would work on stage and that would bring customers back to the theater to see them again: we'll strive to please you every day, says Feste, but any of Shakespeare's company might have said it. Shakespeare employed methods and approaches that would make the ideas of the plays and their effects complex, the characters moving and memorable, and the productions fast-moving, alive, and riveting. Those precepts outweighed the inherited and critical traditions.

Most important for this study, with tragic as well as with comic material

Shakespeare not only disrupts genre conventions, but also leaves us with problems to ponder at the end of the play — problems without easy (if any) solution. Sometimes he even builds the "unsolvable problem" into the fabric of his narrative; sometimes he allows solutions, but not especially desirable ones; sometimes his stories create almost more suffering than an audience can tolerate. Thus he always leaves us, one may say, in the midst of real life: we may have moral precepts, expectations for proper behavior, and religious beliefs, but even firmly held principles of goodness can't always keep us from lingering doubts, insecurities, and irresolution in our own lives. Shakespeare shows us the universal truth of human suffering.

Hamlet: *Shakespeare's Hidden Comedy?*

Hamlet has occasionally come up in discussions of the problem-play idea (see, or instance, Ernest Schanzer). Most scholars and teachers place it among the "great tragedies," and it often tops lists of Shakespeare's best and most important plays (with the usual exception of *King Lear*). It most cagily resists the patterns of tragedy and evokes the greatest range of emotional response: certainly the traditional pity and fear, but many feelings beyond that from admiration to annoyance to disgust to spiritual elation. It may comprise Shakespeare's best efforts at evoking empathy: I once heard that everyone who reads *Hamlet*, regardless of gender, race, or age, becomes Hamlet. We can hardly avoid identifying with him. He has intelligence, and we want to be intelligent; he has big problems, and sometimes we have big problems, too. We, too, want to have the ability to deal with our problems with wit and flair.

From years of the anecdotal evidence of reading, teaching, and discussion with colleagues and friends, I have found that estimation to hold true. Everyone with even the tiniest talent for compassion understands and appreciates what a difficult time Hamlet has, and everyone relates to what a difficult time even he has solving such big problems. But the play creates a great deal of sympathy for other characters as well (Ophelia particularly, and Horatio, too, if we pay attention[1]). It also doesn't leave Hamlet unscathed or untainted: not everyone who reads the play *likes* him, even if we identify with him. He appears at times to indulge in cruelty and selfishness and pride, inappropriate sexual behavior, and maybe murder. Some audiences may well not *want* to sympathize with Hamlet, because they don't want to put themselves in his place: no one wants to lose one's inheritance, avenge a dead father, live amidst treachery, kill one's beloved's father and return home to find her dead, fight a duel against someone who may have a reasonable claim against one's life. Few persons would want a life with that many serious problems. Hamlet's contemplation of suicide, his failure to find an appropriate course of action beyond waiting, and his persistent indecision can bring great pain: they push us out of the created world of drama to the edge of the real, the true, the horrible. Hamlet goes from a situation that looks impossible to one, were it a logical possibility, more impossible yet: he considers vengeance even as Claudius keeps him close, trying to find a means to kill him. But from those difficulties comes the play's magnitude. If we throw ourselves into the experience of the play, we learn from *Hamlet* that others suffer as much as or more than we do. We want someone with Hamlet's problems, his stature, his talents to prevail over his obstacles. At first (or even third) reading he may seem to us to fail. But he succeeds as well as anyone possibly could in his impossible circumstance. In this chapter I intend to defend that point, since it creates the genre problem. The fact that Hamlet does about as well as anyone could, and that he does it with humor and energy, moves *Hamlet* very close to comedy.

Beginning, Again, with an Ending

The old notion that haunts *Hamlet*, both the play and the character, that the tension in the play comes from a protagonist who hasn't the strength of will to make up his mind and act, doesn't hold up to scrutiny. He acts as soon as he can, and for the most part he acts reasonably, if not always successfully. At the end of the play he achieves as much success as he possibly can in a world "out of joint," diseased with selfishness and violence.[2] He brings the world back as close as it can get to justice and safety.

Hamlet finds himself amidst an unsolvable problem. He arrives home from university to find his father dead, his uncle king and married to his mother, and his own proper ascension to sovereignty blocked. At thirty years of age (readers often assume him younger, but the text gives us that figure in V.1.162), having moved beyond youth to full majority, Hamlet should follow his father to the throne. From the apparition — it may or may not be a ghost — he gets a directive to avenge his father. Hamlet understands that directive, but it places him in an irresolvable situation. Old Germanic law required vengeance, or at least recompense, *weregild*, "man-payment," for a death caused by another person. How does Hamlet achieve what his culture would have considered just?

Three problems complicate the act of recompense. First, though Claudius admits privately that he has killed his brother (see Act III, scene 3), he hasn't done so publicly. The people hear that Hamlet Sr. died of a serpent's bite while napping in his garden. The Ghost informs Hamlet Jr. otherwise and demands vengeance. So Hamlet has information contradicting the public report. But can he trust it? The Ghost claims to be suffering for a time in Purgatory to burn away the sins of his life, those which he hadn't time to confess and of which he needed absolution from a priest before he died. Would a ghost, the soul in Purgatory, implying a Christian universe, ask a living person for blood vengeance? Hamlet, a Christian, would have to decline: Christianity forbids blood vengeance ("Vengeance is mine, says the Lord," Romans 12:19). Would Hamlet's father, bound ultimately for Heaven himself, do that to his son, ask him to damn himself for the sake of the old beliefs? We must wonder then about the identity of the Ghost: not the father, perhaps, but a demon out for Hamlet's soul? No one with any sense would trust such a source. Second, the Germanic tradition of blood-vengeance hits a snag in the case of brother-slaying: blood-payment occurs *outside* the family, not within. Though the practice often didn't work out that way (i.e., vengeance did sometimes happen within families), theoretically the family should not kill a man who killed his brother, because they didn't want to sacrifice another after one was already dead and because no re-payment to the family occurs (the family would be paying itself for its own loss). Third, Hamlet's mother, the queen, has married his uncle, deepening the claim Claudius has made to kingship (he is king partly because she is queen), and the people have accepted that claim in Hamlet's absence. Especially with Fortinbras' army hanging about the Danish borders and looking dangerous, the people want strong and dependable kingship, and Claudius, not Hamlet, is present to accept that burden (though he does poorly at it).

So many issues stand in Hamlet's way that we can hardly expect him to kill Claudius either in public or in stealth. What the audience know, Hamlet doesn't know, and Hamlet has only his instinct to go on — hardly enough to depose and execute a king in a time that believed in the divine right of monarchs, that God, not people, chose them. If Hamlet were to act, he would be acting on hunch and dubious information, hardly sufficient to make a decision of such magnitude and potential enormity. Were Hamlet to find indisputable evidence against Claudius, he still would have difficulty arguing a legal right to kill him: religious law and inexact Germanic traditions wouldn't provide firm support, nor would the people appreciate the death of a second king and the obvious murder of a sitting king. Hamlet could bring his charges before the public, but what satisfaction could he get? Claudius now rules the Danish court, and he could dismiss Hamlet's charges and even accuse him of treason, of trying to get the kingship for himself for his own purposes, not through proper ascension, the coronation already having been solemnized.

Hamlet finds himself with few or no means to succeed, leaving him with only one choice: to *wait*. He chooses, reasonably, to wait, because he must wait if he wants to find any proper resolution for the circumstance in which, by no choice or error of his own, he finds himself. No wonder he finds the times "out of joint." No one finds waiting easy, and it creates interesting tactical problems for the dramatist. What can I have this fellow do while he waits, or what will others try to do to him?[3]

Claudius, too, finds himself in a difficult spot. Why does he request that Hamlet stay in Denmark rather than return to Heidelberg? If Hamlet were gone, his continual transition to kingship would go the more easily. But as long as Hamlet lives, Claudius' sovereignty will remain uncertain: the people may at any time reasonably call for Hamlet's return. And Claudius must reason that Hamlet will at least consider what really happened to his father. If Hamlet finds a means to discover the murder, or if Hamlet decides to take the course that Claudius took in killing a king, Claudius risks his life as well as his throne. From his point of view, he must keep Hamlet close and, if opportunity permits, kill him as well. If Hamlet proves docile as Gertrude has, Claudius may permit him to live — at least for a time. But one murder tends to lead to other murders: guilt, pride, cover-ups, worries, the ease of the first murder push one willing to do such a deed to believe it can work again.

Claudius has also, willingly or not, brought Gertrude into his plot. He clearly loves her, and she loves him: she will defend him first at need. When Laertes returns to Denmark in IV.5 looking to avenge his father, Claudius admits simply that Polonius is dead, but Gertrude adds, "But not by him" (129). She loves Hamlet, but would rather give up her son than her husband. We must wonder then when their love began: did Gertrude give in to Claudius' pleas only after Hamlet Sr.'s death, or did they have an affair before hand? Could she have assisted Claudius in the murder? How, for instance, did Claudius find such easy means to get to the sleeping king?[4] The play does not clarify these points for us, but it does give us hints, for instance, the suspicious death of Ophelia.

Ophelia, burdened with the death of her father at Hamlet's hands and what amounts to the banishment of her lover, and without her brother there to comfort her, goes mad. Polonius says of Hamlet, "Though this be madness, yet there is method in't" (2.2.205–206), and one might say the same of Ophelia. Her songs and rants in IV.5 suggest that she knows more than she has said of past events; perhaps Hamlet in his visits to her has revealed his heart, a common but in this case enormously dangerous practice. We learn of Ophelia's death from Gertrude, who enters the close conversation between Claudius and Laertes to announce the girl has drowned. "Drown'd!" Laertes exclaims. "O, where?" (4.7.165). We might expect him to ask "how" or "when" or "by whose hand," but he asks *where* because he can't imagine where it would have happened. And indeed it happened in an unlikely place: a brook near the castle. Gertrude describes the drowning at length:

6. Tragic Problem Plays

> There on the pendant boughs her crownet weeds
> Clamb'ring to hang, and envious sliver broke,
> When down her weedy trophies and herself
> Fell in the weeping brook. Her clothes spread wide,
> And mermaid-like awhile they bore her up,
> Which time she chaunted snatches of old lauds,
> As one incapable of her own distress....
> But long it could not be
> Till that her garments, heavy with their drink,
> Pull'd the poor wretch from her melodious lay
> To muddy death [172–83].

Now who would believe that? Claudius doesn't ask any questions, and Laertes must be too upset about his father's death to notice that Gertrude must have stood by watching and listening to Ophelia sing several songs and gradually slip under a shallow bit of water and die without doing anything at all to help — unless she held the poor lass under. Perhaps Gertrude has done a murder (or a second?) to help her new husband keep his kingship. If Ophelia did know the truth of Hamlet Sr.'s death, either Claudius or Gertrude or both would want her eliminated. Her madness provides opportunity to go with motive. We have a classic murder mystery.

We meet few if any characters in drama smarter than Hamlet — one of the reasons audiences feel attracted to him. But that intelligence puts him in greater danger (Claudius will worry more about him and feel less likely to spare him than if Hamlet were too dumb to figure out what has happened). Hamlet's self-reflection and chattiness also put those others around him in danger, and that fact makes taking action more difficult yet, because anything he does has implications beyond himself. We learn in V.1, if we had doubt, that Hamlet loved Ophelia: he says so quite plainly in a situation where we have no need to doubt him, Ophelia's funeral. If he did tell Ophelia his fears about his father's death, his intelligence failed him there. We may forgive such an error in one so distraught — and one who doesn't know at that point how far Claudius and Gertrude have gone and how far they may yet go. Recognition of that error accounts for his seemingly cruel treatment of Ophelia in Act III, scene 1, in the famous "get thee to a nunn'ry" speech. Nothing has happened to relieve his distress, but he has had time to realize that anything he has told Ophelia (or that she can figure out on her own) places her in grave danger, too: Claudius (and/or Gertrude) will as willingly and more easily murder her than the late king, simply to keep her quiet. Murder leads only to more murder (as we see in *Macbeth*).

The aggressiveness of Hamlet's speech to Ophelia has prompted many and varied critical responses. The tendency to read it as harsh and unfeeling, brought on by madness or dismissiveness, misses the reflectiveness and actual decisiveness of Hamlet's character — when circumstances allow the possibility of decision. Since Hamlet loves Ophelia, and he must suspect her to fall next in line for murder, he must also find a way to get her as far away from himself and Elsinore as possible, ideally to a place where Claudius can't or won't get to her. Reading Hamlet's urgent plea that Ophelia go to a "nunnery" or convent as Elizabethan slang for a brothel implies cruelty indeed. It assumes either that she has given in to him sexually and he has had his fill, so he will simply discard her with no feelings of remorse and no thought for suffering or her future, or that madness has driven him to an outburst that shows a true meanness in his character. The first reading fits partly, in the likelihood of the sexual relationship but not in its satiety; the second does not fit what we see of and hear from Hamlet elsewhere in the play. Hamlet does show concern for others, even Claudius: with more assurance of his guilt and less spiritual commitment, Hamlet could have chosen to kill him outright. But Claudius has no interest in Hamlet's kindness. He will still want Hamlet and anyone close to him dead,[5] so if Hamlet wants to protect Ophelia, where is the only place in the Middle Ages that he can send her that lies beyond Claudius' influence? If she enters a convent, the king would have to breach Church law as well as civil law to get to her; it offers the only place of safety. If she loves Hamlet, he will have a hard time getting her to go: he must do his best to drive her away, to convince her he has got mean, gone mad, or deceived her, so that she will not cling to him and insist on trying to help him. He must make her believe she leaves by her own decision; as long as she remains attached to him, she remains in mortal danger. He must try to get her not to love him and to feel willing to retreat to safety.

The "Hamlet's madness" question seems to me not worth more argument. Hamlet warns his friends that he will act mad as a means to protect himself; he clarifies to Rosencrantz and Guildenstern that he is "but mad north-north-west. When the wind is southerly I know a hawk from a handsaw" (2.2.378–79): he knows danger from safety, predator from prey. When crisis and opportunity come, he can make decisions and act. When he kills Polonius in III.4, he acts with astonishingly quick — if unfortunately wrong — rationality. His thought process would follow a pattern near to this one: someone is hiding behind the tapestry in my mother's bedroom; who would do that? Only the King has the right to enter the Queen's bedroom. It must be the king. I can kill him now and call it an accident, since who but an attacker would be *hiding* there — certainly not the King who may go openly where he pleases? Hamlet doesn't guess that Polonius, whom, as Ophelia's father he certainly wouldn't want to kill, would do something as silly as that. He speaks correctly for his time when he says the tide of fortune has risen against him; he speaks unfairly to call himself a "rogue and peasant slave" (2.2.550). No one could do much better than Hamlet does. There lies the difficulty in calling the play tragedy. Instead, it shows a remarkable psychological heroism. Hamlet maintains his reason, his courage, his love, and his desire to do the right thing all the way to his first command as king, the last words of his life.

The Use of Perspective: Building Tragicomic Character

Perhaps more than any other achievement, the rediscovery of perspective in painting marks the beginning of the Renaissance. We can watch Giotto struggling with it in Italy in the paintings he made early in the fourteenth century: In *St. Francis Receiving the Stigmata* (ca. 1300) he gives us a sense of depth and movement if not of convincing sizes and spacing, but in *The Last Supper* (ca. 1320) he couldn't figure out how to place the apostles around a table and give them the requisite haloes. By the time of Luca Signorelli in the late fifteenth century, painters had largely mastered the lost art. In *Hamlet* Shakespeare gives us the dramatist's mastery of perspective: he creates character parallels and parallel scenes that allow us to see events from more than one point of view, none of which we can call in itself "real," but each of which adds to our ability to see and understand the world of the play much more fully. They add up to a matrix of connections and possibilities that can guide our interpretations and understanding.

Hamlet falls at the center of a matrix of character possibilities, and the other major characters take actions his character could take, too, as he responds to his situation. Other human beings would act very differently in Hamlet's circumstances; Hamlet has difficult choices that another playwright with the same material might have taken in quite different directions and probably would have oversimplified.

How much does Hamlet resemble his father? The play doesn't tell us much about that. We know him warlike: he defeated Old Fortinbras of Norway and won disputed territory that Denmark retains in the time of the play. Hamlet says, certainly exaggerating but still to the point, that Claudius resembles the late King as a satyr to Hyperion: not at all. He indulges in pleasure rather than governing with grandeur and dignity. Was Hamlet Sr. a loving father and husband? His son admired him, but lived away from home, staying at university long past the usual age. His wife may have been cheating on him. The neighboring countries either admired or feared him enough not to attack while he lived. Hamlet may have got intelligence from his father, but he may also have an easier sense of wit and humor and a gentler manner with others, yet he has lived as a prince, not a king. Hamlet could perhaps have grown more like his father as he aged; that course may not have served him or his country well in the long run, as it seems not to fit his character, and it didn't do Hamlet Sr. any good.

Hamlet could become more like Claudius, his uncle, perhaps a more affectionate man than his brother: not two months after the King's death, he has married the widowed Queen, who shows no objections to that course of events but appears quite happy with it. But Claudius has shown himself a schemer and a murderer; Hamlet can dissemble, as we see in the feigned madness and the "Mousetrap" play, but he'd have a difficult time with murder. Hamlet considers committing to that course to avenge his father, but he doesn't find it easy and finally doesn't take it: we wouldn't admire him as much if he did.

Hamlet could become more like his mother: he could simply give in to Claudius, accept him as King, not worry about the manner of his father's death, and fall into place as the simple-thinking heir apparent. In such a case Claudius might still find a means to kill him just to keep himself safe, or he might leave Hamlet alone, seeing in him no threat. We could hardly admire that sort of character either: such a Hamlet might have a pragmatic side, but he would have to lack passion, energy, inquisitiveness, and any sense of right or justice — not our Hamlet. A similar course would move him toward Polonius: he could become a court toady, a flatterer who does and says what Claudius wants him to — an even more ignominious course.

Hamlet could follow the course of Laertes: he could seek immediate vengeance without regard for philosophy, religion, or consequences. Claudius asks Laertes, "What would you undertake/ To show yourself indeed your father's son/ More than in words?" and Laertes answers, "To cut [Hamlet's] throat i' th' church" (4.7.124–26). Laertes has no qualms whatever about violence; he may also have a general moral laxity: when he prepares to return to France, Ophelia warns him not to indulge in the kinds of behaviors he tells her to avoid with Hamlet.[6]

A possible course for our Hamlet would come closer to Fortinbras (an oddly French name for a Norwegian prince, but apt to the character: "strong-in-arm"). Fortinbras may find himself in much the same situation as Hamlet: his father has died and his uncle become king. Rather than stay at home and wait, he gathers an army and goes harrying on his own. His captain lets out that he aims to fight the Poles over an insignificant plot of land, but anyone with any sense understands that he is patrolling the borders of Denmark waiting for the chance to retake the land Hamlet Sr. took from his father, and perhaps more, to rule it as his own: he seeks blood vengeance. Young Hamlet, were he more like young Fortinbras, could raise an army, engage him, and then set off on his own military quests. But our Hamlet doesn't turn to war for its own sake or to gain his own territories; he turns to philosophy, to pursue the course he thinks right. Hamlet's brilliance and even prescience appear in the final scene: as he is dying, he utters, "I do prophesy th'election lights/ On Fortinbras, he has my dying voice" (5.2.355–56). He doesn't mean prophesy in the contemporary sense of "foretell the future": the ancient idea of prophecy still present for Shakespeare's time implied speaking out in an inspired way, diagnosing the present and suggesting action (as the Biblical prophets do), not picking the next Derby winner. Hamlet Jr., King himself but so briefly after Claudius' death, names his successor, and in doing so he saves the Danish court from slaughter — who would believe he has been hanging about for diplomacy? Hardly has breath exited Hamlet's body when Fortinbras enters the court uninvited, no doubt with his army close behind. For all the work of the watch atop Elsinore castle, Fortinbras has made successful entry into Denmark to take what he wants. He gets more. The Danes may not accept a foreign monarch for long, but their receiving him here will save their lives and their country to assert themselves another day. Hamlet has an instant of successful kingship, one far different than his father's but necessary to set the times back in joint.

Finally, Hamlet could also have taken the course Ophelia does: he could have gone mad. Someone close to her has killed her father and made further relationship with her lover impossible, just as with Hamlet. Such a Hamlet, one not strong enough to resist madness, may have committed suicide, but more likely he would have been murdered to keep him from blurting out, in his madness, something the King (and Queen?) didn't want the court to hear: the truth about the late King. Hamlet resists becoming like Ophelia as he resists becoming like Laertes, Claudius, Gertrude, and Polonius. He remains himself at last, the course, however difficult, that we must hope for him and expect from him. He does what we, in his shoes, would have to try to do.

Ophelia, though, presents another problem: she is probably pregnant. When Polonius questions her about her relationship with Hamlet, she admits

> ... as I was in my sewing closet,
> Lord Hamlet, with his doublet all unbrac'd,
> No hat upon his head, his stockings fouled,
> Ungart'red, and down-gyved to his ankle,
> Pale as his shirt, his knees knocking each other ...
> To speak his horrors — he comes before me [2.1.74–81].

He has come to her in her room, half-dressed, with a near equivalent to our modern notion of having pants down, to lament, either truthfully or to act mad, to dissemble, either to throw off Claudius or to drive Ophelia away. What the two of them did after he got there Ophelia doesn't say, other than that he grabbed her wrist and held her for a time, sighed, and finally let her go. Modesty may prohibit her saying more. In Act IV., once Ophelia has gone mad, Horatio, speaking with the Queen and a gentleman, suggests, "'Twere good she were spoken with, for she may strew/ Dangerous conjectures in ill-breeding minds" (4.5.14–15). He may mean that in her rantings she will hint at Claudius' guilt or that she will uncover that she is pregnant: she has lost her father and her lover, and a pregnancy may have been the additional problem too great for her sanity to bear. The Queen, hearing Horatio's warning, says aside, "To my sick soul, as sin's true nature is,/ Each toy seems prologue to some great amiss,/ so full of artless jealousy is guilt" (17–19). She must feel jealous of Ophelia's relationship with Hamlet (Claudius mentions how she dotes on her son), but she suffers also guilt from some other sin, either her "incestuous" relationship with Claudius or knowledge of or even participation in the late King's murder.

Ophelia then sings,

> How should I your true-love know
> From another one?
> By his cockle hat and staff,
> And his sandal shoon [23–26].

The pilgrim allusion must refer to Hamlet (Laertes has gone back to France with far other objects in mind), gone to England at Claudius' behest, obviously as a way to kill him: he is the only "pilgrim," gone to meet his Maker rather than to a holy shrine but also in a sense traveling for his sins (Polonius' death). Which of Hamlet's sins would Ophelia know, beyond her father's killing? Later, after another verse that seems to apply to her dead father, she sings again,

> Larded all with sweet flowers,
> Which bewept to the ground did not go
> With true-love showers [39–40].

She wept for her father and placed flowers in or on his grave, but the tears of her true love — or her tears for her true love — didn't accompany them. From her point of view Hamlet has jilted her as well as gone to his death. Then comes the particularly telling verses:

> To-morrow is Saint Valentine's day,
> All in the morning betime,
> And I a maid at your window,
> To be your valentine.
>
> Then up he rose and donn'd his clo'es,
> And dupp'd the chamber-door,
> Let in the maid, that out a maid
> Never departed more....

> By Gis, and by Saint Charity,
> Alack, and fie for shame!
> Young me will do't if they come to't,
> By Cock, they are to blame.
> Quoth she, "Before you tumbled me,
> You promised me to wed.
> (He answers.)
> So would I 'a' done, by yonder sun,
> And thou hadst not come to my bed [4.5.48–66].

The lyrics suggest that for love she went to Hamlet's bed and left it no longer a virgin. Either he said something to the effect or she believes that because she has done so, he will no longer want to marry her. She has lost him.

Ophelia exits, then returns, and she distributes flowers and herbs, rue for herself and Gertrude (symbolizing sorrow and penitence for their sins, probably sexual),[7] fennel and columbines for Claudius (implying flattery and ingratitude, for the way he felt about his brother). After another reference to her dead father, she adds, singing, "For bonny sweet Robin is all my joy" (187). The robin symbolizes growth and renewal, perhaps a pregnancy image; the name Robin is a pet name or diminutive of Robert, meaning "fame" or "famous one"— in this case likely the potential child of the prince. The songs give Gertrude additional frightening information and another reason for jealousy and concern. If Ophelia has so sinned, so has Hamlet, but Ophelia, unlike Hamlet, has no recourse for action. She has no reason to believe he can or will return; we learn that he will, that he does love her, and that their love will do them no good. At least they will die faithful to each other; given what Claudius and Gertrude have learned, neither Hamlet nor Ophelia had much of a chance of living longer anyway. Gertrude fears perhaps that Hamlet will prove too much like his mother and uncle, but she has missed the chance to learn better.

I will not say that Hamlet could have become like Horatio, but that Horatio serves as a non-royal version of Hamlet. Like Hamlet he has spent much of his life in study, he makes a good friend, and he can act with passion and conviction — unless his convictions lead him to wait, which he, like Hamlet, can do. *Horatio* is "oratio," oration, the voice that must remain behind to tell Hamlet's story. In that service he becomes the best friend for whom Hamlet could ask. Hamlet's voice lives on in Horatio.

Act III of *Hamlet* emerges as one of the most skillfully constructed pieces in the history of drama: it masterfully exploits parallelism to illuminate the value and problem of perspective. The four scenes show us four different versions of Hamlet, depending on from what perspective one sees: scene one gives us Ophelia's Hamlet; scene two shows us Horatio's Hamlet; scene three uncovers Claudius' Hamlet; scene four offers Gertrude's Hamlet.

III.1 begins with Claudius and Gertrude consulting Rosencrantz and Guildenstern in their plot to discover Hamlet's intentions. With Polonius' help they place Ophelia in his way as bait. Hamlet enters with the famous "to be or not to be" soliloquy, contemplating suicide; he still berates himself for failing to act. The speech ends when he spots Ophelia and says, "Nymph, in thy orisons/ Be all my sins rememb'red" (88–89) — if he has taken her virginity, and perhaps she his, she may well have confessed all of his sins as well as her own: Hamlet has done well to avoid other abuses or excesses, given his circumstances. Then comes the "get thee to a nunn'ry speech" speech: from his point of view, he may be trying to save her, but from hers he acts with surprising, vicious anger and probably with madness. When he exits, she laments, "O, what a noble mind is here o'erthrown!/ The courtier's, soldier's, scholar's, eye, tongue, sword,/ Th'expectation and rose of the fair state ... quite, quite down!" (150–54). Ophelia sees madness and potential suicide in Hamlet as we see it in her. Her list also hints at the problem: the words come out of order. The courtier, soldier, and scholar should match up instead with tongue, sword, and eye. When the courtier looks (or leers) but can't speak helpfully and diplomatically, when the soldier speaks but can't fight, and the scholar fights rather than observing and learning to find peaceful resolution to problems, the world has gone awry: it has gone mad. So Ophelia sees their world.

III.2 begins with Hamlet in dialogue with the players about the state of theatrical practice: we see Hamlet as scholar and philosopher. When Horatio enters, Hamlet asks his help to observe the behavior of the King during the play-within-the-play just ahead. The monarchs and other courtiers enter and prepare for the play. Hamlet would verbally spar with the King and Queen, but they avoid his efforts, and he offers Ophelia sexual jests that she tries to deflect. The players' presentation begins with a Prologue followed by a pantomime, which Hamlet narrates (they never get to the speech that Hamlet so carefully helped them prepare). Gertrude objects to the Prologue, because it comes near to the circumstances of Hamlet Sr.'s death. Hamlet identifies the play not as "The Murder of Gonzago," but as "The Mousetrap": his purpose, and the reason he asks Horatio to watch the King's reaction. Significantly, in the play not the brother, but the *nephew* of the King pours poison in the King's ear. At that point Claudius rises, shouts, and runs from the hall. Horatio has noted the King's reaction, but he must know — as ultimately Hamlet must know — that the play has proven nothing: Claudius could interpret it rather as a threat, that the nephew, Hamlet, intends to kill the King, Claudius, not that Hamlet knows exactly how he killed his brother. Hamlet's scholarly ploy, brilliant and dramatic, fails to tell him what he needs not to *guess*, but to *know*. The scholar's eye can't teach the soldier's sword when the courtier's tongue has failed to speak the situation correctly. Hamlet, though at first he believes he has accomplished a coup, will again stop short of acting on it: the scholar in him, the Horatio in him, must note his mistake. He may say, "Now could I drink hot blood,/ And do such [bitter business as the day]/ Would quake to look on" (390–92), but he can't. Horatio's Hamlet is still brilliantly but unsuccessfully trying to learn what to do.

Act III, scene 3, gives us Claudius' perspective. After the play the King repairs to a chapel to pray for forgiveness, but he can't: he knows that "words without thoughts never to heaven go" (98). He wants to pray, but can't because he doesn't really repent what he's done: he has in fact got what he wanted, and he wants to keep it. Hamlet, behind him, poised to strike with his sword, again doesn't commit the deed: not knowing that Claudius isn't really praying, he doesn't want to kill Claudius in the midst of his repentance, thus sending the King to heaven rather than hell. But Claudius' Hamlet speaks there, more than Hamlet's Hamlet: Claudius must suspect that as he would kill Hamlet, Hamlet would as readily kill him, and wishing him not only death, but suffering as well for what he has done. Claudius' Hamlet is more specter than prince, more like his father than like the mad Ophelia or the scholarly Horatio.

Gertrude's Hamlet appears in III.4; he makes her see what she doesn't want to see: the evil in which she has participated. Gertrude wants to believe Hamlet mad, because otherwise she must see him as right: she shouldn't have done what she has done, and she must repent for it. He treats her sins directly and cruelly and would make her face them. She, however, can't see the ghost that stills him from treating her too harshly: what he sees as righteous anger, necessary to turn her toward salvation, she sees as madness, nothing there but the heat of Hamlet's own brain to move him. Hamlet's stabbing Polonius proves, from her point of view, how dangerous Hamlet is; she will concur in Claudius' sending the prince away, probably with an inkling of the King's real purpose in doing so: like Claudius, she does not feel ready to repent — much easier for her to believe in Hamlet's madness. With Hamlet's own final words in the scene, though, we have a hint of truth that Gertrude knows, but that she wants to cover even from herself: Hamlet expects the King to try to kill him, and he prepares for it: "'tis sport to have the engineer/ Hoist with his own petar" (206–207). From Gertrude's perspective Hamlet has turned into someone, like Lord Byron, mad, bad, and dangerous to know. She refuses to see herself in the same light.

The varying perspectives, in some ways oddly comical and in some ways terrifying, can contribute moral or semantic uncertainty or give greater depth and completeness to how we see Hamlet's character, depending on what the reader seeks from them. They make the problems of the play clearer and more poignant as each viewpoint gives us a means to understand the dimensions of character and the nuances of interpretation. The variability of perspective, a productive but unsolvable problem, helps make the play a problem play.

Hamlet observes, Portia-like, to Rosencrantz, "there is nothing either good or bad, but thinking makes it so" (2.2.249–50), an odd observation for someone so tied to philosophy, self-examination, and speculation, to someone we may see and who sees himself in so many ways. Unlike Ophelia, he thinks his way to the best solution he could have reached. When he learns of Laertes' challenge, despite Horatio's warning he readily accepts. He doesn't worry about death, because he doesn't fear it and life has little to offer him. Laertes' death-blow relieves him of the damning option of suicide, and his own counter-blow allows for the uncovering of Claudius' plot to kill the prince. Claudius' poison has killed Gertrude; when Hamlet kills Claudius, he is not avenging his father, but executing Claudius for murdering the Queen. With Gertrude's death on his hands, Claudius is no longer properly King: Hamlet succeeds him and has the right to execute him for a royal murder that he can prove — the whole court know about it. He pardons Laertes — an act of particular kindness, since Laertes is now guilty of regicide — because Laertes was acting on impulses of vengeance Hamlet can understand. Having lost his beloved and his family, and with Fortinbras ready to attack (the Prince himself has seen the army) and probably kill Hamlet along with many of his people, Hamlet has, by waiting to act at the right moment, got himself out of his difficulties.

The play, almost unnoticeably, ends as happily as it possibly could. The sadness comes from the loss of a prince who had wisdom, wit, and conviction from which the world could have learned, and of the young woman who loved him: perhaps they could have made each other happy. But given the break in the Great Chain that occurred with Claudius' regicide, the world of the play could not avoid at least a generation of suffering. Hamlet's choices and action minimize that suffering. *Hamlet* is, at last, far closer to comedy than to tragedy and still a problem to ponder.

Othello: *Culmination of the Horror Play*

Another of the "great tragedies, as we often find Shakespeare's biggest and best works grouped, *Othello* looks like a tragedy in that it has an apparent protagonist of some magnitude who undergoes a terrifying fall — in this case among the most terrifying possible, because he commits an atrocity against the person he loves most at the behest of a character who, like Don John in *Much Ado About Nothing*, but much more so, acts very much like a devil. The problem comes, though, in the means by which the fall happens and in which character we find actually at the center of the play. Othello does have a kind of "tragic flaw" (insecurity and a resulting rashness) and does make several "tragic errors" (the actual notion of *hamartia*), but Iago stands—like Satan at the bottom middle of Dante's *Inferno*—at the center-of-gravity of this plot. He drives the plot and comes closer than Othello to the "chief wrestler," proto-agonist, of the play in that he wants something, goes after it, and for the most part gets it. Othello minds his own business and serves Venice until first love and then a hateful and spiteful enemy get in his way: he has no notion of either as a problem. He, like King Lear, needs to know to "see better," to observe, to make cooler decisions, to gain the ability to know human nature better—something maturity should but seldom does teach us. Othello can do that in war, but he hasn't learned to do it in peace.

Iago has, though, a deep-down anger and meanness of spirit, a deadly combination of enormous insecurity and enormous ego, and he will do anything to anyone to get what he wants.[8] Sadly, he wants nothing really worth getting. He suffers perhaps more than any other Shakespeare character from what René Girard calls *mimetic desire*: he wants something because other characters want or have it, and he fears everyone else wants what he wants or has, so he must subvert, damage, or kill anyone who crosses the path of his desire. He becomes not only the center of action of the play, but also the source of the horror that destroys those it touches. Iago, not Othello, defines the course of the play; Othello gives the play its title because he shows how an essentially good man can fall precipitously (and with astonishingly little reason) when an evil man with spectacular skills of manipulation takes aim to harm him.[9]

Desdemona, like Othello, makes the error of assuming her society has more liberal and accommodating views than it has: she marries the Moor without considering the effect her choice will have on her father, her city, and their associates. The Venetians have no interest in harming Othello, but they have no great love for him, either: they accept him and honor him because he has courage and ability as a soldier and commander and because he defends their city. Without his military successes, they would not so welcome him, and they will perfectly happily damn him for his crime despite what he has accomplished—neither they nor we can forgive him for murdering Desdemona. Othello, caught up too much in the ego boost of Desdemona's love—or at least her adoration—fails to think through their choice to elope. As a much older man from a different culture, he should know better than to make such a rash choice, but Desdemona's love briefly disarms any rational reluctance. The marriage angers and ultimately kills Brabantio: he believes both his daughter and his new son-in-law have betrayed him. He feels that way partly on parental grounds—the elopement surprises and insults him, since he would believe he had the right to bestow his daughter as he chose — and partly on racial grounds: he will invite a foreigner, a Moor, into his home for dinner and conversation, but with no expectation that the man, particularly a man so unlike his daughter, will steal Desdemona from him. The young woman apparently doesn't know her father very well, nor does she know her husband well: she would hardly believe he could kill her for a supposed infidelity she has not committed. Nor does the father know the daughter well: he has failed to observe the direction of her affections. The murder of Desdemona isn't Classical tragedy, but contemporary horror.

Michael Cassio makes a similar youthful and nearly fatal error in trusting Iago. Iago must have a great deal of charm and an incredible talent for dissembling — as does the traditional Christian devil — but the others help him by paying him little careful attention. How can Cassio not know that Iago will feel cheated in not gaining the appointment as Othello's Lieutenant? Apparently he doesn't notice that obvious likelihood; despite his having less experience and fewer accomplishments than Iago, Cassio remains caught up in his own concerns and pays no real attention to what Iago has lost and to Iago's real character. He, like Desdemona, and like King Lear, doesn't really observe. Knowing that he doesn't hold drink well, he allows Iago to talk him into drinking anyway, an indiscretion that nearly leads to his own death as well as contributing to Desdemona's. Shakespeare never flinches from showing how disaster can come from seemingly small — but bad — decisions.

Emilia, while a relatively minor character — and a relatively good one — plays a major part in the downfall of the principals. As badly as Iago treats her, she remains sufficiently in love with him to do what he says — unthinkingly — even when it can serve no good purpose. She observes that "the Moor's abus'd by some most villainous knave" (4.2.139) but can't or won't make the leap to recognizing that knave as her husband; she obstructs her own vision. Her providing him the handkerchief that Othello gave Desdemona allows Iago to put just enough pressure on Othello's diseased ego to drive him to sickness and deadly violence. Emilia, trying to be a good wife, misplaces her duty, trusting a monster, and so contributes to murder, and she herself suffers murder for it, a penalty far greater than anything she deserves. This world has no inkling of justice or mercy; it punishes unmercifully for errors small or large, especially those characters who have had the opportunity to learn better, to avoid the bad situations in which they find themselves, but have ignored the clues that should have taught them better. Iago preys on those who trust him, both those worthy of better treatment (such as Emilia) and those who allow themselves to be led with incredible ease to acts of murder (Roderigo gives in more easily and stupidly than Othello).

Othello, at last, foregrounds Iago more than it does Othello because he

6. Tragic Problem Plays

most fully embodies the play's major problem; Othello's self-absorption weakly mirrors his self-obsession, and obsession all-consuming in Iago. The other characters serve as fodder for Iago's hatred, for the monomaniacal character who must always come first: the great disease that for Shakespeare's world (and that Milton later told so completely and powerfully) began with the Fall of the rebel angels from Heaven, continued with the Fall of humans in the world, and that plays out daily in the writhings and wailings of our internal worlds when every thought turns to self and self-aggrandizement.[10] Othello commits the murder of his beautiful and faithful young wife because a "devil," a man who has good traits but who has brought himself to a collapse of character into hatred and unprovoked vengeance, has driven him to it. Yet he acts willingly and so remains culpable. Othello sins as Milton's Adam and Eve do, but in an act of violence rather than one of pride and envy and gluttony. The interpretive difficulty with *Othello*, what moves it toward problem play, is that it comes closer to horror play than tragedy. We conclude the play with the sense that none of its horrors had to happen; they do because most people don't pay attention. The man who drives the action has eschewed nobility of character in exchange for envious self-absorption that leaves him in a perpetual state of desire for vengeance against anyone over whom he can gain control — the very evil of Satan, a living figure in Shakespeare's time and the father not only of lies, but of all terrors. The charm by means of which he leads us on the path to horrific acts adds to the terror — the reason so many readers at first encounter believe Satan the hero of *Paradise Lost*. "First-wrestler," perhaps, but a long way from hero...

Once again, while we know little of Shakespeare's personal thought, how he stood philosophically on the perennial human issues or those of his time, we know from his work what he *thought about* and what troubled him in human behavior. His plays repeatedly show that when we try to control others' thoughts and decisions, when we obsessively pursue our own desires at others' expense, when we fail to think through problems but act rashly instead, when we pursue civil conflict rather than mutually rewarding peace, and when we forget fidelity and duty we court disaster for ourselves and our world. We dare not expect happy endings on this earth even if we act virtuously, but through love and kindness and humor and courage and mercy we may provide ourselves and others happy moments on the way; we should hope at last for redemption, but we ourselves haven't the strength to bring it to pass; we must remain vigilant, since the natural world — and the humans in it — will often not forgive even small errors of judgment or action. Most of those points come into play in *Othello*, but in a sequence of such bad choices by so many characters that the action slides down a long, slow slope from potentially noble love and victory to sickeningly and avoidably base jealousy, exploitation, and violence.

The Steady Fall of Iago

The fall of Iago has already begun before the play commences, in the appointment of Cassio rather than Iago to Othello's Lieutenancy, and we find his reaction to the fall-in-progress in full swing in the first scene of the play. In Act I, scene 1, Iago has duped Roderigo to help him begin his vengeance against Othello. They meet around midnight in front of Brabantio's house to rouse him with the news of his daughter's elopement with Othello. Roderigo gives his name, but Iago cunningly does not: he shouts loud warnings and insults from the shadows:

> Awake! What ho, Brabantio ...
> Look to your house, your daughter, and your bags!
> Thieves, thieves! [1.1.78–81].

and

> Your heart is burst, you have lost half your soul;
> Even now, now, very now, an old black ram
> I tupping your white ewe. Arise, arise! ...
> Or else the devil will make a grandsire of you [87–91].

and

> I am one, sire, that comes to tell you your daughter and the Moor are [now] making the beast with two backs [115–17].

His comments, racist, lewd, alarming, of course frighten a man who didn't even know that his daughter had gone. Iago hopes that the elopement and Brabantio's anger will bring on an attack against Othello; they don't, partly because Othello and Desdemona together convince the Duke that the young lady has married of her own choice and partly because Othello has served the Duke so well as a naval commander: Venice depends on the freedom of its waterways. Roderigo, not Iago, will bear the burden for rousing the city against Othello: Iago plays both sides of the fence, continuing to claim to Othello his loyalty and service while enlisting others to trouble his every step.

Meanwhile, he continues to exploit Roderigo, who believes he loves Desdemona, though Brabantio had thrown him out when he tried to court her. Roderigo believes, then, that he must hate Othello. Iago continues to borrow money from him and to use him to provoke violence and trouble. In IV.2 Iago sets him on to the murder of Cassio, but, Roderigo argues, rightly, "I do not find thou dealest justly with me" (173). Roderigo gets gradually angrier at Iago until the villain finally exclaims, "Why, now I see there's mettle in thee.... Give me thy hand, Roderigo.... I protest I have dealt most directly in thy affair" (204–208). He praises Roderigo's courage (of which he has little)

6. Tragic Problem Plays

and urges him on for the profit he (Roderigo) can make of it—the benefit from Cassio's death would come to Iago, not Roderigo, since he wants vengeance on him, too, for taking the office he wanted. The irony comes in how easily Iago manipulates Roderigo: the devilish way by which he overcomes the minimal scruples of a stupid man prepares him for the subtler means by which he overcomes the better man, Othello. That he also does by fairly simple and common means: sexual jealousy. He expects that ploy will work, because the emotion works on him: he suspects (with no reason or likelihood), or says he suspects, that his wife has been unfaithful to him with both Othello and Cassio. The statements read more like an excuse than a fact, but they say much about Iago: he can and will delude himself as well as anyone else. While he must have shown some valor as a soldier to have won Othello's trust, he devotes the events of this play to unrelenting and nearly unparalleled dissembling, showing no courage or honor whatever.

"I hate the Moor," Iago says to himself, "And it is though abroad that 'twixt my sheets/ [H'as] done my office" (1.3.386–88). Has Iago really heard that, or does he make it up as an excuse, or does it come from paranoia? Cassio, if her were not in sufficient danger already, meeting Iago and Emilia with others on the quay in Cypress blithely greets Iago, then turns to Emilia:

> ... Welcome, mistress.
> Let it not gall your patience, good Iago,
> That I extend my manners; 'tis my breeding
> That gives me this bold show of courtesy ... [2.1.96–99]

and without waiting for an answer, he kisses Emilia. As so often in Shakespeare's plays, a bit more reticence would have served him better. Once Cassio has fallen from Othello's favor as a result of his drunken fight with Roderigo (whom Iago has set on Cassio), Iago will help him get to Desdemona to plead with Othello for his forgiveness. Desdemona way over-pleads the case. Othello is ready to hear, but Iago uses what he learns to spark Othello's jealousy and fan its flames, and Desdemona's excess works right into his plan. While nearly every other character praises "honest Iago," Iago uses increasingly cunning and invasive advice to create and repeatedly abrade the wounds that lead them to thoughtless and bloody precipitousness.

Lured by Iago into drink and violence, Cassio laments, "Reputation, reputation, reputation! O, I have lost my reputation! I have lost the immortal part of myself, and what remains is bestial" (2.3.262–65). Cassio, of course, gets it wrong: he has not lost his immortal soul, though he has lost some social status that he must find a way to regain if he would have his career prosper. He places his soul in danger, though, by dealing with Iago: misplaced trust can lead to endless suffering. Iago disagrees with what Cassio says, but not to set him straight; instead, he aims him down a far worse path by hiding falsehood amidst truth:

> As I am an honest man, I had thought you had receiv'd some bodily wound; there is more sense in that than in reputation. Reputation is an idle and most false imposition; oft got without merit, and lost without deserving. You have not lost reputation at all, unless you repute yourself a loser. What, man, there are more ways to recover the general again [266–72].

He tells the truth about the nature of reputation, often unsubstantiated or simply wrong. He lies about his own honesty and doesn't admit the difficulty Cassio will have in regaining good standing: he prepares Cassio for the psychological excess that will contribute to Othello's and Desdemona's demise. He praises Cassio for winning the fight rather than counseling him against excess. He galls and gulls Othello through similar half-truths: "As I confess it is my nature's plague/ To spy into abuses, and [oft] my jealousy/ Shapes faults that are not" (2.2.146–48) — by pretending not to want to defame Cassio he leads Othello to "force" him to confess Cassio's faults. In Roderigo he contributes to the fall of a man with little goodness; he aims higher with Cassio, but not yet as high as he will go.[11]

Iago dismantles Othello systematically. He says, "Good [God] the souls of all my tribe defend/ From jealousy" (3.3.175–76), but he finds Othello soft to that attack and pursues it skillfully and relentlessly. He drives Othello mad so that he doesn't even notice he himself has caused Desdemona to drop the offending handkerchief, drives him to an apoplectic fit in IV.1, and in the end to deadly wrath — as Emilia calls it, the "serpent's curse" (4.2.16). Othello loses all sense of decency and honor, perhaps even lying to Desdemona about the source of the handkerchief to make her feel even worse about it. "It is the cause, it is the cause, my soul;/ Let me not name it to you, you chaste stars,/ It is the cause" (5.2.1–3), whispers Othello to himself as he prepares for murder. He refers to Desdemona's infidelity, but a grammatical parsing of the line shows the real cause: the error and weakness in Othello's own soul. He cannot bear his own jealousy. Iago has found him out and exploited him to death. Resorting to the murders of Desdemona and Othello by proxy, that is by Othello's hand, Iago has fallen nearly as far as a human can fall — of all Shakespeare's characters, perhaps only King Lear falls lower. He shows no interest in saving his soul; he commits to silence, refusing to confess at the end of the play, in hope of saving his body.

With his last act in the play Iago kills his own wife. We do not see his death. A great and unstated fear at the end of the play must lie in what will happen to Iago. Dare we fear he may yet escape and that we may find him loose in the world? Many of the horror movies of our time end with the monster seemingly stopped, caught, or dead, but still at large.

Othello falls: while he has a strong exterior, he has a surprisingly fragile internal life. He can't muster the strength to resist either Iago's cajolings or his own wrath. Driven by Iago, he falls quickly and easily to murder and suicide, in Shakespeare's world to damnation: hardly the fall of a tragic hero, particularly since he falls failing to accept his own culpability. Desdemona dies willingly, with forgiveness on her lips. That may present a kind of love, but it doesn't help Othello. Iago, starting lower on the Chain of Being than Othello, falls at great length in steady steps by his own doing: he commits a kind of suicide not of body, but of the soul. He answers the question "How far can a person fall?": as far as he's willing to fall, until he dies. And perhaps, in a Christian universe, further yet...

The Unredeemed Death of Desdemona

More than any other event, the murder of Desdemona by the person she loves and trusts most turns the play from tragedy to horror. Neither the principle characters nor the world of the play gain knowledge or understanding from the deed. They have only the inexplicable Iago, who hates and kills perhaps as much for the sake of hatred as for what he gains from his manipulations, which promised little and turn out to bring nothing of worth — again that great evil, *dissembling*. The citizens have if anything deepened their xenophobia as a result of Othello's actions, and they have lost their best naval commander. Cassio will lead them now, but while he has shown himself no Iago, he has given no reason for anyone to see him as a new Othello, an advisable choice for military command. Desdemona remains true to her last breath, but her loss produces emptiness, not any sort of revelation. Can a play that leads nowhere useful and that supplies no recognition and redemption produce a catharsis?

Having killed Desdemona, Othello fails to recognize his own culpability, and he mis-assigns the reason for his own erratic behavior and horrific violence: he has given away his free will, the essence of the Christian soul's functioning in a fallen world. After faith in God and in the redemption offered by Christ, the central principle of Christian thought is free will: God has given us the ability to choose, and we must keep ourselves vigilant to choose well rather than poorly. Without his making them explicit, those ideas pervade Shakespeare's plays. To do him justice we must appreciate the centrality of the Christian worldview and daily Christian experience in the lives of the Elizabethan and Jacobean English. We must sorrow not only for death, but for damnation through actions that the characters chose for themselves, misled though they be.

Emilia arrives in the final scene not in time to save Desdemona, but in time to swear her innocence: "she was chaste; she lov'd thee, cruel Moor;/ So come my soul to bliss" (5.2.249–50). The best Othello can do is sorrow for himself:

> ... O ill-starr'd wench,
> Pale as thy smock! when we shall meet at compt,
> This look of thine will hurl my soul from heaven,
> And fiends will snatch it....
> Whip me, devils ... [5.2.272–77].

and finally

> I have done the state some service, and they know't....
> ... I pray you, in your letters ...
> Speak of me as I am; nothing extenuate,
> Nor set down aught in malice. Then thou must speak
> Of one that lov'd not wisely but too well;
> Of one not easily jealous, but being wrought,
> Perplex'd in the extreme; of one whose hand
> ... threw a pearl away
> Richer than all his tribe ... [5.2.339–348].

He gets most of both speeches wrong. Desdemona wouldn't damn him; he would damn himself, and has done so. No one need hurl him from heaven; like Milton's fallen angels, he has jumped. He doesn't want anyone to speak of him as he is or was: he wants them to remember the good and brave service he did. He did not love too well; Desdemona did. Iago drove him to jealousy with incredible ease — not the reaction of one who really loves, but of one who possesses and desires to keep possession. The "pearl" he threw away refers not only to Desdemona, but also to his soul: not a conclusion Desdemona would have wished. They both chose poorly, but they both felt love, at least of a sort; we do not choose whom we love — love comes upon us by circumstance and as it will. Neither Desdemona nor Othello gains any redemption from that love. No one will learn from either their love or their deaths, and nothing good can come from them.

In the world of this play love itself has fallen, and that may be the greatest fall of all. Where love has died, horror reigns, and there we find the lurking problem at the beginning, middle, and end of *Othello*.

King Lear: His Heart Burst Smilingly

Audiences have always found Cordelia's death at the end of *King Lear* almost too shocking and painful to bear, so much so that the play verges, like

6. Tragic Problem Plays 167

Othello, on horror rather than tragedy. Shakespeare swerves there from his major source: Raphael Holinshed in his 1587 *Chronicles of England, Scotlande, and Irelande* has Cordelia live to restore Lear to his kingship and later follow him to the throne. In 1681 Nahum Tate rewrote Shakespeare's ending so that Cordelia survives and marries Edgar — that version of the play persisted on the English stage until nearly 1840, more sustainable for patrons. Lear experiences perhaps the worst pain a human can feel, and one wonders how an actor can play Cornwall and the blinding of Gloucester. At the end of *King Lear* the world of play exists in a kind of flux, lacking resolution or direction. Kent, following a masterful blood-letting of the principals, says he must soon follow his master in death. Albany and Edgar, neither exactly prepared for kingship, must sort out who will rule and how. With their defenses down, we must wonder if the British forces have entirely put down the French invasion, launched though it was by Cordelia's good cause, to rescue her father. Tragedy often requires the cleansing of an entire generation, sometimes two, before anyone or anything can put the world right. The world of *King Lear* has nearly, but not entirely, reached that point.[12] We have but remnants of the younger generation, and they may not have the strength to bring peace. If catharsis comes at all, it occurs only in bits and pieces, as fear and pity remain to trouble the ending of the play and beyond.

In *Seneca and the Idea of Tragedy*, Gregory Staley explains Sir Philip Sidney's ideas of tragedy: its "essence ... lies ... in its cognitive power: It 'openeth,' 'showeth forth, 'manifest[s],' and 'maketh us know.' ... [I]t constitutes a vivid revelation," has the "power to open wounds" and is "epistemological rather than therapeutic" (18) — not entirely in line with Aristotle's idea of catharsis, but awfully fitting for *King Lear*. Shakespeare's play opens many wounds without suturing them by any means other than the end of the play. Stephen Medcalf among others has argued for Cordelia as a Christ figure: her realism, love, forgiveness and sacrifice give us a way to read the play as something other than horrific disaster. Once again, we have no reason to try to free Shakespeare of Christian intention or of allegorical method — we need not see a whole work as an allegory to find useful allegory in it. Allegorical reading alone doesn't resolve the problems of the play, but it allows audiences a means to integrate what we learn from the play in our own lives, particularly for Christian readers, but also for anyone who believes that from the study of bad decisions and their horrific results we may learn to avoid similar errors in our own lives.

In that sense *King Lear* parallels the Old English *Beowulf*. While the hero is not Christ, we may see him as a Christ-figure who points to what humans may accomplish, but, without Christ, however brave and strong, we will always lack the capacity to offer redemption and salvation. From *Beowulf*, as potentially from *King Lear,* we may learn to endure, persist, show courage, avoid rash action, use what strength we have, forgive others (especially family members or close associates) who choose poorly and do what we can to help them — those messages apply as powerfully to non–Christians as to Christians, as powerfully in realism as in allegory.

A. D. Nuttal argues that, at the moment of the King's death, "the very intensity of Lear's joy increases our sense of his error [in believing Cordelia lives] and so deepens the pathos" (309). Much of what we know we know by contrast.[13] Lear's hope that Cordelia lives will not let go of us. Like Lear, we think we know when someone is living or dead, but we cling to the hope that something good can and will happen. The fact that Lear can't let Cordelia go, and that we can't either, intensifies the feeling of loss and the unwillingness to accept that such a small act as Lear's temper tantrum in Act I can ruin many lives and destroy a society. Lear's death may provide a sense of relief and release — at least his suffering has ended — but it may instead just deepen the sadness at our recognition of waste. Lear's abandonment of his position of power leads to his own loss of strength, his madness, and his family's complete demise: what greater fear can we take with us into old age, when strength and wit and breath itself must finally fade? We want hope, not fear; tragedy is supposed to cleanse us of fear, not deepen it.

In addition to its pathos, *King Lear* has some of Shakespeare's most scorchingly sad, yet wickedly witty humor, and it has an ending that resists catharsis — or allows, perhaps instead, for minor catharses followed by additional, and even deeper, wounds. With Cordelia's death, we have lost the best of this world; much of what we do with the end of the play, then, depends on how we view Lear's death (if we want a hint of redemption). Harold Goddard has suggested that *King Lear* is *The Tempest* in hell, and *The Tempest* is *King Lear* in heaven. The humor of the play can't relieve us of this world's hell by taking into the realm of comedy, nor does a certain catharsis cleanse us of hellish suffering. Bu the hell of this world doesn't eliminate the humor that can still provoke a degree of wisdom, if we attend to that wisdom where we find it.

As in *Twelfth Night* we see in *Lear* "what is and is not"; in II.3 Edgar, disguising himself as poor Tom the beggar, says, "Edgar I nothing am" (21) — not entirely correct, since enough of what Edgar was remains so that in the end of the play he may face his brother, avenge his father, and look ahead with Albany to the future (however bleak) of their people. Many characters in *Lear* act as both what they are and what they aren't: Lear becomes a shadow of himself; Kent reappears as Caius to continue to serve his king; the daughters who proclaim their love for their father have none, and they may not even be Lear's daughters, at least not "natural" or "legitimate" daughters. Edmund convinces Gloucester that Edgar, not he, is plotting the Earl's demise: "[I never got him]," Gloucester exclaims angrily, and just so easily Edmund has reversed Gloucester's notion of who is the bastard son. Lack of firm identity leads to dereliction of duty, and so the world plunges into chaos and war. We end the play, as usual, with problems: can wit get us to useful wisdom, can anyone set this world straight, and can we find any way to read Lear's suffering as cleansing or redemptive? The play both is and is not, in the old sense, *tragedy*.

One of the most remarkable and understated events in the play occurs in III.4, as Kent has joined Lear and the Fool on the blasted heath amidst the storm. "Pour on, I will endure" (18) says Lear to the uncaring universe. Kent finds a mere hovel for shelter and suggested Lear enter to get out of the cold. "I'll go in," he says, but he stops to let the Fool enter first: "In, boy, go first.— You houseless poverty—/ Nay, get thee in; I'll pray, and then I'll sleep" (25–27). Lear commits an unusual act for any king, particularly such a proud one: he thinks of another first, despite his own suffering, and urges toward what relief they can find someone else who suffers too: Lear has learned, perhaps for the first time, compassion, the appreciation of the feelings of another. That small step in kindness, followed by the desire to pray, represents an enormous step in wisdom—but too late to change the course of events he set powerfully and unstoppably in motion.

Sophomoric Wit, and Wisdom Won Too Late

I use the term *sophomore* here not as we do for second-year college students, but as the Greeks did, to indicate the irony of the "wise-fool"—*King Lear* has at once the wittiest, wisest, and saddest of Fools, and what the Fool says to Lear contributes to the tension of how we understand the characters and how they reach their ends.

The Fool "replaces" Cordelia in the action: when she leaves, he appears, and after she has returned, we see him no more. What Cordelia tries but fails to accomplish with Lear through directness and rationality, the Fool must instead manage through pointedly true but carefully roundabout wit. When Lear springs on his daughters the request to tell him how much they love him, the elder two easily gush—and as easily lie. Lear expects something "more opulent" from Cordelia, which she will not deliver:

> You have begot me, bred me, lov'd me: I
> Return those duties back as are right fit,
> Obey you, love you, and most honor you.
> Why have my sisters husbands if they say
> They love you all? Happily, when I shall wed,
> That lord whose hand must take my plight shall carry

> Half my love with him, half my care and duty.
> Sure I shall never marry like my sisters,
> [To love my father all] [1.1.96–104].

She does tell Lear she loves him, but she doesn't gush in the way he expects. She doesn't *obey* him: faced with the choice of obedience or truth, Cordelia chooses truth, which doesn't go far enough to feed Lear's ego and probably embarrasses him in front of the court, whom he has just led also to expect more. In a fit of temper he banishes Cordelia — his extension of the tragic error he makes in abdicating and dividing his kingdom — and then banishes Kent similarly. He has made the aged person's frightening error: he has dismissed those who love him and cast himself at the mercy of those who don't. While Kent returns almost immediately, and Cordelia will return with an army supplied by her husband, Lear has done sufficient damage that they can't repair it. He has broken the Great Chain of Being right at the top.

The Fool can't fix Lear's problem, either, but he can help him, if the King wishes, to understand it. Part of the experience of tragedy as a genre comes in the protagonist's recognition that he has caused his own fall; Lear gets some recognition, but not all. As Cordelia has spoken truth, so must the Fool, but in a way that Lear can (and will) understand. Wisdom may not come soon enough to prohibit error, but it may at least provide compensation and, if luck allow (in King Lear it doesn't), it may point toward remedy. Kent points Lear to the first step, but again too bluntly, Cordelia-like: "See better, Lear" (line 157). But Lear must come to recognition slowly and through the terrifying gate of madness. "I am a man/ More sinn'd against than sinning," Lear asserts in III.2.59–60; he's right, but the world doesn't care. Fortune will turn its wheel, and the magnitude of suffering may well exceed that of the error that caused it.[14]

The Fool has a privileged position from which he may to an extant say what he wants, as long as he entertains. Lear will threaten to beat him when he goes too far, but the King quickly realizes the truth of what he hears, truth he has refused to hear from Cordelia and Kent. The Fool offers Kent his coxcomb, the symbol of his profession, for showing himself the greater fool "for taking one's part that's out of favor" (i.e., for coming to Lear's defense now that power lies with his daughters instead). He will also call Lear a fool:

> That lord that counsell'd thee
> To give away thy land,
> Come place his here by me,
> Do thou for him stand.
> The sweet and bitter fool
> Will presently appear:
> The one in motley here,
> The other found out there [1.4.140–47].

"Dost thou call me fool, boy?" Lear asks, and the Fool replies, "All thy other titles thou has given away, that thou wast born with." Lear was born a fool, the Fool says, and from all his possessions no one has taken away his foolishness: it has grown to its worst as Lear has reached his point of greatest weakness, when wisdom only could help him. No one has counseled Lear to give away his lands and power: he has made his own bad decision. He can blame no one but himself for his foolishness, but he can learn to know foolishness when he finds it.

The Fool's advice, much like that of Polonius to Laertes in *Hamlet*, though pithier, comes too late to help Lear, but perhaps not his audience:

> Have more than thou showest,
> Speak less than thou knowest,
> Lend less than thou owest,
> Ride more than thou goest,
> Learn more than thou trowest;
> Leave thy drink and thy whore.
> And keep in a' door,
> And thou shalt have more
> Than two tens to a score [1.4.118–27].

The speech "translates" essentially thus, through far less succinctly, so we can see how much the Fool has packed into a few words:

> Don't let others know how much you have; then they won't want to steal it. Don't tell all you know: reserve your knowledge for when you need it. If you lend, keep enough in reserve for your own needs. Save your strength, since you never know when you'll need that, too. Learn everything you can, even more and other than you believe to be true: you may unexpectedly need that sometime, too. Stay home: don't go out to drink and visit prostitutes. If you do all that, you'll not only have saved your money, but you'll have gained some wisdom about how to stay out of trouble.

Nearly all Shakespeare's characters in all his plays could stand to hear and follow that advice, however cliché, yet Lear responds to it with "That is nothing, Fool," essentially the same response he gave Cordelia's realistic expression of her love for him: he still hasn't learned to understand his errors. As for the "nothing," the Fool quips, "so much the rent of this land comes to": perhaps you will come to understand what *nothing* means, because now you have nothing. As with the characters in *Much Ado*, Lear has failed to note, to see, but in Lear's case that failure costs him everything, the reason we have usually seen *King Lear* as tragedy, which we equate with sadness. This play goes way beyond sadness, and its once noble protagonist has lost the traits that would have made his fall magnificently terrifying rather than horrifically pathetic. "A bitter Fool," Lear observes (136): yes, indeed.

More bitterness lies ahead. When Goneril confronts Lear with the intent to reduce his retinue, Lear, stunned at what he considers insubordination, asks "Who is it that can tell me who I am?" "Lear's shadow," the Fool answers (1.4.230–31). Goneril chastises Lear further, adding "As you are old and reverend, should be wise" (24); the Fool will add, more bluntly yet, that if Lear were his fool, he would have him beaten. "How's that?" asks Lear: "Thou shouldst not have been old till thou hadst been wise" (1.5.43–45) — the Fool's line cuts to the heart. Regan will add in II.4.147–50, "[S]ir, you are old.... You should be rul'd and led/ By some discretion that discerns your state/ better than you yourself" (i.e., do what I tell you). Lear can do nothing about that now, and he has no one strong enough to help him. He has determined and begun his descent, and that of anyone attached to him, into terminal suffering. The Fool sings,

> Fathers that wear rags
> Do make their children blind,
> But fathers that bear bags
> Do make their children kind [2.4.48–51].

Since Lear has given his money bags to his daughters, he can expect no more kindness from them, and he will get none: the way of the world, and Lear has learned it too late.

"Degenerate bastard," Lear shouts at Goneril (1.4.253), and there he has perhaps got the problem right. The Fool has already hinted at it: "For you know, nuncle,/ 'The hedge-sparrow fed the cuckoo so long,' That [it] had it head bit off by it young" (1.4.214–16). Maybe Goneril is Lear's bastard daughter,[15] not legitimate; maybe Regan is, too, and Cordelia also — perhaps he had more besides — and the fledglings of other birds eat the remaining parent. The issue of bastardy comes up in the very first scene of the play, and it taints the action of the play in its entirety. What does legitimacy mean and imply? What does bastardy mean and imply? Has the Fool already referred to it in the advice-rhyme that I have quoted just above, suggesting that we will far more likely have good fortune raising legitimate children than bastard children, who, as the result of our excesses and infidelities, will embody the wages of our sins? That concern not only troubles the main Lear plot, but also entangles Gloucester and his sons in the parallel subplot.

The Gloucester Subplot and the Dark Side of the Force

The most important problem-play key for *King Lear* comes in the what happens to the Earl of Gloucester as a result of the betrayal by one son and the tenacity of love from the other. Act I, scene 1, begins with Gloucester introducing Edmund to Kent, explaining his illegitimacy and the "good sport" in his begetting. Edmund can't inherit his father's title, which will go to the legitimate son, but he can still assume some prospects. Kent speaks kindly to Edmund and offers "I must love you, and sue to know you better" (line 30): he offers, essentially, to do what he can for Edmund because of his friendship with Gloucester. But why does Gloucester come particularly to Kent, of all the members of Lear's court? The world of the play suggests that a penchant for evil may go along with bastardy, but what if Kent may have a willing sympathy for Edmund because he too is a bastard, namely Lear's illegitimate son?[16] As an earl and a trusted companion of Lear, he would make a perfect role model for Edmund: someone who has managed to win a title through faithful service despite his illegitimate birth.

But Kent has no opportunity to help Edmund because Edmund won't wait to get what he wants or serve a lord to earn it: he wants wealth and power immediately, and he will get it by deception, by dissembling, by deceiving the father and brother who have loved and trusted him. The circumstance of Gloucester's sons parallels but does not strictly follow that of Lear's daughters. Lear gives away his power, and Edmund tricks Gloucester's from him. Lear has failed to see, and when the sorrow and weakness of his position become clear — when he does see — he goes mad. Gloucester fails even to look clearly at what Edmund tells him about Edgar; though he has no reason to suspect anything ill of Edgar, the ploy shows his gullibility, and he pays with the loss of his sons and the loss of his eyes. Edmund has learned that dissembling works: one need only make an assertion with apparent confidence, the inattentive father will believe, and fortune follows.

Edmund also learns from the political discussion between his father and Kent that tensions may exist between Albany and Cornwall, the husbands of Lear's elder daughters, allowing him an opportunity through current tensions to rise even further, if he can get himself skillfully aligned with whoever has the likelihood of gaining more power. Both of Lear's elder daughters fall in love with him, probably because of a mutual love of power and attraction to those who boldly take it. Affection comes into play for Gloucester, who loves both his sons, but Edmund hasn't any more regard for his father than the elder daughters have for Lear: "Love's not love/ When it is mingled with regards that stands/ Aloof from th'entire question," says the King of France, who happily takes Cordelia as his wife despite her lack of dowry: Edgar shows that same attachment to his father, and Kent and Cordelia show it for Lear, but genuine love otherwise appears little in the world of play: desire for wealth, power, and position replaces it, bringing disaster to all concerned.

We see too little love in this world; a world with little love turns quickly to a world full of torment. Kent loves Lear, and though Lear accepts the disguised Kent back into service (does he really not know that Caius is Kent?), neither Kent's nor Cordelia's fidelity to the King can save him. Edgar continues to love Gloucester, and he tends the blind old man with care and selflessness. Edgar's love can't save Gloucester physically — the trauma has done too much damage — but he can salvage something of his spirit at the last. He plays the ruse with his blind father and takes him to the cliffs of Dover nominally to jump and commit suicide, but Gloucester merely falls on flat ground: Edgar has kept him safe. Finding himself still alive, Gloucester must learn patience yet: "Henceforth I'll bear/ Affliction till it do cry out itself/ 'Enough, enough,' and die"; Edgar agrees and adds, "Bear free and patient thoughts" (4.6.75–80). In V.2 he must repeat the lesson as Gloucester tires almost beyond endurance: "No further, sir, a man may rot even here," says Gloucester; Hamlet-like, Edgar responds, "What, in ill thoughts again? Men must endure/ Their going hence even as their coming hither,/ Ripeness is all...." "And that's true too," Gloucester concludes, committing finally to one of the play's great themes.

The message of enduring suffering builds through the second half of the play. "O gods! Who is't can say, 'I am at the worst'?/ I am worse than e'er I was" (4.1.24–25), says Edgar when confronted with his blinded father, and "O side-piercing sight!" (4.6.85) he exclaims on seeing the mad Lear with weeds and flowers in his hair. Edgar, like Hero in *Much Ado*, serves as a kind of Christ-figure,[17] but, in a far sadder play, with no power to fix what the world has ruined beyond healing: "As flies to wanton boys are we to th'gods," observes Gloucester: They kill us for their sport" (4.1.36–37). Edgar has, though, the power to forgive, but that forgiveness can't save. In fact, it probably contributes to Gloucester's death. Edgar explains to Albany the effects on his father of the truth:

> I ask'd his blessing, and from first to last
> Told him our pilgrimage. But his flaw'd heart
> (Alack, too weak the conflict to support!)
> 'Twixt two extremes of passion, joy and grief,
> Burst smilingly [5.3.196–200].

The last phrase has considerable import in how we read the end of the play and thus the play as a whole. Gloucester dies suffering physically, but in his last few moments he has got the son who loves him back again. He dies as happily as he might, given the horror of the events he has experienced.

How should we read the parallel events in Lear's last moments? He hangs on a thread between life and death, joy and despair:

> ... No, no, no life!
> ... Thou'lt come no more,

6. Tragic Problem Plays

> Never, never, never, never, never.
> Do you see this? Look on her! Look her lips,
> Look there, look there!

Having assured himself that Cordelia has died, before he expires he either wants to believe she lives or actually believes it — we as audience can't know. The uncertainty, the wavering, twists the audience to writhing, and Lear may die in the sickest delusion or, like Gloucester, in an instant of joy believing that Cordelia lives. That belief more than his own life would grant him an instant's redemption. If Lear's heart has burst smilingly, the emotion-complex changes; the smallest shred of hope relieves his self-punishment. If he dies believing her dead, his last instants drown in the grotesque weight of his sins. Either way, patience has failed. Thus the power and the problem of *King Lear*...

In Act III, scene 2, Lear shouts to the storm,

> Blow, winds, and crack your cheeks! rage, blow!
> You cataracts and hurricanoes, spout
> Till you have drench'd our steeples, [drown'd] the cocks!
> You sulph'rous and thought-executing fires,
> Vaunt-couriers of oak-cleaving thunderbolts,
> Singe my white head! And thou, all-shaking thunder,
> Strike flat the thick rotundity o' th'world!
> Crack nature's moulds, all germains spill at once
> That makes ingrateful man! [1–9].

He rails, as Gloucester might do as well, for what he wants to believe his children have cost him. More so than Gloucester, Lear must blame himself, and his inability to do so contributes to his madness. Lear, unable to command in his former kingdom, instead as uselessly commands the elements to strike the world flat. The passage has phallic images, a pregnancy image, and an image of sperm spilled on the ground: anything so that humans stop creating children, Lear suggests, the source of our problems.

We must not, Shakespeare suggests, seduce ourselves into believing the sole source of our problems lies in others: we must take responsibility for our actions and think before we act. Rashness leads to disaster that temperance can avoid. Lear never acquires that wisdom — all the more shocking then, that Cordelia returns, and the reason he sees her as both "spirit" (4.7.48) and "fool" (5.3.306): she returns for a lost cause, simply out of love, and he can't believe she has done it. "I am a very foolish fond old man,/ Fourscore and upward" (4.7.59–60), he admits, far to old to have fathered a daughter, and for the abuse of such indiscretion he feels himself "bound/ Upon a wheel of fire" (lines 45–46). The wheel turns, never releasing Lear, burning him all the way to his last breath. He never frees himself of self-obsession: "I am mightily abus'd; I should ev'n die with pity/ To see another thus" (52–53). Sadly, though Cordelia has learned compassion, it can do her father little good: "Mine enemy's dog,/ Though he had bit me, should have stood that night/ Against my fire" (35–37). Where she would save the father who wronged her, her sisters — if they be her sisters — will kill each other over a murderer who loves neither and tries to use both to gain more power. When Kent and Cordelia (his faithful children who represent honesty and rationality) attend Lear together, he briefly regains his wits, but they do not have time to save him: "We are not the first/ Who with best meaning have incurr'd the worst./ For thee, oppressed king, I am cast down" (5.3.3–5), Cordelia laments as she is taken off to be hanged. Her compassion can't save her, either, but it allows her to know that she is dying because she has tried to do the right thing: some small compensation for her. Unlike her father, she has not become a fool in her own eyes.

I'm not sure that the knowledge the characters have gained, perhaps too brutally pathetic, is enough to allow us tragedy's catharsis. Has Lear's heart, like Gloucester's, burst smilingly? Either way, the world has taken its revolution through utter darkness; whether it offers a blink of light I don't feel certain. The play ends with Lear's soul-rending "Howl" in our ears and an unsettling feeling of what it must mean to have killed, if indirectly, one's own child. Not even Othello, who kills his young wife, and certainly not Hamlet, perhaps complicit in if not responsible for the death of his beloved, suffer that much. I know of no bigger problem than that.

7

History and Romance
Problems of Love, Adventure and Language

As I mentioned at the beginning of the book, beyond those plays scholars have called problem plays most of Shakespeare's other plays display some kind of genre hybridization, and they also present lingering, troubling ideas that resist resolution. This final chapter will consider plays that with respect to genre fit most closely with history or Romance, but that apply compelling elements of comedy or tragedy or, in the case of *Love's Labour's Lost*, that don't want to move quietly into anything identifiable at all. Once again the genre transgressions lead us to the problematic ideas that urge our consideration and interpretation.

1 Henry IV: *Not Exactly Like the Sun*

While we need not doubt that Shakespeare thought of this work as a History play, not comedy or tragedy or Romance, he had still to introduce elements of drama to make it compelling and entertaining. He had, then, while staying essentially true to what his audience would have understood as significant characters and events of their past, to use humor, the potential for marked rises and falls, and adventure to build a play that audiences could admire and enjoy. In *1 Henry IV* he provided aspects of all three, comedy, tragedy, and Romance, with undertones of commentary on each; together they make the play more than a recitation of history, something different, more embracing, than any one of the genres alone: more niggling than comedy, more raucous than tragedy, more critical than Romance, less judgmental than we may expect: a play set in history that raises problems.[1]

1 Henry IV deals very little with Henry IV; it focuses instead on the emergence of Prince Hal as king-to-be. King Henry creates the background problem: having usurped the throne and called for the murder of Richard II, and having contributed to the distance that now stands between himself and those men who helped him gain the crown, he begins (and ends) the play as an unsympathetic figure. As we follow the play, we want a better king, and while Prince Hal stands in line for succession, he gives us little more reason than he gives his father to have great expectations. Much as he did with Hamlet, Shakespeare created for Hal a matrix of possibilities, a number of directions his character could take. While the audience know that he will become Henry V, one of England's most heroic and admired kings, the structure of the play and the other characters leaves for him a sufficient number of possible directions to make his course dramatic and interesting. The play matches him repeatedly with Hotspur: his father wishes he could claim that the two were exchanged at birth, as he admires Percy and deplores the behavior of his son. That pairing leads them to one-on-one conflict on the field of battle, the young hero (Hotspur) versus the young scoundrel (Hal) — there Shakespeare holds not to historical accuracy, but to dramatic power, as their conflict makes excellent theater and provides an enormous lesson on courage, judgment, duty, generosity, and our ability to change for the better.

The problems in this play come from the mutability of character, an important idea in literary, religious, and philosophical considerations in Shakespeare's time, and its comic and nearly proto-tragic elements, which invade the sense of the story's history. Hal has so many possible directions that he may take. He could remain a wasteful, self-indulgent, burdensome prince with little potential for proper kingship. He could become like his father, a proud but pragmatic usurper. He could become more like his younger brother John, a dutiful, useful, and unquestioning servant to his father. He could become another Mortimer, from his father's point of view a traitor who will fall in line with other rebels and violently split the kingdom through political upheaval and war. He could become another Hotspur and try violently to take the crown for himself. Worst of all, he could become another Falstaff.

Critical (and popular) opinion on Falstaff has varied as much as that on any character in the history of theater. Some readers love him for his good humor, his realistic views on heroism, honor, and nobility, and his ability to turn every situation into a party and every failing to an advantage. Harold Goddard has warned that "Sir John runs away with us as some critics think he did with the author" (Vol. 1, 161). I find the idea monstrous. Not only has he no sense of duty, but he has no real kindness nor any sense of basic decency: when Hal requires that he raise a company of soldiers to help defend the King in civil war, Falstaff allows anyone with money to pay his way out of service, then keeps the money and drafts men too old, weak, sick, or improperly accoutered to fight and places them in the front lines to die defenseless — unforgivable behavior, however apt he may prove with a joke.

We do, of course, see Hal take the proper direction, defending his father, abandoning Falstaff, and dispatching Hotspur. His offer to face young Percy in sole and equal combat to determine the result of the conflict — and the fact that Hotspur doesn't accept that challenge — proves him the better gentleman, their combat proves him the better soldier, and his return to duty, both as son and as prince, proves him the better man for monarch. He will make a far better king than his father has or than Hotspur or Mortimer would have, but can he make of himself the hero-king the world of the text needs?

Before even his handling of Falstaff, the first problem with our interpretation of Hal as prince and man comes in how we respond to his speech at the end of Act I, scene 2. He knows he must reject his current friends and behaviors, but we must wonder about the motivations both for those friendships and for the rejection to come:

> ... Yet herein will I imitate the sun,
> Who doth permit the base contagious clouds
> To smother up his beauty from the world,
> That when he please again to be himself,
> Being wanted, he may be more wond'red at
> By breaking through the foul and ugly mists
> Of vapors that did seem to strangle him.
> If all the year were playing holidays,
> To sport would be as tedious as to work;
> But when they seldom come, they wish'd for come,
> And nothing pleaseth but rare accidents....
> My reformation, glitt'ring o'er my fault,
> Shall show more goodly and attract more eyes
> Than that which hath no foil to set it off.
> I'll so offend, to make offense a skill,
> Redeeming time when men think least I will [197–217].

The speech presents enormous problems for interpreting Hal's motivations and actions both before and after he makes it: it rings of hypocrisy. It brings to mind for me comedian Nipsey Russell's satirical joke that he observed to a Christian friend who criticized his behavior: "To be forgiven for our sins, the first thing we have to do is sin." Hal not only excuses himself to himself for what he recognizes as base behavior by asserting that he will look all the better in the future for having looked bad in the past, but also, despite recognizing his current behavior as bad, he commits to even more of it before succumbing to some future "reformation."

The difficulty comes, then, in how to interpret both his subsequent actions and the reasons for them. Goodness and worthiness come not from calculation about how to look good, but from one's trying to understand what they mean and how to achieve them and committing to the better behaviors and thoughts necessary to reach those goals. Hal announces to the audience his insincerity. He allows Falstaff and his friends to rob a group of travelers on the road to Gadshill (a euphemism for "God's Hill") so that he and Poins may in turn rob Falstaff and disgrace him — perhaps funny, but hardly a joke with any dignity and one potentially dangerous, at least to the travelers. Hal later pays back the money that Falstaff stole, but that doesn't recompense them for the fear they would have experienced: they hardly know they are being robbed by an incompetent. Then at the beginning of II.4, the famous Boar's Head Tavern Scene, the Prince and Poins play a joke on a poor serving boy: they sit in opposite rooms and call repeatedly to him, so that he doesn't know which way to go to serve them.[2] That exchange makes the Prince look mean, not funny. The "play" Hal enacts with Falstaff later in the scene complements and inflects the kind of childish cruelty we see at the beginning of the scene. Falstaff, whether he plays himself, the Prince, or the King, keeps trying to win Hal's affection and preferment at the expense of their other friends. Playing the part of the Prince as Hal plays his father the King, Falstaff argues for himself thus:

> That he is old, the more the pity, his white hairs do witness it, but that he is ... a whoremaster, that I utterly deny. If sack and sugar be a fault, God help the wicked! If to be old and merry be a sin, then many an old host that I know is damn'd. If to be fat be to be hated, then Pharaoh's [lean] kine are to be lov'd. No, my good lord, banish Peto, banish Bardolph, banish Poins, but for sweet Jack Falstaff, kind Jack Falstaff, true Jack Falstaff, valiant Jack Falstaff, and therefore more valiant, being as he is old Jack Falstaff, banish not him thy Harry's company.... [B]anish plump Jack, and banish all the world [2.4.467–480].

The Prince answers, of course, "I do, I will," and he will. Hal faces a test that he must pass to move from youth to adulthood. He must banish not only Falstaff, but the part of himself that resembles, follows, or feels attracted to Falstaff. Whatever fun Falstaff provides as a wit and drinking companion, he steals, lies, misleads, damns his friends, and drags Hal down from any chance of becoming the King we want and need him to become. We must not mistake the humor or "comedy" of this scene for some silly notion of "comic relief": it shows exactly what Hal must leave behind, anything that keeps him from his duty and from the refinement of his character. The fact that he sees Falstaff as a friend, and a beloved one at that, makes his maturing all the more difficult. When he sees Falstaff as he believes lying dead on the battlefield, Hal says, sorrowfully and perhaps even wistfully, "Poor Jack, farewell!/ I could have better spar'd a better man" (5.4.103–104), but he immediately adds, "O, I should have a heavy miss of thee/ if I were much in love with vanity"—of all of Hal's sins, he has at least freed himself of that one.

Hal's refinement we see only at the Battle of Shrewsbury in Act V. While the King acts dishonorably[3]—"The King hath many marching in his coats" (scene 3, line 25) explains Hotspur to Douglas, who believes he has just killed Henry, and "Another king? they grow like Hydra's heads" (5.4.25), exclaims Douglas when he finally finds the real King—Hal fights bravely, honorably, and successfully. He saves his father's life by driving off Douglas, and he essentially wins the battle for his father when he fights and kills Hotspur. He treats Hotspur respectfully even in death, and he allows Falstaff the brief glory of claiming to have killed him on the field: "For my part, if a lie may do thee grace,/ I'll gild it with the happiest terms I have" (5.4.157–58). While hardly purged or purified, Hal has at least shown his potential for heroic kingship without losing his generosity or sense of play.

Falstaff, significantly for our understanding the problem of the play, hasn't learned any better: he has no hint of "reformation." "I'll follow, as they say, for reward," he says as the battle winds down. He intends to maintain the sham that he, not Hal, killed Hotspur, and he imagines himself gaining thereby and so reforming: "If I do grow great, I'll grow less [i.e., I'll lose weight], for I'll purge and leave sack, and live cleanly as a nobleman should do" (162–65), but of course he won't, as we see in *2 Henry IV*. Falstaff remains Falstaff, though the Prince may not remain Hal. The truer Falstaff is the one who betrays Hal on the battlefield, giving the Prince a bottle of sack rather than a weapon when he needs one, the one who argues to himself that honor can't fix a broken leg or salve the pain of wounds, that honor is no more than a word one applies to the dead, not the living: "Therefore I'll none of it, honor is a mere scutcheon. And so ends my catechism" (5.1.140–41). When a person's religion becomes the abandonment of honor, anyone honorable must abandon him. As Falstaff eschews honor, hardly even understanding it, Hal embraces it, having finally experienced it. His honor does not, though, remain unwavering: that problematic instance we will see in *Henry V*, and the question of right and honorable behavior and right an honorable kingship remains the problem that nudges *1 Henry IV* in the direction of *problem play*.

Henry V: *Fighting, Wooing, and Dying*

As Shakespeare built his portrait of the great heroical king and the astonishing events of his life, he sought to simplify and specify the traits necessary to successful kingship: head, heart, hand, and tongue. This play focuses on the spectacular emergence of *tongue*, the ability to speak well, and the problem of sincerity in the person in whom all those traits meet. The essence of this play comes in its grand speeches, whether the King delivers them to his soldiers or as soliloquies, but also in its shadowy opening scene and in the cynical irony that undermines the otherwise pleasantly comical scenes with Katherine, Princess of France. The soliloquies seek understanding, justification, and resolution, and the speeches to the army aim to spur a bedraggled force on to one more victory against a foe at once proud and honored and yet, in a world at the very beginning of modernizing warfare, astonishingly incompetent. The play has elements of Romance — martial adventures and Henry's love-interest in Princess Katherine — near-epic and tragedy in the brash magnitude or Henry's military operation that becomes instead tepid pathos in the execution of Bardolph, sexual comedy in Katherine's attempt to learn English, as well as the historical elements of Henry's life and victories.

In some ways the most important parts of the play — beyond Henry's speeches — come in the Prologue and Epilogue. The pre–Miltonic call for the "Muse of fire," the theatrical reference in the "wooden O," the images of the air filled with arrows and "proud hoofs" of horses leaping over plots of time and Henry striding through the whole like a young Mars dragging "famine, sword, and fire" behind him build pace and epic scope. The opening rush reins to a quick halt with the machinations of the Archbishop of Canterbury and the Bishop of Ely as they plot to get Henry into war so that he won't take the time to relieve them of rents upon which they have counted for years. Thus the King's adventures hinge on the encouragement of men motivated by greed, not by divine right or the good of the country or the people involved. And after all Henry's successful adventures and the well of hope he brings back to England, the Epilogue pulls us to a similar stop by reminding us that the King's "glory" lasted but a "small time": "This star of England" blessed by Fortune "[b]y which the world's best garden he achieved" died young, leaving an infant king in his stead,/ "Whose state so many had the managing,/ That they lost France, and made his England bleed." For all the play's energy, humor, and high tone, the audience will not leave it happy; it ends in a tone of distinct melancholy, Fortune's wheel having turned, a country bereft of its hero and wondering about its honor. As with every other human endeavor, Shakespeare raises the problems that go with grandeur, heroism, and martial honor, marking them with transience and a thoroughly medieval *memento mori*.

But Henry outspeaks even the choric opening and closing. Of all of Henry's speeches the one that lingers most problematically comes in Act V, scene 2, as the King woos Katherine in direct and common prose:

> Now fie upon my false French! By mine honor, in true English, I love thee, Kate;
> by which honor I dare not swear thou lovest me, yet my blood begins to flatter

me that thou dost — notwithstanding the poor and untempering effect of my visage. Now beshrew my father's ambition! he was thinking of civil wars when he got me.... But in faith, Kate, the elder I wax, the better I shall appear.... Put off thy maiden blushes ... and say, "Harry of England, I am thine.... Come, your answer in broken music; for they voice is music and they English broken; therefore, queen of all, Katherine, break thy mind to me in broken English.... Upon that I kiss your hand, and I call you my queen [220–251].

He kisses her despite her diffidence, and he adds

O Kate, nice customs cur'sy to great kings. Dear Kate ... [w]e are the makers of manners ... and the liberty that follows our places stops the mouth of all find-faults, as I will do yours [268–73].

Does Henry really love Katherine, and does he expect her to love him, or does he woo by calculation to make France the more fully his, stopping her objections by "stopping her mouth"? In addition to his victories, winning the Princess makes him more clearly heir to the current French King, and their children become clearly the heirs of both England and France — should their power hold. The character question comes down to a matter of Hal's sincerity, not a problem easily solved, as actors may play the scene variably to much different effects, and modern audiences have greater trouble with the idea of love happening so quickly than would medieval — Shakespeare seems to fall right in the middle, where we would expect him, urging us to see the situation not as simple, but as dubious and interpretable. Do we mind a calculating and businesslike king, or do we insist on a chivalrous and honorable hero-king?

The *Henry* plays deal with politics, but gingerly: they make political points (rule, if God has chosen you so, openly, generously, participatorially, and in your own lands, it suggests).[4] The speech with the most important political implications comes in Act IV, scene 1: the famous "ceremony" speech. Henry may not get everything in it right, but the political point has weight that no English poet could have expressed before Shakespeare's time:

> Upon the King! let us our lives, our souls,
> Our debts, our careful wives,
> Our children, and our sins lay on the King!
> ... What infinite heart's ease
> Must kings neglect, that private men enjoy!
> And what have kings, that privates have not too,
> Save ceremony; save general ceremony?
> And what art thou, thou idol Ceremony? ...
> 'Tis not the balm, the sceptre, and the ball,
> The sword, the mace, the crown imperial....
> Not all of these, thrice-gorgeous ceremony,
> Not all of these, laid in bed majestical,

> Can sleep so soundly as the wretched slave [who] ...
> Sweats in the eye of Phoenix, and all night
> Sleeps in Elysium ... [230–274].

The monarch gets the pomp and ceremony of office, but also the worries of a nation: Henry has that partly right. He tells Katherine (and the audience) how little he loves ceremony and how much he prefers campaigning, so we may suspect that as king he gains little that he really wants. That the slave sleeps in Elysium, however, he has wrong: beyond the trials of campaigning he has never known want or privation. We may too easily sympathize with Henry here: Shakespeare complicates our sympathies by showing at once what Henry suffers and what he never will suffer. As kings go he has less pride and makes fewer demands than most; he has a hint of the common touch and can speak with anyone; he remains a man of his station with the blindness that accompanies it — one of the really interesting human problems in the play.

That speech of course echoes the discussion he has just had with the soldiers Bates, Court, and Williams the night before the battle of Agincourt. Williams has made the point that "if the cause [of the battles] be not good, the King himself hath a heavy reckoning to make, when all those legs, and arms, and heads, chopp'd off in a battle, shall join together at the latter day and cry all, 'We died at such a place'" (4.1.134–38). The King reminds him and the others, "Every subject's duty is the King's, but every subject's soul's his own" (176–77): true enough, in Shakespeare's time if not so unquestionably for ours. Shakespeare then contrasts the seriousness of the point with comic business: as the argument continues, in the dark where identities are hard to determine, Henry nearly gets himself in a tiff with Williams; they exchange gloves as a token that they will fight each other later when opportunity permits; Henry later gives Williams' glove to Fluellen, to get the over-garrulous Welshman a box on the ear — a typical Prince Hal kind of joke, funny but inappropriate to the circumstance. He quickly turns serious again, though; alone, he prays, whether with true intent or not one can't say,

> Not to-day, O Lord,
> O, not to-day, think not upon the fault
> My father made in compassing the crown!
> I Richard's body have interred new,
> And on it have bestowed more contrite tears....
> Five hundred poor I have in yearly pay,
> Who twice a day their wither'd hands hold up
> Toward heaven, to pardon blood ... [4.1.292–300].

In religious terms he has nominally done the right thing, but far too late to make up for Richard's death, and his act of generosity may amount, really, to more of an act of self-interest: to gain God's grace in his quest for France.

When he learns that the English have indeed won the day's battle and thereby the war, he insists, "Praised be God, and not our strength for it!" (4.7.88), and when he learns the monstrous losses of the French compared to the small number of English soldiers killed, he adds, allowing those numbers proclaimed, "but with this acknowledgment,/ That God fought for us.... Let there be sung *Non nobis* and *Te Deum*.... (4.8.119–123). The speeches show a repeated tension between the noble and the common, the sacred and the profane. Today's audiences will have a harder time with this aspect of Hal than would Shakespeare's time with its belief in the Divine Right of kings and in God's direction of battles, but once again we may well see Henry V as more calculating than admirable, more political than spiritual.

The most famous of all the *Henry V* speeches, the St. Crispin's Day speech of IV.3, shows a similar and greater tension between the sacred and the profane. When Westmerland wishes they had even a few more soldiers to help against the vast French army, Henry answers,

> What's he that wishes so?
> My cousin Westmerland? No, fair cousin.
> If we are marked to die, we are enow
> To do our country loss; and if to live,
> The fewer men, the greater share of honor.
> God's will, I pray thee wish not one man more....
> Rather proclaim it, Westmerland, through my host,
> That he which hath no stomach to this fight,
> Let him depart, his passport shall be made,
> And crowns for convoy put into his purse.
> We would not die in that man's company....
> This day is called the feast of Crispian;
> He that outlives this day ...
> Will stand a' tiptoe when this day is named....
> Then will he strip his sleeve and show his scars,
> And say, "These wounds I had on Crispin's day." ...
> And Crispin Crispian shall ne'er go by,
> From this day to the ending of the world,
> But we in it shall be remembered —
> We few, we happy few, we band of brothers,
> For he to-day that sheds his blood with me
> Shall be my brother; be he ne'er so vile,
> This day shall gentle his condition ... [18–63].

Henry plays the honor card to win the affection and revive the energies of his army for one last pitched-battle, and it works. He offers those who fight and survive gentility: he will raise all to the status of nobility. He can't make them equals, but he can call them equals to get them to fight. He does. They do. They win, only to find another contrast between nobility by name and honor in behavior: during the battle some of the French army have ridden into the English camp and slaughtered the boys and the livestock they attended. "Kill the poys [sic — Welsh dialect] and the luggage! 'Tis as arrant a piece of knavery ... as can be offert" (4.7.1–3), exclaims Fluellen. Learning of it, Henry in sympathy responds, "I was not angry since I came to France/ Until this instant" (4.7.55–56) — rightly so, indeed, as the enemy, having considered themselves the soul of chivalry, have committed a heinous deed of cowardice. The anger quickly passes from Henry's thoughts, though, replaced by praise of God, as he then learns of his victory. The flower of French chivalry has fallen largely to the prowess of common English bowmen. The contrasts create and foreground the difficulty: how exactly should we understand this Henry? As Fluellen and Gower wait for Henry to learn of the camp massacre, they talk of how Alexander the Great killed his friend Clytus. Gower remarks that Henry has never done such a thing, but Fluellen partly corrects him: Henry has "turn'd away" Falstaff — Fluellen, though, praises Henry for doing it. He has cast off not a real friend, but a dangerous element of waste and sloth, a ghost of himself past.

Has Henry, through the course of the three plays, shown himself to gain strength of character, to accept and fulfill his place in the world with heroism and commitment to duty and right, or does he emerge as a simple pragmatist, enjoying what he can while he can and then moving lightly to the next lark, whether it be a highway robbery or pitched battle in France for the kingship of two countries? There the play moves toward the Mirror-for-Magistrates tradition, asking us to examine our notions of rule.

But in many ways we may call the Henry cycle language plays. Henry V rules well when he speaks well; Henry IV fails to keep civil peace because he spoke more than he could deliver, and once he won kingship, he couldn't retain the loyalty of his one-time followers or win by charm or rhetoric the allegiance of more diffident — or even offended — countrymen. When Henry Bolingbroke offers the rebels amnesty, he can't make them believe he means it; when Hal turned Henry offers his dead-weary soldiers brotherhood and nobility, both in practice and in memory, they can't wait to fight for him, even against impossible odds — and they win. The language of rule works when it moves in the realm of inclusiveness and mutuality, not in division or exclusion — a powerful lesson for which Shakespeare's time was hardly ready, but that marks the modern world for perhaps its chief innovation in the history of human thought.[5] This play, like the other *Henry* plays, winds its way transgressively among history, Romance, and comedy, leaving us inspired by its language but troubled by the problems of character it refuses to solve.

Cymbeline: Would You Do That to Your Wife?

With its mix of Romance, comedy, history — near tragedy — and pastoral, Cymbeline represents a blend of generic vectors. Joan Hartwig describes *Cymbeline* as a "romantic comedy in which the young lovers are thwarted by parental hostility" (100), but she also stresses its "bewildering complexity" (61). Like Hamlet it exploits a "multiplicity of perspectives" (Hartwig 84) to address the problem of "the limitations of human vision" (86), and it asks poignantly how far we should go in forgiveness.

The play raises a number of productive but problematic questions. Why is it *Cymbeline*: to what extent does he emerge as title character, since anyone watching (or reading) the play must see Imogen as its hero? Critics have excused Posthumus' bargain with Jachimo as standard stuff of medieval Romance, but as much as Shakespeare happily borrowed from the Middle Ages, he shows the distinctly different sensibilities of a Renaissance man. So how can we accept such a rash, stupid, and nearly disastrous (almost tragic?) wager? The play throws great weight on the problems of obedience, proof, vengeance, and judgment, matters more serious and varied in an age of increasing freedoms and self-determination than much of what we learn from earlier Romance.

A number of critics (Tennyson or Coleridge, for example), though notably more of past generations than in recent times, have loved either the play or Imogen, finding them among Shakespeare's most beautiful or admirable creations. Certainly Imogen shows a nearly supernatural devotion to a husband who may not deserve her, but do we want a hero/heroine so willing to die at her husband's hands for the sake of his ego and someone else's murderous dissembling?

Dissembling begins even before the play begins, and it persists as a problem in the world of the text: neither the Queen nor her son loves or respects Cymbeline; they are simply using their positions to try to gain power (the Queen, notably, is experimenting with poisons). Listening to the Queen, who largely directs the King's decisions, Imogen observes "O,/ Dissembling courtesy! How fine this tyrant/ Can tickle where she wounds" (1.184–85) — everyone seems to recognize that truth of their characters except Cymbeline himself.

Typically Shakespeare observes both the problem of dissembling and the possibility that in some instances it may have merit. Pisanio, an unwitting passer of poison (literally) to Imogen and (figuratively) to Posthumus, must dissemble or else commit murder: he spares Imogen despite her husband's command to kill her, proving himself the better servant for disobeying, but placing Imogen in little better position in his attempt to do her good. Her own dissembling allows her to find service with an ethical Roman general and to reunite with her long-lost brothers. She has goodness, pluck, and resourcefulness, but even she lacks any powers of close observation: she mistakes the dead body of Cloten for her husband's largely because of the clothing and some basic similarities of build. Few characters in the play make the effort to observe at all: they jump to rash conclusions. Philario tries to warn Posthumus not to jump rashly to conclusions about Imogen's supposed infidelity, but Posthumus only too readily believes in his wife's fall and allows himself to turn toward deadly wrath. He should have known better than to lie to his wife, recommending Jachimo to her when he knows the fellow a cad. When the truth of Imogen's fidelity comes out at the end of the play, Posthumus forgives his Italian "fiend"/"friend": "Kneel not to me./ The pow'r that I have on you is to spare you;/ The malice towards you, to forgive you. Live,/ And deal with others better" (5.5.417–19) — that judgment Imogen and Cymbeline might as easily have passed on him. "Pardon's the word to all" (5.5.422), says Cymbeline at last, finally getting the idea right, but he needs quite a while to get there. Eager to pass judgment on Belarius for kidnapping his sons ("The whole world shall not save him"), Cymbeline must first hear and process the old lord's advice: "Not too hot./ First pay me for the nursing of thy sons" (5.5.321–23). Fostering happened relatively commonly in the old world, and Belarius has at least raised Guiderius and Arviragus to be brave, true, loving, honest, and not acquisitive.

Cymbeline has already recognized his folly toward Imogen: "Heaven mend all!" he prays aloud (5.5.68), a sentiment that caps the Jailer's prayer at the end of V.4, which places more responsibility on human action: "I would we were all of one mind, and one mind good. O, there were desolation of jailers and gallowses! I speak against my present profit, but my wish hath a preferment in't" (lines 203–206). What would do him harm in the short term would do everyone good in the long term, and he and we would all gain "preferment," a better lot in life, if we could learn to treat one another with kindness and generosity. Imogen forgives Posthumus unquestioningly — probably a happy ending for most of Shakespeare's audience, but undoubtedly a troubling one for our time and perhaps for Shakespeare himself. He often stresses the significance of forgiveness, mercy, even to those who don't deserve it. Posthumus has made himself a war hero, but he has yet to make himself a trusting husband.

Having learned mercy and perhaps a glimpse of patience, Cymbeline can finally top off the play with a word of piety: "Laud we the gods" (line 476), he says, and he concludes also a peace with the Romans wherein he will pay the tribute he has denied. He hopes now to maintain a lasting allegiance and peace, having learned the bitterness of war even in victory. Neither he nor his world can count on long-lasting peace, but they can aim for it, believe in it, and even strive to keep it. Placing these last words appropriately in the mouth of the monarch, Shakespeare allows a play that has foregrounded selfishness, attempted murder, kidnapping, and war to step lively toward a nearly happy ending. We need now for the "angelic" Imogen, after the events of the play, to forgive her husband indeed: not so easy to do as to profess. And we need the world to have learned better from its errors — much to ask, but exactly what drama must ask of us, as Shakespeare knew.

The Tempest: *A Shipwreck and a Dangerous Swan Song*

Hallett Smith notes that *The Tempest* hasn't much plot, but "it contains more songs than any other play in the canon" (1609–10). In some ways it more resembles masque or pageant, or even a Classical play (it sticks closer to the Aristotelian unities than most of Shakespeare's plays) than it does Shakespeare's other plays. It makes its themes pretty plain: our need for recovery from trauma, patient endurance, forgiveness. "The rarer action is/ In virtue than in vengeance," Prospero says in V.1.27–28, and Stephano repeats a line Shakespeare has used elsewhere, "Thought is free" (3.2.123): we may use our free will to find a way to resolve ourselves with the world. The final scenes drain the power of magic from the world and replace *Romance* with hope for *romance*: Miranda and Ferdinand *may* have sufficient strength in their love to make the world better than had the previous generation: we must depart this world *hoping* for that result. The natural and the grotesque — along with our own sin — struggle for supremacy, but music, endurance, and love may win out, at least for a time.

And, ah, once again the problem of an ending: the conventions of Romance let us easily get past the improbabilities of Prospero and Miranda's survival and of the passage of Alonso's ship so near the remote island that Prospero can use his magic to effect resolution, but, thinking practically rather than romantically, how can we accept Prospero's abandoning his wand and his book and readily returning himself to the mercy of those who show themselves unrepentant and apt to serial murder? I treat this play here not because of a question of its genre — the exotic setting, love theme, use of magic, and mixture of danger and wistfulness nearly assure that we may call it Romance — but because of what it does with its genre in the problematic conclusion.

Romance turns here to a thoroughly practical and probably unwelcome conclusion: because we live in a world of people, we must learn not only to forgive, but also to forget, and the latter may prove much harder and much more dangerous. We must, at last, trust one another, knowing that many if not most people will at one time or another break that trust.

Based on the racial and political tensions of our time, and particularly on an American sense of guilt by association, readers will sometimes impose on *The Tempest* critical diatribes on racism and colonialism, as if Shakespeare were somehow speaking for the civilizing value of European colonists on other peoples. Such ideas, while certainly worthy of academic and public dialogue in our time and of necessity part of our own social criticism, have little if anything to do with Shakespeare's play. Shakespeare deals powerfully with feelings of guilt in many plays, notably in *Macbeth*, *King Lear*, *The Winter's Tale*, and *Cymbeline*, but the remarkable point about guilt feelings in *Tempest* isn't their presence, but their absence: Antonio and Sebastian seem remarkably — and dangerously — free of them. They express no repentance for what they have done — and what they have considered doing — though Prospero confronts them with it. One suspects they will as likely try it again.

Yet Prospero must return to Milan without the powers he has had and learned so well to use. He must place himself once again at the mercy of others who would usurp his place. He abandons his best means to defend himself against them, and he gives up his daughter to a young man he must trust to treat her well and faithfully, though she may not make for him the best political match that his father might have hoped for. Prospero must trust that love will sustain them and that repentance and contrition will restrain his murderous brother.[6] The world of play, full of trouble, like ours, may not have sufficient means of love and goodness to surmount those problems.

Prospero also shows no guilt about using Ariel and Caliban as servants — perhaps the main problem for contemporary readers if they don't read the play carefully and in the context of Shakespeare's time. Ariel attends Prospero as a kind of indentured servant, and we may easily forget that Prospero treated Caliban well until he tried to rape Miranda, merely a child. When Ariel's work is done and Prospero has provided for his daughter, returned to his God-given duty, and forgiven those who have wronged him, he frees Ariel, and he leaves the island to a Caliban now perhaps ready to appreciate it and to understand the difference between noble and scurrilous action: having come to recognize the difference between the learned Prospero and the drunken foolishness of Stefano and Trinculo, he follows Prospero's final command with

> Ay, that I will; and I'll be wise hereafter,
> And seek for grace. What a thrice-double ass
> Was I to take this drunkard for a god,
> And worship this dull fool! [5.1.295–98].

7. History and Romance

I believe he means it and that his character has changed with the wisdom he has gained. Shakespeare makes Caliban less "savage" than are the nominally noble Sebastian and Antonio: they give no evidence of having learned better. With the benefit of wisdom and the opportunity for grace, they may still turn to murder to gain what they don't deserve. Caliban will now possess the island that he has learned to deserve, one of the main points of the play, and one that turns it a touch away from "problem play" and toward "Morality play."

When Prospero gives away his daughter in marriage and commits himself to break his staff and drown his book, he not only potentially places himself once again in the scheming hands of his murderous brother, but he also loses the comforting presence of the person he loves most in the world. He gives away his chief solace, recreation, and perhaps vocation: he must, since she has her free will, too. In case we didn't get the point sufficiently, Shakespeare creates doubles in the Alonso/Sebastian story: another lesser brother willing to kill his elder to gain power. The Stefano/Trinculo/Caliban plot to kill Prospero again mirrors a general human problem: while they pose little danger to a Prospero with magical power and full awareness of their activities, even such persons as they could create danger outside the enclosed world of the island — all the more so old self-proclaimed foes who now once again lack what they want (and for which they were willing to kill). They now, too, suffer a loss: have they the capacity to think generously as he does? Perhaps with reason Prospero says that subsequently every third thought will be on his own death....

Other Romances, either those in prose for reading (from the Middle Ages or Renaissance or beyond) or recitation or those for the stage, drift or bolt into problematic endings. Thomas Malory's *Le Morte D'arthur* has, of course le morte d'Arthur, Arthur's death, unless one continues despite Malory's warning to read Arthur as the King *who shall return*— though that reading also presents its interesting problems. It also has the unfulfilled love between Guinevere and Launcelot. *Sir Gawain and the Green Knight* has its own problematic ending: having succeeded as well as any human can hope to succeed, Gawain has still made his errors; while we may readily forgive him for them, he may not forgive himself— and Camelot will fall anyway. In Chaucer's "Knight's Tale" (which Shakespeare used for *The Two Noble Kinsmen*) Arcite wins the battle, but dies, and Palamon eventually wins they hand of their beloved Emily, but does she feel happy about that result? Tasso's *Gerusalemma Liberata* tells how the Christians deliver Jerusalem, but they concluded their siege with the slaughter of thousands of innocents and lost the city again a generation later. Even in our time J. R. R. Tolkien's *The Lord of the Rings* (which he thought of as a Romance) ends ambivalently (those who claim it has a simple happy ending have simply failed to pay attention): though the quest to destroy the Ring concludes successfully, Frodo does not succeed—

he can't get himself to drop the Ring in the fire — and he has only a brief future in the Middle-earth he helps save. Nominally he leaves because of the sword wound he receives on Weathertop, but he actually leaves, I suspect, because the failure of his own moral strength at the moment of Doom proves too much for him. So Romance as genre promises no happy ending or future. Neither should we assume or expect one — though we may hope for it — for *The Tempest*.

Beyond what Prospero loses and may lose, the audience must now deal with what we have lost: Prospero. He tests the young couple for obedience and goodness, but only briefly and very gently. He gives Ariel the freedom that few other masters would have granted him, and even the duties he imposes on the nature spirit are occasional and light — not so great a burden for someone who had been locked in a tree perhaps forever had Prospero not come along and had the power to save him. Most of all we learn Prospero's knowledge, kindness, wisdom, and understanding. When the pageant he has prepared to entertain Miranda and Ferdinand disperses and he notices that Ferdinand looks troubled, he offers,

> You do look, my son, in a mov'd sort,
> As if you were dismay'd; be cheerful, sir.
> Our revels now have ended. These our actors
> (As I foretold you) were all spirits, and
> Like the baseless fabric of this vision ...
> Leave not a rack behind. We are such stuff
> As dreams are made on; and our little life
> Is rounded in a sleep [4.1.146–58].

The couple leave him respectfully, as he finds himself troubled by where his thoughts have lead him. What he has created here he will soon lose the ability to create ever again. He can summon no more images. He will have to depend, like the rest of us, on mere words. Images designed to display the greatness of love and fidelity need not trouble anyone; they should inspire. But the loss of greatness, whether in something physical or in something imaginative, leaves us face to face with mortality: everything earthly, regardless of its power and glory, must pass away. We don't know where, if anywhere, we go when this life passes; we may go from the sleep from which we rise at birth to another sleep, of which we will know nothing: an aching sorrow for someone who has lived life with passion and pursued with all his heart the passion to create. The most famous lines are among Shakespeare's most often misquoted: "We are such stuff as dreams are made *on*." Someone we don't know is making dreams upon us, imposing an imagination and a course of action not our own: I suspect Prospero says so not because he believes so, but because he fears so. He wants free will; without it his mercy means nothing.

What if what we strive so hard to make doesn't come from us, but from someone else who may make dreams — and nightmares — upon us for his, her, or their own amusement, not for any good it does us? What if, at last, our ounce of free will has only the power to laugh or cry at what some far greater power wreaks on us? Were it true, that idea would leave us with a great sorrow indeed, not only for the magician, not only for the playwright, but for anyone who takes time to consider the lines, the great problem that clouds the ending of *The Tempest*.

Love's Labour's Lost: *The Problem Play Without a Problem*

Love's Labour's Lost defies genre — Nuttall credits it with a "convulsive disruption of genre" (95). H. B. Charlton asserted that it has "small importance in establishing the line along which Shakespeare's comic genius grew" and that it avoids complications (270) — he also notes the significant if underplayed aspect that it features a king "who runs away from public life on a hare-brain scheme without even so much foresight as to appoint a deputy" (271), an error that in other plays leads to tragedy. The main plot has little action, and the whole play works almost as if it were the play-within-a-play, a nearly allegorical piece that helps illuminate some incompletely referenced "real" story. The play has some clear purposes: the "constant questioning of convention" and the exposure of a "shared experience of the mutability of life," as Alexander Leggatt notes (87–88), and in its "critical, comic testing of love and language" (79) it exposes the problem of ridicule and mockery in the guise of wit (82) and our mutual comical vulnerability (71). It pokes fun at the stiffness of convention and how blithely we can permit ourselves to make silly vows. It skewers wit for mockery's sake and makes a fool of nearly everyone in the play. In its love elements it has aspects of Romance, but the romances fail, and it has nothing that we would call adventure. In its use of wit in comes near to comedy, but it has no happy ending — nor has it an unhappy ending, other than the death of the King of France, whom we haven't met and who dies offstage and distant from the matter of the play. If we may call *Troilus and Cressida* an *anti-*, then we should probably call *Love's Labour's Lost* a *not-quite-anything*.

Love's Labour's Lost has four men who make a silly vow and break it even as they make it. The immediately meet four lovely ladies, share some occasionally searching but mostly silly wit, and then must wait a year to see if anything will come of their possible romance. "That's too long for a play," says Berowne (1.1.878), and he's right with respect to this play, though Shakespeare wrote many that take place over a longer time period. The play presents a problem because it presents no real problems, no twists and turns for the characters to navigate or solve, other than, as the King of Navarre says, "Our wooing doth not end like an old play: Jack hath not Gill" (1.1.874–75). Despite its lack of action, the play concludes with the longest single scene in all of Shakespeare's drama (931 lines). No one seems to have learned the danger of swearing on his honor: the characters break their vows readily, then as readily swear new oaths. They're not even nice, so they rouse little sympathy. Only Don Armado, the braggart soldier, full of pompous locutions and malapropisms, has learned anything, though I'm not sure exactly what it is: after almost getting in a sword fight with Costard because of the clown's rude treatment, he finds, "For mine own part, I breathe free breath. I have seen the day of wrong through the little hole of discretion, and I will right myself like a soldier" (5.2.722–24). He gives his reason for not fighting as that he has no shirt to which to strip down so he can fight freely, and his declaration of wisdom comes after the announcement of the Princess's father's death — one shouldn't duel, perhaps, in a state of mourning. Later Armado admits to having vowed to Jaquenetta "to hold the plough for her sweet love three year" (883–84); he leads the final song that warns of cuckoldry and cold weather and celebrates a servant's stirring a pot of warming ale, and he gets the last words in an entirely anticlimactic ending: "The words of Mercury are harsh after the songs of Apollo. [You that way; we this way.]" He must take up farming, the other men if they want their loves must also keep new vows, and all must part after a sad message — all exit with no more ceremony or resolution than that. The play has gone nowhere except, notably, perhaps teaching the men to avoid rash vows — not a bad lesson as far as it goes.

What should we make of *Love's Labour's Lost*? I conclude this study with a few thoughts on it partly because I have less to say about it than about the other nominal problem plays of the first four chapters, but next to them it creates the greatest problems for interpretation, though not necessarily for performance. I suspect an audience could find a good performance of the play quite enjoyable, except for the minor chord with which it closes. We need not doubt what it "means," but we may well wonder why Shakespeare did it and what he wanted it to accomplish.

As *Twelfth Night* in a way rewrites *A Comedy of Errors*, *Love's Labour's Lost* rewrites parts of *Much Ado About Nothing* and *The Taming of the Shrew*. As with Beatrice in *Much Ado*, in *Love's Labor*'s "the women find it necessary to put wit to one side if love is to be established on a serious basis" (Leggatt 82) — or at least the suggestion appears. Whether the loss of wit would do this world any good we don't know: it hasn't much else to recommend it, and maybe we should lampoon silly conventions and even sillier behaviors until we replace them with something more real and productive — and honestly dutiful. The "acting" that through twists and turns of character and cattiness brings Katherine to Petruchio's side in *The Taming of the Shrew* keeps the ladies in *Love's Labor's* at a safe distance until the men can find a means to approach them. When they do, they try to win the ladies through dissembling, and the ladies resist them by the same means. The men must learn that vows mean something before they can safely keep vows to maintain love for a lifetime: so the ladies warn them. The ladies thereby appear wiser, but not necessarily kinder than the men.[7] Have they learned anything, or do they show us anything we didn't already know? Neither the men nor the women show us they have got anywhere through the course of their interaction.

One of only four plays for which Shakespeare constructed his own plot (along with *A Midsummer Night's Dream*, *The Merry Wives of Windsor*, and *The Tempest*), *Love's Labour's Lost* seldom gets stage time and draws little critical interest — and largely for good reason. But it can work on stage much as contemporary musicals do. It allows for some broadly comic performances, mixes in possibilities for music and (bad) dancing, and has quite a bit of successful humor: no plot elements get in the way of various displays of wit and foolery until the final movement of the final scene. Hearing of her father's death, the Princess must immediately return to France. She resists the King's efforts to get her in "the latest minute of the hour" to commit to a relationship first: "A time methinks too short/ To make a world-without-end bargain in" (5.2.788–89). Each of the four ladies imposes a combination test/penance on her gentleman. The Princess requires that the King observe an ascetic life for a year in a "forlorn and naked hermitage/ Remote from all pleasures of the world" (795–96); if he has not changed his mind, he may ask her again to marry, as she will have spent the intervening time in mourning (he may, of course, change his mind). Rosaline requires that Berowne, the wittiest of the gentlemen, work for a year at a hospital trying his best to cheer the sick with his jests. Katherine requires of Dumaine that he get "a beard, fair health, and honesty" (824–25) — essentially that he grow up. Longaville gets something more hopeful from Maria: "At twelvemonth's end/ I'll change my black gown for a faithful friend" (833–34): he need only wait and she will accept him. "I'll stay with patience, but the time is long," he harrumphs. All must learn — including the ladies, though they seem not entirely to realize it — that, as Rosaline says,

> A jest's prosperity lies in the ear
> Of him that hears it, never in the tongue
> Of him that makes it ... [861–63].

Therein we find the play's major theme, clearly stated and significant, if not delivered with astonishing artfulness.

But the characters have yet to practice what they preach. The men "fall in love" with the greatest of ease, and they can't even tell apart the women whom they respectively court: as a joke, the ladies cover their faces and exchange jewelry, and each man courts the lady who wears the jewel he recognizes, not bothering to check her identity beyond that. They fail the simplest of external and material tests, and having sworn that they have just courted the women they love, they find themselves again forsworn. Responding to Berowne's charge that, while the men have failed, the ladies have deceived them, the Princess excuses herself and her companions with

> We receiv'd your letters full of love....
> And in our maiden council rated them ...
> As bombast and as lining to the time;
> But more devout than this [in] our respects
> Have we not been, and therefore met your loves
> In their own fashion, like a merriment [5.2.777–784].

We thought you were courting in jest, just spending the time, so we didn't take it seriously, she explains. Do we believe that? And when the noblemen make rather cruel fun of the Nine Worthies play that Holofernes, Armado and the others try to put on for them, the ladies don't stop or even chide them. "This is not generous, not gentle, not humble," Holofernes complains (5.2.629), and he's right: the scene brings to mind the *Pyramus and Thisby* of *A Midsummer Night's Dream*, with the courtiers' jokes at the expense of the rustic players.

There Theseus at least tries to say something the players may take as kind; when the Princess in *Love's Labour's Lost* responds to Armado's complaints that the nobles keep interrupting his speeches—"sweet chucks, beat not the bones of the buried.... Sweet royalty, bestow on me the sense of hearing" (661–6640—she asserts "we are much delighted" at his efforts, but she may as likely be speaking sarcastically as honestly.[8] She has already dismissed Costard for delivering Pompey poorly, and she encourages the King to allow the play though he has already commanded against it, knowing it will go poorly. She argues,

> Nay, my good lord, let me o'errule you now.
> That sport best pleases that doth [least] know how....
> Their form confounded makes most form in mirth,
> When great things laboring perish in their birth [515–520].

The nobles will find fun in joking about the poor quality of the players—more fun, in fact, the Princess suggests, than if the players were to perform well. She jests at what must be Armado's accent or his overblown delivery, "'A speaks not like a man of God his making" (526): should we say a man isn't a man because he suffers from an overblown sense of his worth? If so, everyone in this play must suffer the audience's laughter not from the brilliance of their wit, but from their blindness to their own faults. Wit leads often to emptiness and seldom if at all to wisdom in *Love's Labour's Lost*: all the characters end up lost. Love's labor, such as they have spent it, has gained nothing for anyone. Shakespeare repeatedly calls attention to the words *fool*, *wit*, and *mock*, and as he does in *Measure for Measure*, he repeats the name *Pompey* as well — in this case in the Worthies play, rendered by Costard, despite the fact that Pompey isn't among the Nine Worthies. Shakespeare's audience thought of Pompey the great as a source of civil conflict, and the clowning in this play leads to conflict rather than to self-discovery — a typical Shakespearean warning.

Funny moments do occur in the play, though, and they also serve thematic purposes. As the play begins the King suggests that by asceticism and study he and his friends will win fame that will "grace us in the disgrace of death," that will "regist'red upon our brazen tombs ... make us heirs of all eternity." The solemn declaration misses the point of ascetic life and study: to free one of concern over the world's opinions. To encourage them, he calls them "brave conquerors," though if they keep their vow they will hardly leave his garden, and all swear not only on their honor, but that he who breaks the oath will suffer "eternal shame." From the beginning Berowne notes not only that the vows are too hard to keep, but that they must all fail in them immediately, as the French Princess awaits in embassy. Berowne takes his swearing as a jest and even expresses doubts about its simplest part: retreat for study. "What is the end of study, let me know," he asks, and the King answers, "Why, that to know which else we should not know"; "Things hid and barr'd (you mean) from common sense," Berowne wryly replies. But the King misses his point: "Ay, that is study's godlike recompense" (1.1.55–58). What the men lack of common sense they won't gain from study. When Berowne makes a fuller case against study, which the King again defends as protective against "vain delight," he answers that "all delights are vain, but that most vain/ Which, with pain purchas'd, doth inherit pain" (71–73): why provoke pain that leads to nothing but more pain? And shortly he continues: "Small have continual plodders ever won,/ Save base authority from others' books" (86–87) and

> So study evermore is overshot:
> While it doth study to have what it would,
> It doth forget to do the thing it should;
> And when it hath the thing it hunteth most,
> 'Tis won as towns with fire — so won, so lost [142–46].

Berowne, wisest of the men—and that's not saying much—gets right that study goes awry if it ignores the very ends it seeks, but he too gets the purpose wrong: whatever contemporary movies may say, study doesn't serve as a means to woo sexual partners. Again he's right when he says that, given the tenor of the vows, they all must forswear themselves repeatedly: "Such is the simplicity of man to hearken after the flesh," Costard observes (1.1.216). Ascetics, too, must occasionally eat and sleep, and these men have hardly trained themselves to ascetic discipline. At the end of IV.3 Berowne makes a lengthy case to show that now they *must* and *should* break their vows ("cheat the devil," says Longaville, and "salve for perjury," says Dumaine). He argues that the original vows, "to fast, to study, to see no woman"—constitute "treason 'gainst the kingly state of youth"; "abstinence engenders maladies"; they shall find in study nothing more excellent than the "beauty of a woman's face," so in the vow not to see women they have forsworn their true books; therefore, in their case, "it is religion to be thus forsworn."

The argument, while funny for its undermining of logic, does nothing more than excuse what they have already done without noting that thereby they have given up their honor: keeping a sinful vow is a sin, but was the vow sinful or merely silly? In II.1, when the King tries to welcome the Princess and yet explain he has sworn an oath not to admit women to his court, she replies, "our Lady help my lord! He'll be forsworn." "Not for the world," he responds, but she can already see better: "will shall break it, will, and nothing else." She means both that he will in fact break it willfully, with full intention, and that *will*, a pun for sexual desire (Shakespeare famously uses it so in Sonnet 135), shall drive him to break it. Not only will he break it, but he will follow Berowne's reasoning that he not only will, but must; he might as well have listened at first to Berowne: "Necessity will make us all forsworn" (1.1.149). In forswearing they do, from the audience's point of view, suffer "such public shame as the rest of the court can possible devise" (130–31): not only should they all have known better, but what they really need is something useful to do rather than wasting their time on silly vows to begin with. Perhaps they learn that lesson with the announcement in V.2 of the death of the King of France; the intrusion not only of their own foolishness but of general mortality on their artificial world, plus the withdrawal of the ladies to mourn, may strike them back to sanity—the purpose of this kind of humor throughout the play. Berowne has already made the point to which his humor returns us: while "necessity" will urge them to break their vows, "every man with his affects [passions] is born,/ Not by might mast'red, but by special grace" (1.1.151–52). That's as close as Shakespeare gets to a specifically religious and doctrinal statement: only Grace can save them from the effects of breaking their oaths as well as from their natural tendency to sin.

7. History and Romance

As he so often does, Shakespeare uses malapropisms here not just for humor, but to point toward his thematic concerns. When Dull says that he "reprehends" rather than *apprehends* Costard, and when Costard admits to the "contempts" rather than the *contents* of Dull's warrant, we get the sense of contempt that accompanies licentious, rash, or inappropriate actions: in the tragedies those errors lead to horrific results, and Shakespeare seems to want us to remember that. The similar humor of Don Armado's overblown diction (along with his name's pun on the lost Spanish *Armada*) strays a bit from the typical *miles gloriosus*: while he shows no wisdom or courage, he may be the only character by the end of the play to have learned better. The Princess shows a kind of false modesty about her beauty that parallels Armado's self-importance: she, too, has much to learn that, unfortunately, only the sadness of mourning may teach her. She has come to Navarre essentially to cheat the King: her father wants Aquitaine without paying the money he owes to get it. The King, while he would like to get his money for it, has no great interest in keeping it, and he may prove willing to give it away given the lure of the Princess's beauty. He may not have the moral strength to resist, and if she fully understands what she's asking — she does seem a very smart character — she may lack the moral strength not to ask for something she may well know is wrong, simply because her father wants it. There we may discern the subtle humor of Horatian satire directed at both the King and the Princess.

The funniest bits come not in the gentlemen's failed dissembling as Muscovites or in the clowns' failure to present the Worthies (except, perhaps, in the casting of little Moth as Hercules), or even in the way the supposed lovers repeatedly insult one another, or in the satire of wit and courtly foolishness, but in Moth's satire of the nobles' ignoble behavior: the smallest character makes the biggest points. When Armado asks, "Comfort me, boy: what great men have been in love?" Moth answers, "Sampson, master; he was a man of good carriage ... for he carried the town gates on his back like a porter; and he was in love" (1.2.64–72). The story of Samson, of course, would give no comfort to Armado, if he knew it, because though Samson dies heroically, he dies horribly: not something that will appeal to the character, but Moth makes the point nonetheless. And when Moth is delivering his performance as Hercules in V.2, he recites, "A holy parcel of the fairest dames/ That ever turned their — backs — to mortal views!" (160–61). Berowne corrects him that he was supposed to say *eyes*, not *backs*, but the embedded stage direction is clear: the ladies aren't paying any attention and have turned their backs on him, so that they will not follow the play — they could indeed have acted more graciously. They don't get his message. In his next passage he makes a similar emendation in his lines: "Out of your favors, heavenly spirits, vouchsafe/ Not to behold...." Berowne again corrects, "Once to behold," but too late. The audience has again got (but the ladies haven't) the point that the ladies show no interest, not even polite attention, to the spectacle performed, however ineptly, for their benefit. The men have repeatedly referred to the ladies as *heavenly*; among the virtues they have and show, kind condescension isn't one. The satire shows both the ladies and the men of court out of touch with common human feeling; neither wit nor foolery nor self-importance will help any of them find that virtue. Some level of ascetic study may, but that too will probably fail unless it leads them to learn and practice basic human decency: the major theme, I think, of this play.

The purpose of study should hardly be, as Berowne's argument suggests, to break an oath; nobility does not allow license for insulting others. We should make oaths to keep them, not to break them, or not make them at all. Sometimes only patient service proves goodness. *Love's Labour's Lost* leaves no doubt of those ideas that Shakespeare wanted us to consider. Its world does, though, leave us little if any nearer to the *practice* of those ideas, and Shakespeare loves to lead us to the crux that lies between theory and practice. He leaves us there with the major problem of this play.

* * *

Though I end my analysis of problem plays here, I believe the approach of this book may offer a helpful means to consider the problems of some of the other plays, *Romeo and Juliet, Titus Andronicus, Timon of Athens, Coriolanus*, and *The Winter's Tale* particularly.[9] The troubling of genre makes them, also, more interesting by swerving them away from standard expectations and simple readings. *Romeo and Juliet*, for instance, as I have remarked in the Preface, should by pattern have turned out a comedy: a play full of some of Shakespeare's best witty wordplay, hinging on a marriage that should happen but that circumstances temporarily thwart — but the thwarting becomes permanent. The play's wrenching ending chucks us into the throes of youthful mortality, as Poe would tell us the most horrifying and so most moving — and so most poetic — of human experiences. It comprises a filled and buffed version of *Pyramus and Thisby*, with characters who attract our full sympathy because of their passion, candor, and realism. The break in the Great Chain happens in the comedy section, but it produces escalation, moves toward melodrama, and escapes just short of tragedy — no less sad than tragedy, but with the resolution that the warring families will at last make peace, as they should have done through the marriage rather than after their mutual loss. The play leaves us only one solution, repeating two of Shakespeare's most important messages: avoid blood feud and civil conflict, and allow love to take its course. The useful theme hardly mitigates the tremendous sense of needless loss.

7. History and Romance

Can we say in *Timon* that prodigality followed by misanthropy, perhaps a "tragic flaw," can lead to a seamless and continual tragic error sufficiently to create what Aristotle would call proper tragic pleasure? By the end of the play Alcibiades wins some sympathy, and Flavius shows a sense of unselfish duty; both leave some hope for the world of the text, but doesn't that kind of ending produce melodrama rather than tragedy? Melodrama can certainly provide dramatic pleasure — many of our casual entertainments rely on it — but it seldom has the power of Shakespeare at his best, in tragedy or "dark comedy" or Romance. The biggest problem we have with Timon, I think, comes from the likelihood that Shakespeare never entirely finished it: it lacks not tonal, but narrative and emotional completeness.

Coriolanus nominally betrays his people, but he remains oddly true to his own sense of ethics and social order, smudged by the dangers of a bruised ego — little enough to point the play toward tragedy. His death comes as an anticlimax, somewhere amidst deserved absurdity, moral and civic disaster, and a heroic if distorted obsession to try to do the right thing.

The Winter's Tale, largely Romance, with elements of "tragicomedy," especially in the merciful reunion with which it concludes, suffers (like *Cymbeline?*) from outrageous coincidences of plot. Once more a bit of allegory helps: Perdita, the "lost one," reminds us to hope for more than we deserve. But in Leonatus's reunion with his wife and daughter, has mercy gone too far in *Winter's Tale* — not too far in a religious or allegorical sense, but too far in a dramatic sense, so that we can't accept it as possible and appropriate in the world of the text? If *The Tempest* is *King Lear* in Heaven, perhaps *The Winter's Tale* is *King Lear* in Purgatory.

So much more to say... But, as Byron would write,

> the heart must pause to breathe,
> And Love itself have rest.

* * *

So much of what we teach in literature courses has to do with lexical, structural, and semantic analysis, what literary works mean and how they do what they do, that we may easily neglect an equally important aspect of the literary experience: how they make us *feel*. Part of what makes problem plays problem plays comes from the ambivalence with which they conclude — and yes, of course I know the danger in generalizing audiences' emotional responses. My point here: to be true to works of art of any sort, we must always raise that question and then try to understand and deal with our answers.

We must be willing, too, to deal with instances where meanings and our feelings about texts may differ or clash, or where texts resist meaning to create more complex feelings. What John Keats wrote about Shakespeare in a letter of 1817, his idea, nascent but intriguing, of negative capability, an author's willingness to dwell in uncertainly without insisting on reasoning out a single solution to a problem, remains important to reading and appreciating Shakespeare's approach and accomplishment. Ambiguity may at times annoy us — it may even create displeasure and leave us unsatisfied with a work as an intellectual and aesthetic experience — but it can contribute to its living, breathing qualities, allowing us to live in it and work with it, to find it real, provocative, and continually exciting.

Often culturally, particularly these days but to some extent always, we don't necessarily like problem solvers — ironic, because an important part of our learning jargon focuses on the "problem-solving skills" we supposedly teach and encourage. We often prefer the problem creators. We call them important, believe them brilliant, and elect them to public office. They will find problems even where we have none, allowing us to feel better about the complexity of situations — whether they have such complexity of not. The problem solvers we brush off as "facile," "ignorant," or "moralistic." We don't want to believe an easy solution has eluded us. With the Civil Rights Movement in the United States in the 1950s and 1960s, much of mainstream white America said to Black leaders, yes, we sympathize, but you must accept that change happens slowly: be patient. Leaders such as Martin Luther King, Jr., insisted, "If not now, when?" And they were right to insist. The solution stood there in front of everyone as clear as it could possibly be: everyone, regardless of race, gender, orientation, age, or physical abilities had and deserved the same unalienable rights. The embarrassing complexity came in getting the general population (especially those in power) to *accept* that idea, not in the idea itself. We needed *not* to wait.

We admire the men and women who proposed and insisted upon that solution more in retrospect than we did at the time. Often the most lauded artists, like the most lauded social theorists, raise the problems, uncover them, or find new ways to look at them. Only the very few solve them, and when they do, audiences tend either to hate them for it or simply to ignore their solutions. Shakespeare didn't make his solutions, when he found them, explicit, so we tend to ignore his ideas rather than to hate him for them. He often raised the most difficult of human problems, and he seldom resolved them explicitly because he wanted his audience to ponder them, not reject him. Where he did propose to solve them, he gave us solutions we feel unwilling to accept or to practice, because they involve stunningly simple notions that prove enormously difficult to practice. We must avoid exclusive self-centeredness and pride; we must practice compassion and kindness, but with the willingness to make difficult judgments when others, even our friends, do wrong — or when we do ourselves, even if that means making recompense.

We must keep to our duty, establish loyalties to which we will remain willing to adhere. We must understand that sometimes the problems of the world prove too great for humans to solve, and we must simply accept and endure the presence of and results of perplexing and troubling circumstances. As Alexandre Dumas put it at the end of *The Count of Monte Cristo*, we must wait and hope. We must build selves we can believe in and honor the achievements of those who differ from us. To have a society, we must make and keep honest bonds and avoid making or demanding dishonest ones. We must live, love, gain friends, remain faithful, endure, and, when the time comes, die.

None of those ideas requires brilliance to understand; each requires goodness, resolve, and fortitude to practice well. Shakespeare points to those solutions without making them simplistic or pedantic. He shows them as the foundations of living. "Shakespeare's mind refuses rest," A. D. Nuttall wrote (147); when we read him, we must not let our minds rest, either, nor our hearts.

The term *problem play*, despite its recent fall from favor, has, I think, quite a good deal of value both for more casual readers and audiences (if such a person exists anymore for a Shakespeare play) and for students, critics, or scholars. If we look at where and how Shakespeare swerves from expectations of genre and where interpretation leads us to questions rather than answers, we find a good deal of what, I think, he wanted us to find. The problem play steps gingerly back from happy endings. It refuses the grand steps of Classical tragedy and snatches away catharsis. It "plays" with historicity to get down to troubling bits of character and the dubious (or ambiguous) reasons behind historical choices and events. It makes love in Romance a dubious commodity and saps the heroic glory from adventure. It allows characters to talk, vow, fall in love, and accomplish exactly nothing — not even completely *noting*— in the process. It democratizes the theatrical experience and it democratizes life, because it brings everyone in equally and gives everyone the same potential range of problems, challenges, potentials — in the current parlance, *issues*. So many writers have recognized Shakespeare as the "poet of real life" because his characters have our problems, regardless of who they are, when or where they live, and in what social stratum we find them. Not every audience member finds every character and every problem interesting, but anyone and everyone can find somebody in the plays who feels familiar and real.

Those characters' problems remain real, and in our efforts to understand them we carry them with us after the play has ended and often for the rest of our lives.

Chapter Notes

Preface

1. In *Simply Shakespeare*, a book largely targeted at students, Toby Widdicombe says that examining Shakespeare's plays through the lens of genre has the following advantages: it allows one a useful means to compare and contrast Shakespeare's plays and to compare and contrast his plays with those of other playwrights; it allows the reader to follow changes in his technique over time; it focuses attention on the value of mixed forms; it allows the reader to appreciate Shakespeare's work as part of a tradition rather than simply free-floating original plays (115). I believe the point applies as well to detailed "professional" critical analysis as to introductory study.

2. H. B. Charlton wrote in 1938 that "[a]ll plays are problem plays, in so far as in every play one starts with persons of a certain disposition involved in a certain situation, and the play is the dramatist's solution of what the inevitable outcome must be" (*Shakespearean Comedy* [New York: Macmillan], 209). In that sense all literature is problem literature. I will explore here how Shakespeare "transgressed" boundaries of dramatic genre to raise problems with which he wanted his audience to grapple.

3. Occasionally critics have used the term *tragicomedy*, but I don't find that one extremely useful, as I'm not sure what it means. Does it imply a play with a happy ending or funny bits but also sad or scary elements? In that case don't we mean melodrama? We could apply a similar portmanteau for nearly all of Shakespeare's plays, as he regularly mixes genres to fit his purposes. For a useful and informative discussion of the issue with respect to Shakespeare's plays, see Joan Hartwig's *Shakespeare's Tragicomic Vision* (Baton Rouge: Louisiana State University Press, 1972). While Hartwig discusses the late plays that I consider Romances, she comments especially helpfully on the variety and complexity of emotional responses, particularly catharsis, to mixed-genre plays.

4. I won't cover all the plays, but will aim at a good sampling; I believe further work may produce valuable readings by addressing nearly all the plays so.

5. For a full discussion of this idea that comes from Plato and Aristotle and that persists through the Middle Ages and Renaissance and the eighteenth century, see Arthur O. Lovejoy, *The Great Chain of Being: A Study of the History of an Idea* (New York: Harper, 1936). Relating to everything from the structure of the Ptolemaic universe to the esoteric philosophy of alchemy, the hierarchy of angels, and the order or "degree" of humans, animals, and even plants and minerals, this central structure informed for a very long time philosophical and artistic notions of the deep-down structure of the universe.

6. In her chapter on *Measure for Measure*, Garber writes that while that play "has always been controversial, exciting a great deal of critical and directorial interest, and puzzlement," critics have given it "unhelpful and unhistorical labels like labels like 'problem play' and 'dark comedy'" (563). I find dark comedy at least partly helpful: critics have used it or *black comedy* regularly enough recently, for instance in reference to Kurt Vonnegut's or Thomas Pynchon's novels. *Problem play*, as I discuss in this book, certainly isn't a term that we have any record of Shakespeare's using, but it does pretty exactly describe what he *does*: he repeatedly and

successfully plays with genre conventions and leaves his audience with all sorts of problems to contemplate.

7. What Tennenhouse wrote about the histories we may reasonably extend to the other genres as well: "I want to consider if there is not something wrong with the categories we use to read the chronicle histories, since this designation of genre does not seem to come to terms with the way Shakespeare uses the materials of chronicle history when he sets them forth on the stage.... But chronicle history is not the only genre that reveals something amiss with conventional genre categories.... Shakespeare seems to have been unwilling or unable to write a romantic comedy" (3). The questions Tennenhouse raises about power may lead to similar questions about the issues Shakespeare foregrounds in other kinds of plays: order, duty, fidelity, friendship, envy, revenge, desire, love.

8. Louis B. Wright and Virginia A. LaMar call *The Merry Wives of Windsor* "the most English of Shakespeare's comedies" (*The Folger Guide to Shakespeare* [New York: Pocket Books, 1969], 246). We may as readily call *The Comedy of Errors* Shakespeare's least English or most Roman comedy. Both arrive at pretty happy conclusions—except for Falstaff in *Merry Wives*, and he gets off with lampooning, but nothing worse.

9. See *Anatomy of Criticism: Four Essays* (Princeton: Princeton University Press, 1957), especially essays one and four.

10. Quotations from Shakespeare's plays will come from *The Riverside Shakespeare*, ed. G. Blakemore Evans, et al. (Boston: Houghton Mifflin, 1974).

11. Professor Bache used to say that in Shakespeare's plays "everybody is everybody else." While I have always found that statement provocative and helpful in reading the plays, I'd rather say that "everyone is like everyone else," or, better yet, Shakespeare wants us to compare and contrast characters, so he creates many pairs or complexes of characters that urge us to use one to understand another. I don't think that kind of dramatic construct takes away from the playwright's "realism"; I think we do the same sort of thing in life: we may say, for instance, "She's like my sister, but really more like my friend Jane." We naturally move to compare and contrast to understand the persons we meet, even though that process does to some extent limit our ability to see each person as an individual—a general human limitation, perhaps. For more on Professor Bache's work see his books: *Measure for Measure as Dialectical Art* (West Lafayette: Purdue University Press, 1969;) *Design and Closure in Shakespeare's Major Plays* (New York: Peter Lang, 1991); *Shakespeare's Deliberate Art*, coauthored with Vernon P. Loggins (Lanham, MD: University Press of America, 1996).

Chapter 1

1. He also accuses Chaucer of bigotry in the Prioress' telling of the Hugh of Lincoln story; one may better say that the Prioress shows it. We don't know if Chaucer felt that way or if he is perhaps satirizing a character who feels that way and should know better—I suspect the latter.

2. Shylock has given Launcelot a positive reference to Bassanio (2.2.112–13), but probably to help waste what he has lent him (2.5.48–50). "The Moor is with child by you, Launcelot," says Lorenzo in 3.5.39.

3. An example of that sort appears in Boccaccio's story of Ser Ceperello in *The Decameron*.

4. Everyone else in the play has made Shylock an outsider. Bassanio has tried desperately to become an insider. Antonio began as the ultimate insider, but by the end of the play, with Bassanio married, he has become, like Shylock, an outsider: he has become secondary in a relationship where he once was primary, Bassanio's provider, and I suspect, were we to see the world of the play after the events we witness, Bassanio and Portia would tire of him soon enough.

5. *Shylock Is Shakespeare* (Chicago: University of Chicago Press, 2006), 6. Gross identifies Shylock as a double of his author, a "means to articulate his doubt, desire, and rage, his troubled solitude as author, his wish to put his audience in its place" (172), interesting if impossible to show of Shakespeare rather than of the subsequent writers who have treated and responded to Shylock. While connecting character and author may prove both dangerous and interesting, the play clearly doubles Shylock with Antonio: "Antonio abhors Shylock because he catches his own reflection in his face" (Goddard 88). And one may connect both to Shakespeare: all practice a kind of merchantry; Shakespeare had to hope that the authorities would continue to allow him to practice his trade, which some factions wanted to

outlaw; he had to give his pound of flesh to his audience and to his company, who probably both required of him deals he would rather not have made (i.e., plays he would rather not have written). Who knows to what extent he felt welcomed or excluded, honored or reviled, free to practice religion as he saw fit?

6. Students who resent the father's imposing that bond often suggest that he had "control issues," that even after death he can't give his daughter, however wise, the freedom to use her judgment and choose for herself.

7. The caskets also have sexual implications. Each man who attempts the game honestly tries to win Portia, a wife, and the one who chooses wisely gets her picture and then her person. Who chooses the gold gets death; sex with death leads only to death. Who chooses the silver gets a picture of an idiot, i.e., of himself, since he has risked so much only to end up with no sexual partner. What do you get when you have sex with yourself? As one of my students once replied, "A mess." Who wisely—or luckily—chooses the lead box gets Portia, and where does sex with Portia lead? As two other students answered, "Love!" and "Babies!" As Benedick wryly observes, "The world must be peopled." Choosing a sexual partner/mate requires that one give and hazard all he or she has, not just in our world of pandarean diseases, but always, because of the depth, commitment, and personal and social importance of the marriage bond.

8. Color and its implications, inside and outside, play a significant part in the casket game. While contemporary readers, especially Americans, have a hard time separating any color symbolism from racial issues, the stronger influence for Shakespeare's audience is the physiological theory of the our humors. Portia may be reacting more through an unwillingness to have a "melancholy" husband more than to racial perceptions, or Morocco may represent a double for Shylock, an immediate and perpetual outsider in the world of the play because of his difference, his "otherness."

9. The word *sad* in Shakespeare's time and for a good while after may mean "serious" rather than melancholy, but I take the darker meaning as more apt here.

10. A. D. Nuttall in *Shakespeare the Thinker* feels quite certain on this point: "Antonio ... is a homosexual, virtuous Christian," yet Shakespeare "respects the love of Antonio for Bassanio. [Antonio] is an outsider, but he is a good outsider. His love for another man is not set in contrast with his Christian virtue but is instead the strongest example of Christian goodness in the play" (255 and 257). I do think that the likely (though not the only) possibility; in our time we tend to sexualize bonds that Shakespeare's audience may not have understood so unequivocally. A homosexual Antonio would in some way find himself an outsider in Shakespeare's time, but in a society less bent on labeling he would have remained more an insider for his extensive business connections and range of financial influence.

11. Just so we don't miss the importance of the idea of the nature of the bond, when the jailor comes to get Antonio in III.3, Shylock uses — and emphasizes — the word *bond* six times in the space of thirteen lines.

12. At a public lecture a lawyer mentioned to me the principle of *presumption of intent*: e.g., if a person shows up at a closed business with the tools of burglary in hand and has perhaps discussed with others the notion of breaking and entering to steal, the legal system may prosecute him as if he had committed the crime. A lawyer may have a difficult time proving the intention in court, however. I have seen no evidence for such a law in Shakespeare's time, but neither did they have a presumption of innocence. Given the desire to punish in what most authorities saw as a sinful world, we may suspect that everyone watching the courtroom drama would simply assume that Shylock intended to torture Antonio if not outright kill him.

13. In the last few years I have had an increasing number of students who say something to this effect: "Shakespeare was obviously a bad man, since he wanted another bad man like Bassanio to win the love of such a good woman as Portia." They miss the obvious satire and irony of Shakespeare's character creation.

14. As we first meet Portia in the beginning of I.2, she laments, "My little body is aweary of this great world"; an echo of that line appears in *Macbeth*, 5.3.22, "I have lived long enough," and 5.5.48, "I gin to be a-weary of the sun"—an unlikely character double for her. Portia's sadness or boredom parallels Antonio's less murderous demeanor (though all three contribute to the death of someone who stands in the way of their intentions), but as with Macbeth and Antonio both, how do we read the future of a character with an inherent strain of melancholy?

15. We could call the play anti–Romance, unlike *Pericles* and *Cymbeline* which, although

they have their problems, reasonably well follow what Romances typically do. A Romance need not have a happy ending, but it must take place in a world where romance is possible and potentially worth having. The problem with *Merchant* comes in there: do we see any romance in the play that we trust, that looks worth a chance of survival and happiness?

Chapter 2

1. The 1609 Quarto labeled the play a "Historie"; the First Folio calls it a "Tragedie"; *The Riverside Shakespeare* places it among the comedies; it uses the subject matter of medieval and Renaissance Romance.

2. Haydock suggests, aptly I think, that we may see *Troilus and Cressida* helpfully as a "parodic and satiric reaction to the composite genre that had come to embody the highest aspirations of Renaissance poetics, the romance epic" (249); in some ways it responds more, I think, to Spenser's *Faerie Queene* than to Chaucer or Henryson. Spenser shows both good and bad knights, but focuses on the good finding virtue; Shakespeare suggests how rarely we really do seek virtue as the foundational experience and quality of our lives.

3. D. W. Robertson considered the poem another instance, in greater magnitude, of Chaucer's *de casibus* tragedy, informed by Boethius ("Chaucerian Tragedy," *Chaucer Criticism*, Vol. 2, ed. Richard J. Schoeck and Jerome Taylor [Notre Dame: University of Notre Dame Press, 1961], 86–121. Reprinted from *English Literary History* 19 (1952): 1–37. I see it more as Romance Epic, a grand tale of failed love amidst war, with its own catharsis, but lacking for any character the kind of fall and recognition typical of great tragedy.

4. "*The Testament of Cresseid*: Introduction," *The Poems of Robert Henryson*, ed. Robert Kindrick (Kalamazoo: Medieval Institute Publications, 1997).

5. I find an interesting pun here, as the word suggests both "pity" and "piety."

6. "Introduction," *Testament of Cresseid*, ed. Denton Fox (London: Thomas Nelson, 1968), 23. Fox observes later (45), considering the leprous Cressid, that Henryson has "skillfully introduced a walking corpse onto the stage"; the dramatic allusion may have a buried reflection of Shakespeare's treatment, but it the image aptly embodies the *memento mori*— and its constant medieval connection to worldly appetite — that Henryson places clearly in our imagination as the play ends.

7. *Shakespeare's Troy: Drama, Politics, and the Translation of Empire* (Cambridge: Cambridge University Press, 1997), 95 and 92.

8. *Parlement of Foulys*, lines 90–91.

9. The same pun occurs also in 1.2.190, where Pandarus describes Antenor as a good man of "shrowd wit." Having captured him, the Greeks will exchange Antenor for Cressida at Calchas request, and the exchange will initiate the death of Troilus and Cressida's romance.

Chapter 3

1. For an excellent introduction to the critical views until 1930, see William W. Lawrence, *Shakespeare's Problem Comedies* (New York: Macmillan, 1931). For instance, he notes the general lack of sympathy for Bertram ("a cad, a liar, and a coward"), but the wide-ranging opinions of Helena from Shakespeare's "loveliest character" (Coleridge) to someone who ignominiously plots in "woman fashion" [sic] for a "selfish end" (John Masefield), even a "schemer and a harpy" (32–35). Among recent critics Marjorie Garber is perhaps kindest to Helena, calling her "a young woman equipped with patience, ingenuity, and good sense" (617) — though I wonder about the "good sense." Nuttall, perhaps the critic kindest to Bertram, notes that Bertram feels unfairly trapped by Helena's plotting and naturally resents not only her pursuit but the King's judgment that he must marry her: surely because [m]arriage is a serious business ... one must "be allowed some say" in his or her own marriage partner (247–48). Of course Shakespeare's audience would have understood all about arranged marriages, especially among the elite classes. In our time any young person, especially one eager for freedom and a chance to make a mark in the world, must sympathize with not wanting to get forced into a marriage that he or she would find odious. Lawrence also quotes Barrett Wendell on the play as a whole, that while "other works of Shakespeare ... are more painful," we find "none less pleasing," and "no other work of Shakespeare's ... in conception and in temper seems quite so corrupt...." (37). Lawrence concludes by finding the play "artificial in effect," believing that Shakespeare "never put his whole heart and

soul in it," yet he believes that in the end nothing can "alter the impression that things come out right. Virtue triumphs in the end over the baser elements of human nature; the purity and devotion of Helena shame the cruelty and neglect of Bertram" (76–77). I find the conclusion — and all the parts leading up to it — much more problematic than that. Goddard calls it "Shakespeare's least satisfactory play" (38), but I must disagree there, too: I think it does what he set it up to do. Before postmodernism sought to change our opinions of meaning and clarity, we tended often not to like art works that lead us to doubt and even painful pondering, preferring, in Frank Kermode's term "a sense of an ending." But Shakespeare, though an Early Modern rather than a Postmodern, left us in this play with an unsatisfying ending and many honest but unpleasant — and perhaps unsolvable — problems to consider.

2. The name *Parolles* suggest a number of possibilities: coming from Medieval French *parole*. it means "word" or "speech" or "the spoken range of language." I don't know how to say the name correctly, as Shakespeare would have said it; the few metrical clues in the text suggest either "pə-ROLL-əs" or even "PER-ə-ləs," as in *perilous*. As a standard *miles gloriosus* the character represents words without the deeds to back them up or the kind of companion most perilous to an impressionable but headstrong youth, one who through bad advice can lead him to peril. *Helena* suggest Helen of Troy, possibly on his mind from the contiguity of *Troilus and Cressida*: *All's Well*'s Helen, rather than having been kidnapped, pursues her man with the fleet-footed tenacity of an Achilles. And Bertram makes an assault on the chastity of *Diana*, in Roman myth the chaste goddess of the hunt. The name *Bertram* comes from a compounding of Germanic roots "bright" and "raven," rather an oxymoron, as the raven appeared most commonly among the "beasts of battle," those scavengers that eat the dead after human carnage — hardly a typical association with brightness.

3. See Stephen Greenblatt's *Shakespeare's Freedom* (Chicago: University of Chicago Press, 2010) for an interesting if somewhat brief discussion of the tensions between order and autonomy in Shakespeare's world and work.

4. The Countess is the closest we have to a "good" person in the play, but, sadly, despite having good intentions and a fair degree of power, she has little to no effect for good on the other characters. In I.3, where she explains that Helena's father left his daughter in her charge, the Countess says Helena "may lawfully make title to as much love as she finds. There is more owing her than is paid, and more shall be paid her than she'll demand" (lines 102–105). Helena does make that claim, and she gets it from the Countess, but not from Bertram, from whom she demands it.

5. Again and again Shakespeare returns to the motif of dissembling, willfully misleading someone: even if one does it for ostensibly good motives, and even if the results seemingly turn out well, he leaves us with a sense of doubt about whether by deceiving we can ever reach personally, publicly, morally and ethically acceptable results. He makes the point explicitly in *Much Ado About Nothing*.

6. In Act IV Helena uses the phrase "all's well that ends well" twice, and at the end of Act V the King uses variants of it twice: Shakespeare obviously wanted the phrase to ring in the minds of his audience as we depart the play.

7. Marjorie Garber observes, "Although it is conventional to say that a comedy ends in marriage, Shakespearean comedy seldom does. Instead it ends in the promise of a marriage" (185); the audience may assume the marriage will take place, but, as with what Shylock would have done at the razor's edge, we *don't really know* the outcome. Shakespeare plays with our assumptions of narrative as well as theme.

8. The Latin maxim "*Nemo ante mortem beatus dicendum*," derived from either Aeschylus or Sophocles or both, comes to mind: no one should be considered happy/blessed before his death. The end of the play isn't an absolute ending: if the world of the text went on, the characters would have to deal with the results of their actions and choices. No episode in life, not even death, has a complete ending as long as others remain alive to benefit or suffer from one's actions. And any given moment of happiness may precede another of problem or disaster — like the ancient fairy tales, traditional maxims may as often express the sorrows as the joys of life.

9. Sometimes we oversimplify notions of *theme*: *love* and *honor* are by themselves not themes, but ideas or motifs. *Motif* implies a repeated element, such as love or honor; *theme* implies a clear expression of an idea that holds a work together: lack of fidelity in love, particularly to a good and worthy beloved, can

ruin our lives and the lives of others, or failure in our duty to our nation or our family can, more easily than we wish to believe, bring ruin to that nation or family.

10. In V.1, when the King is about to apprise Bertram of his plan for the young man to marry Lafew's daughter, Maudlin, Bertram says that he remembers the girl "admiringly, my liege/ At first I stuck my choice upon her, ere my heart/ Durst make too bold a herald of my tongue.... Thence it came/ That she whom all me prais'd, and whom myself,/ Since I have lost, have lov'd, was in mine eye/ The dust that did offend it" (lines 44–54). He asserts that he couldn't love Helena partly because he already loved another. The King allows that argument as a partial excuse of Bertram's behavior; I would not, because I don't believe him. We don't see him any less eager to depart his mother's court for love of that young lady, and he never mentions her or any lovelonging anywhere else in the play. Love of Maudlin doesn't stop him from trying to seduce Diana, and it doesn't stop him from lying for most of the rest of Act V. His assertion looks awfully like just one more attempt — unfortunately Parollean — to get himself out of trouble, in this case with the King whose previous command he ignored.

11. Bertram has also said that, regardless of the opinions of other characters in the play, he doesn't find Helena beautiful: "In such a business [choosing a spouse] give me leave to use/ The help of mine own eyes" (2.3.107–108). Lafew can't understand his diffidence: "These boys are boys of ice.... Sure they are bastards to the English, the French ne'er got 'em" (lines 94–95).

12. Like the ancients and medievals before him, Shakespeare liked the "rash decision" or "rash judgment" motif as a means to precipitate horrific if not tragic results. Lear banishes Cordelia in the midst of a tantrum, and Othello elopes with Desdemona without thinking through the social implications of marrying her without her father's consent. Macbeth, on the other hand, in a more traditional tragedy, murders Duncan not with complete *sangfroid*, but certainly with premeditation and knowing the deed wrong.

13. Shakespeare's use of Paris as the setting for Bertram's unwilling marriage may suggest a small, sly allusion to the Paris of the Troy tale, whose kidnapping of Helen leads to the Trojan War.

14. When Bertram enters the war in Florence, he prays to "Great Mars," not to God (3.3.9). The play conspicuously includes references to Classical deities and lacks any direct references to Christianity.

15. If he means a cancer, then the King faces danger indeed. Would Shakespeare have thought a single draft could cure a cancer, or would he have felt willing to employ such an unlikely motif other than ironically? If he means a benign cyst, then perhaps the King, like other characters in the play, is overdramatizing himself, and no wonder Helena's attention and miraculous medicine can cure it, perhaps by placebo effect. If it means a boil or festering wound, it suggests a wasting away, either from inside corruption or outside infection, apt metaphors for the state of mind and behaviors of several of the characters, particularly Bertram and Helena.

16. For an interesting comparison see *As You Like It*, Act IV, scene 1, lines 106–108, where Rosalind says in comic dialogue with Orlando, "Men have died from time to time, and worms have eaten them, but not for love."

17. Note that Parolles casts virginity as a lexical feminine: apparently he either believes that only women care about it, or, as something peevish and resistant to male desire, it must apply only to females — or he intends to assault her virginity and so casts her virginity as a direct offense against himself as well as nature as a means to get her to yield.

18. Some audiences, particularly in my experience young American readers, express disgust at the idea of deference to order and rank in Shakespeare's world. They forget the deference they readily show to the rich, to powerful corporate chiefs and potential employers, to movie stars, to physicians, lawyers, coaches, and the persons they have formally or informally chosen as the leaders of their own "peer" groups, which often have as firm a hierarchy as any society with nominal class distinctions. Since Shakespeare comes before the time of the birth of "human rights," he makes an especially modern move in allowing the kind of class mobility we see in some of his plays (such as this one), and he makes a thoroughly medieval and Renaissance move in raising questions of the extent — though not the existence — of free will in human experience.

19. Note, for instance, *Romeo and Juliet*, *Coriolanus*, *Julius Caesar*, and even *Twelfth Night* and *The Tempest*.

20. The King further praises Bertram's father for his "good melancholy," i.e., seriousness

of thought and sober judgment — again, traits Bertram needs to learn. Almost an oxymoron, that simple trope highlights a problem in the world of the play: the lack of (and need for) cool judgment to accompany both compassion and mercy.

21. Contemporary audiences must remember that despite current usage, the word *prophet* in Shakespeare's context — as in nearly every pre-twentieth-century context, means not foreteller, but one who by divine inspiration sees and can speak out the problems at hand, what the prophet's own time needs to know and understand. In that sense of the word, we can see Lavatch as a prophet rather than a sage, because while he lacks virtue and any useful knowledge or wisdom, he does reflect the problems of the more important characters in the world of the play.

22. Once again Shakespeare shows the danger of dissembling as Diana presents the King's ring and a riddle to the court at Rossillion: however good her intentions and the results she achieves, she nearly meets disaster by them, and she too may end up like Helena, choosing a husband who doesn't love her and who finds himself forced to marry her.

23. The double-ring game also recalls *The Merchant of Venice*: the rings, both of which have got where the person who gave them didn't intend them to go, affirm the relationships of the persons involved in their return, but possibly not to their long-lasting good.

Chapter 4

1. See her introduction to *Measure for Measure* in *The Riverside Shakespeare*, Boston: Houghton Mifflin, 1974, page 145. Barton also mentions that, though in Shakespeare's plays that we may more readily identify as comedies we find some kind of newer and better society arising at the end of the play, nothing we can identify as better happens at the end of *Measure*.

2. As with so many of Shakespeare's plays, issues of power accompany issues of authority. Goddard adds, "The effect of power on those who do not possess it but wish that they did, Shakespeare concludes, is scarcely better than on those who do" (66). *Measure for Measure* deals especially with that problem: whether or not I believe I am corruptible, should power come to me, I will fall. Not only Angelo demonstrates this point; however much the hangman Abhorson may resent having the uninitiated tapster Pompey imposed on his "mystery," Pompey takes to it readily enough: if once an unlawful bawd, why not better a lawful hangman? Pompey's rapid career change and the pretty rapid failure of Angelo's moral scruples show Shakespeare playing with the tensions of those stuck in "rigid ideals of conduct" (Barton 546) and those only too eager to shift from one objectionable behavior to another, the tensions that underlie the problems of this play. The "problem play" problem in *Measure* comes for Ernest Schanzer in that the audience and not the characters have doubts about their "moral bearings" (6): the characters have their own notions of right or wrong, but we, the audience, will call them into question and ponder them.

3. In a 1570 bull Pope Pius V had excommunicated Elizabeth and called on all good Christians to depose the Protestant "heretic" from the English throne. In 1588 Pope Sixtus V renewed the excommunication, claimed the Queen unfit even to live, and called on her subjects to bring about her chastisement upon threat of punishment if they failed to try. That declaration grants plenary indulgence to anyone who were to participate in arresting Elizabeth and her adherents and delivering them to Catholic authorities for judgment. Plenary indulgence offers full remission of temporal punishment for sins committed; the odd suggestion in this case is the implication of remission for actions (that might in some instances been recognized by the Church as sinful) *before their commission.*

4. "[H]ence shall we see/ If power change purpose: what our seemers be" (1.3. 53–54).

5. Stephen Greenblatt calls *Measure for Measure* "Shakespeare's comedy of substitutes and substitutions" (6). Shakespeare used that strategy often either directly or metaphorically. Here the substitutions sometimes create prove gruesome but useful, but other times they create what Jeanne Addison Roberts calls a "horizontalizing of the Chain of Being." When the Duke substitutes Angelo for himself, and when he suddenly raises Isabella from postulant to the level of Duchess, he makes a move that to modern audiences may seem liberatingly iconoclastic levellings of class, but to Shakespeare's time they would have appeared as dangerous challenges to God's ordering of the world.

6. For instance, I don't think Shakespeare was suggesting Angelo is *bad*, but that pride in one's own virtue can easily turn to hypocrisy

and abuse, especially if we come to believe ourselves above human weakness.

7. See scene 2, lines 261–82. The speech uses tetrameter, unusual for Shakespeare when a noble person speaks. Some of the lines prove difficult if not impossible to parse, and in one especially troublesome spot, some scholars have proposed lines must be missing, as the syntax evades interpretation. Some of the lines simply aren't very good poetry. But the thematic substance of the speech weighs heavily on the whole play, summarizing the problems both in what the Duke says (which is largely right) and in what he proposes to do (which may well be wrong).

8. In an interesting and comic exchange Escalus examines the tapster Pompey about the bawdy house where he works and the youths who frequent it. Pompey replies that if the law prohibits all fornication and prostitution, then Escalus must be ready to "geld and splay all the youth of the city" (lines 230–31). In an odd and particularly Shakespearean use of repetition, Escalus speaks Pompey's name twelve times in the course of thirty-six lines despite the small role the character plays in the whole, thus calling particular notice to the name. I have discussed this occurrence with several scholars; one suggested the name repeats *pomp*, satirizing courtly excesses as silly, formal parallels to the silly, private excesses of the bawdy house. But the powerful characters of *Measure for Measure* notably eschew pomp, though Angelo may treat his own dignity of office too seriously. I suspect Shakespeare wanted to make sure that his audience had in mind Pompey the Great, who came from a provincial if influential family to rival Julius Caesar for supreme power in Rome. Pompey's political machinations precipitated a civil war, and ultimately he lost what he had gained and was assassinated in Egypt, where he had gone hoping for help to mount another counteroffensive. In many plays Shakespeare warns his audience about the horrors of civil conflict — he seems not only to have had a troubled fascination with the Wars of the Roses, but also to have foreseen the English Civil War on the horizon. In *Measure* he is perhaps suggesting that Vienna has fallen into dissolution, and in the Duke's absence Angelo may turn it into a police state; both excesses of leniency and harsh constraint may lead to rebellion, and rebellion may lead to civil war — the hint of problems with the King of Hungary furthers this idea. Shakespeare's audience, for whom Caesar was one of the Nine Worthies and a major historical figure both for his accomplishments and his violent murder, would have understood the reference to Pompey as foreshadowing more and more intense civil violence and strife that extended throughout one's own country and beyond its borders. Once again the comic scene has serious thematic import, sufficient for Shakespeare to repeat it in III.2, where Lucio asks "noble Pompey," arrested again, if he finds himself "at the wheels of Caesar ... led in triumph" (lines 43–44). Lucio then repeats the name *Pompey* twelve times in twenty-five lines, where he teases him for his pimping and imprisonment. Here the motif calls particular attention to punishment for improper behavior, but also inconsistency in the public execution of justice, though Lucio will later get his measure for measure, through the Duke's punishment for his own sins. Another of the better instances of humor comes when the Provost bids Abhorson take Pompey as his assistant executioner. Abhorson resists, "A bawd, sir? fie upon him, he will discredit our mystery" (4.2.28): he sees his role, his class, his guild soiled by the addition of a pimp.

9. The Duke observes, "This is a gentle Provost: seldom when/ The steeled jailer is the friend of men" and "There is written in your brow, Provost, honesty and constancy; if I read it not truly, my ancient skill beguiles me" (4.2.86–87 and 153–55). While he judges the Provost aptly for his kindness, the jailor like the Duke hates the execution of unpleasant duties, and the Duke has shown his judgment suspect by allowing Angelo any additional public (or private) authority. Neither leadership skill nor sturdiness of character proves easy to display or to maintain.

10. In Act V, when the Duke gradually unfolds the workings of his plot, Escalus supports Angelo with sufficient readiness that he will order the torture of Isabella for publicly denouncing him and "Friar Lodowick" for his part in the plot. He will also taunt Angelo, once his guilt comes to light, though he has so recently defended him: "I am sorry, one so learned and so wise/ As you, Lord Angelo, have still appear'd,/ Should slip so grossly, both in the heat of blood/ And lack of temper'd judgment afterward" (5.1.470–73): he might have said the same, not about his own passion, but about his own judgment.

11. Isabella shows little realistic compassion even for Marianna. Learning of her experience with Angelo, rather than wishing that Mari-

anna may find a better love, Isabella offers instead, "What a merit were it in death to take this poor maid from the world! What corruption in this life, that it will let this man live!" (3.1.231–33). She sees death as a better option than trying to improve one's life, quite a morbid view for someone as youthful and vibrant as Isabella.

12. As he so often does, Shakespeare raises issues of honor repeatedly in *Measure*. He treats it from the viewpoints of several characters and with several different kinds of implications. Noble or powerful folk have a public honor they must maintain, and poorer or less influential folk have a private honor on which their souls depend. Shakespeare doesn't say whether they are right or wrong, but in their insistence he does urge the question of what we believe honor means and what we must or should do to keep it — if it means anything at all, anything more than an excuse for doing what we already wanted to do.

13. The word means here "unfortunate."

14. Chaucer's Troylus, but not Shakespeare's, suffers from this same irony, and the difference drives the exploration of character (and how an audience judges it) in separate ways. Chaucer's Troylus wins some sympathy, Shakespeare's none. Angelo might, like Chaucer's Troylus, except the change in himself and try by it to become a better person. Love — or lust — leads Shakespeare's Troilus to even greater selfishness, not to any self-discovery; Angelo does worse: he mutes the self-discovery and acts abominably to exploit it and then cover it up.

15. The image recalls Francis Bacon's essay "On Studies," where Bacon wrote that "some books are to be tasted, others to be swallowed, and some few to be chewed and digested." Not all books deserve our full attention, but some we want to make fully a part of ourselves and our thinking. Angelo chokes on a prayer that part of him wants and part of him rejects.

16. "Alack, when once our grace we have forgot,/ Nothing goes right — we would, and we would not," Angelo adds in 4.4.33–34: we want to do well, and we want to do ill, but with either intent everything will go badly once we have lost touch with goodness. The lines serve thematically and foreshadow the problem that ends the play: has the Duke, in his idea of mercies, and despite his time disguised as a friar, forgotten grace?

17. After his marriage, offstage, Angelo returns again to beg for death: "I am sorry that such sorrow I procure... That I crave death more willingly than mercy:/ 'Tis my deserving, and I do entreat it" (474–77). He expresses no resolution whatever to the marriage and doesn't respond to the Duke's command, "Love her, Angelo!" (526). The Duke believes her worthy of a good marriage because he believes in her virtue: "I have confess'd her" (527). No one seems to worry that the Duke hasn't the power of confession and absolution nor that the marriage of a "good" woman to a man now proven "bad" bodes ill for their futures.

18. When she pleads Marianna's case for mercy to Angelo — Marianna must beg her twice — she opines, "My brother had but justice,/ In that he did the thing for which he died," and she adds in specific defense of Angelo "Thoughts are no subjects,/ Intents but merely thoughts" (lines 448–49, 453–54). If someone pushes her, she will plead eloquently enough, but without her heart in it.

19. "Sir, your company is fairer than honest," the Duke tells him (4.3.175).

20. After what he's done, he still focuses exclusively on himself: "Marrying a punk, my lord, is pressing to death, whipping, and hanging" (5.1.522–23). The Duke sentences him to all of them, but has remitted all punishments but the marriage (519–20). Apparently the Duke views the punishment of making him a cuckold enough (516–17).

Chapter 5

1. Discussions in college literature courses often turn to the nature of evil. I find that more often than not today's students don't believe in it, especially if they have lived somewhat sheltered lives: they believe no one does evil willingly, that persons who perform dangerous or harmful acts simply misunderstand what they're doing. Shakespeare, like Milton after him, has characters who deliberately perform evil, and he seems to have believed that kind of thinking and action part of the range of human experience. In Christopher Marlowe's *Doctor Faustus*, the title character, having by means of a spell called the devil Mephistophilis, bravely — or foolishly — asserts, "I think hell's a fable." Mephistophilis replies, "Aye, think so still, till experience change they mind." I suspect Shakespeare is making that same point, though in a more quotidian setting, through Don John.

2. We never learn the purpose, extent, or significance of the war. Shakespeare uses the

reference to it to allow us to see Don Pedro's party as brave and successful soldiers and to set the tone of the world of the play as one of conflict. When Leonato asks him about losses, Don Pedro replies, "Few of any sort, and none of name." The passage may call to mind Henry V's tally after the Battle of Agincourt, it may show the general practice of the nobility after battle, or it may show a kind of disdain or lack of concern toward those men who did lose their lives, since it shows an interest only in titled persons.

3. Both Benedick's first and last names suggest sexual puns. His name is not *Benedict*, which translates as a "well-spoken word" and suggests a prayer of a blessing — a good match, were it so, for Beatrice, whose name means "blessed one" with perhaps a pun on *beatus rictus*, "blessed mouth," or one who speaks blessedly.

4. There Benedick utters one of the themes of the play: if we err, we must do better, and indeed he tries. In V.1. 199–200 Don Pedro says something similar: "What a pretty thing man is when he goes in his doublet and hose and leaves off his wit." He refers to Benedick who at Beatrice's urging has challenged Claudio to a duel for wronging Hero. Don Pedro, though, has failed to learn what Benedick is learning: choices bear consequences, and wit doesn't cover up everything.

5. In *Shakespeare's Comedy of Love* Alexander Leggatt calls attention to the insecurity and anxiety behind the aggression in the exchanges between Beatrice and Benedick; we should also note the aggression behind the insecurity and anxiety in Claudio. His youthful success in battle doesn't translate to success in romance, which must come from love rather than hasty pursuit.

6. Shakespeare would have known the Latin but probably not the Greek sources.

7. Ovid's metamorphoses happen because of excesses: sometimes but not always those of the victim. Minerva changes Arachne into a spider because of her excess of pride in her weaving talent, but Daphne becomes a laurel tree because of Apollo's excess of desire to possess her. We differ not so greatly from the animals and objects of the world, Ovid suggests, and the gods treat us sometimes kindly and sometimes miserably. We must simply accept the human lot and try to find our way to balance, generosity, acceptance, and piety.

8. Titania will echo Puck's epithet in 2.1.61, after Oberon has called her "proud Titania."

He has no right to what he asks, the Indian boy for whom Titania now cares because his mother, her votress, has died, but that doesn't keep him from his making his demand. He assumes she will and must comply, but Titania resists. Oddly, she seems at the end of the play not only to have given in to him, but fully to have forgiven him. In a kindlier way, then, this subplot echoes the Hero and Claudio story in *Much Ado*: forgiveness wins out even if it doesn't constitute justice.

9. This theme undergirds not only this play, but much of Shakespeare's work. Here everyone but Theseus seems to recognize that truth, but, perhaps since he doesn't, no one else can do much about it.

10. See Stephen Greenblatt's *Shakespeare's Freedom* for a discussion of "Shakespeare's growing skepticism about the claim for autonomy that he had made" with respect to this play and others.

11. How often have we heard (or felt or said), "I will die without her/him? *MSND* presents that problem, which Rosalind in *As You Like It* tells us doesn't hold up, in fact, in a specific and troubling way.

12. Shakespeare's Catholic reference makes an anachronism, of course, but he includes it to touch his audience in a particular way. Theseus as King/Father offers Hermia only a slightly less odious option; he seems kinder, but not much kinder, and Hermia finds no help at all in the additional choice.

13. Shakespeare's second daughter seems to have married against his wishes, and based on his will, we can guess that he disapproved, intending to leave her little or nothing.

14. See her introduction to the play in *The Riverside Shakespeare*.

15. Though Shakespeare's time and the authors who influenced him either believed in love at first sight or knew its value as a literary motif, Sonnet 130 suggests that Shakespeare clearly knew the difference and enjoyed playing with it.

16. Earlier Toby has referred to the joke as "our pleasure and his penance, till our very pastime, tir'd out of breath, prompt us to have mercy on him" (3.4.137–39).

17. Sir Toby, not a very good friend, though he wants Sir Andrew to court his niece, doesn't even get his name right, but calls him "Agueface" (1.3.43).

18. "[A]n ass-head and a coxcomb and a knave, a thin-fac'd knave, a gull": the insults may refer to Andrew (my suspicion), whom

Toby perhaps insults for being stupid, proud, and cowardly, or to Sebastian, who has given them both injuries when the attacked him, thinking they were setting on Viola/Cesario.

19. Feste calls her so, presumably for turning down a good marriage offer, mourning overmuch, and keeping Sir Toby despite all the trouble he causes.

20. "Observe him [Malvolio] for the love of mockery," Maria suggests.

Chapter 6

1. Historically writers have often neglected friendship-love as a topic to explore, but Shakespeare does not. The sonnets deal with it, and both good and bad "friends" appear in Shakespeare plays (see, for instance, *Love's Labour's Lost, Much Ado About Nothing, 1 Henry IV*, and *Othello*).

2. In Greek terms Claudius, by murdering his brother, has created *miasma*, the blood pollution that comes from intra-familial violence and that invokes the wrath of the Furies, destructive not only to those involved, but often those anywhere near the inciting act.

3. Roland Frye notes the connection between "Christian prince" Hamlet and "virtuous heathen" Edgar in *King Lear* (137): both understand endurance, waiting, readiness, virtues regardless of time, place, heritage.

4. For an interesting exposition of this idea in fiction, see John Updike's *Gertrude and Claudius*.

5. I suspect the only thing that keeps Horatio out of harm's way is that Claudius doesn't notice his closeness to Hamlet; the King probably believes he has come to Elsinore to celebrate his and Gertrude's wedding.

6. One recent film version has Ophelia finding condoms in Laertes' suitcase.

7. Ophelia also gives Gertrude a daisy and would have given her violets had they not "wither'd all when my father died" (lines 184–85); the flowers symbolize dissembling and unfaithfulness. Ophelia apparently knows more yet about Gertrude.

8. His name, like several of those in *Othello*, carries heavy irony. *Iago* is Spanish for James, and according to Spanish tradition St. James the Apostle appeared on a white horse in 844 to Ramiro I at the battle of Clavijo to help him defeat the Moors on the way to the *Reconquista*. Tradition terms St. James *Matamoros*, "Moor-slayer." Ironically, like a devil rather than an apostle, Iago has the ability to rouse dangerously aggressive anger in others.

9. In Chapter III of *J. R. R. Tolkien: Author of the Century*, Tom Shippey has an interesting discussion of Tolkien's use of the concept of evil in *The Lord of the Rings*: it can come from inside or outside, a failure or absence of good within ourselves but also a malignant force outside ourselves intending to harm. Shakespeare, I think, shows much the same notion; the characters in *Othello* struggle with both.

10. C. S. Lewis makes an interesting and pertinent point in his *Preface to Paradise Lost* about the Devil and self-absorption. Many readers on first encountering the epic believe Satan its hero: he has great speeches, makes arguments about freedom, self-determination, and resisting tyranny. But with whom would one want to have lunch, Adam and Eve or Satan? Adam and Eve talk about God, Creation, angels, animals, the Garden, dreams, sex, each other, and the way the mind works — anything and everything. Satan talks about himself and his wounded feelings; that would quickly grow stale, even unendurable — exactly Milton's point. Satan's error isn't so much pride as self-obsession. We see the same error, with all its destructive power for self and others, in Iago.

11. Though he shows admirable traits, we can hardly call Cassio a good man: he treats Bianca, regardless of her social status and sexual habits, abominably.

12. One of the critical problems in working with *King Lear* — indeed, with a number of Shakespeare plays and with many works of the Old World and some of the New — comes in the difficulty of establishing which text of the play to use. As Marjorie Garber amply explains, "Many recent Shakespeare editors have concluded that there are *two* extant viable versions of the play the Quarto (1608) and Folio (1623) differ in serious and significant ways, so some contemporary editors have tried to 'unedit' the play to return it to a less 'impure' form" (651–52). Garber continues, "In my observations on *King Lear* I will continue to include scenes and passages that have become customarily associated with the play over the years"— she chooses the Folio as primary source but adds material from the Quarto where she finds it helpful or necessary (652). At the risk of studying a text that no on has ever played on stage, I prefer for both teaching and studying to include all the material that may have once formed part of King Lear, so I

use the reconstructed, longer versions of plays where I can find them. Printed versions of the play may differ because editors (or printers) were working from the imperfect memories of actors or from scripts shortened to play in a more tolerable length of time; I want to have access to everything that Shakespeare wrote, that he may have wanted to include in an "ideal" or complete texts from which a company of players might make their own deletions to present the play as they thought best. I would rather include too much than omit something Shakespeare might have thought useful or even essential, but there, I repeat, I give only my own preference for study and teaching, not a rule that I think editors must follow.

13. Back in the nineteenth century Thomas DeQuincey made a similar point about the knocking at the gate and the Porter's speech following the murder of Duncan in Macbeth. Macduff's knocking and the Porter's humor invade the black silence that follows the horrific act, providing an extreme contrast; the contrast calls us back from shock to recognition of the real monstrousness of the deed.

14. The Fool calls Fortune "that arrant whore" who "ne'er turns the key to the poor" (2.4.52–53)— rich folk, not poor, declaim against changes of fortune, since the poor rarely see a change for the better— and Kent will ask, "Fortune, good night; smile once more, turn thy wheel" (2.2.173). It will keep turning, but for the worse.

15. We get further hints of this suggestion. "Are you our daughter?" Lear asks (1.4.218); the Fool says that Lear should have been smarter than a snail, who knows better than "to give [his shell] away to his daughters, and leave his horns without a case" (1.5. 30–32)— the horn image hints of cuckoldry, that another man fathered Lear's daughters; "Woe, that too late repents," Lear says at Goneril's disrespect— he may refer to his own whoring, from which his daughters have perhaps sprung.

16. I first heard this idea from Professor William Bache of Purdue University back in the 1980s; it has always seemed to me to bring many strands the play sensibly together. It also urges us to ask the same question of the other parent/child relationships in the play. The play presents many images of cuckoldry and infidelity as well. Has Lear any legitimate children? What happened to their mother(s)? Does he love Cordelia best because she has treated him best or because he loved her mother better than the mothers of the other daughters, if they weren't in fact the same woman? How can free will overcome whatever determinacy lies in bastardy?

17. The end of the play has several Christian images: the dead Cordelia carried in by Lear in a kind of reverse piéta; Cordelia as Christ-figure again, hanging from a tree, then in Lear's hopes on the verge of resurrection; Lear as well, having killed the slave that hanged Cordelia, saying, "I am old now,/ And these same crosses spoil me" (5.3.278–79) as a kind of Peter having denied Christ and now atoning, and Kent as the faithful disciple who will follow his master in death as in life: "My master calls me, I must not say no" (5.3.323).

Chapter 7

1. In *Shakespeare's Ideas* David Bevington observes about *Richard II* and the Henry IV plays that "Shakespeare refuses to give final judgement [sic], even though he freely appeals to our sympathies as the story unfolds. His job as dramatist is to present opposing sides with sympathy and insight, inviting his audience to be enlightened and entertained by the clash of ideologies" (53); the key comes, I think, in suspending judgment, since we don't see so much competing ideologies as competition for power and over who has the right of succession and why— and what that will mean to the country.

2. Professor Bache first pointed out to me the importance of hearing this passage rather than reading it silently. The two men repeatedly call "Francis!" to get the boy to come to them, and he repeatedly answers "Anon," trying to get to them as quickly as he can. The attentive listener will hear "France is anon": however stupidly Hal behaves at this point in his life, the audience must remember that his heroic adventures in France are anon, that is, they lie ahead for him and for his country. Again Shakespeare succeeds in creating a complex emotional scheme by contrast: silly jokes versus extreme martial heroism. We must recognize, though, that Hal's future behavior as Henry V doesn't excuse his bad behavior as Prince Hal, however much he may urge us to believe that.

3. Laurie Maguire in *Studying Shakespeare* describes the *Henry IV/Henry V* sequence as Shakespeare's means "to develop (in theory) and demonstrate (in practice) this postmedieval and unsacramental concept of kingship, in which

persons become to those in power a form of currency" (97). Amidst the growing wealth and power of merchantry in Shakespeare's time, he used many plays to address this problem — though I'm not sure the Middle Ages were free of it.

4. Leonard Tennenhouse in *Power on Display* suggests that "chronicle history uses the same strategy to produce political order out of political conflict as romantic comedy uses to reinforce the dominant rules of kingship. Both represent patriarchal hierarchies in a state of disorder ... creating two bases for authority, and thus competing hierarchies of power, which only the monarch can hold together in harmonious discord" (73). I think Shakespeare in the histories is questioning not the notion of hierarchy, but how those who come to power (or may come to power) either use it or find a means to inveigle or murder their way into it. The best they can do, often, is to reach a discordant harmony, something like Orsino's "dying fall." Human flaws leave us little more success than that, and Shakespeare never simply affirms quality of monarchy.

5. Marjorie Garber says of *Henry V* that "we are asked to approve ... a spectacle of victory, and a concept of kinship, that is finally only an idea, precariously achieved and too easily lost" (408). I'd suggest that Shakespeare doesn't so much ask us to approve it as to think about it: where it succeeds and where it fails, why it might have worked — temporarily — for a Henry V, but may fail miserably for someone else in a different time and circumstance. In Shakespeare's time Queen Elizabeth could move an army or a people with a fairly direct and relatively simple speech because she had come to inspire awe and devotion. But a generation after Shakespeare the deposing of Charles I, a monarch who could not move his people by mind or heart or tongue, plunged the English into Civil War.

6. He is "Prosper-O!" He may prosper; he may not.

7. The men's vows include punishments for breaking them that apply not only to themselves, but to others who know nothing of them: the King's document specifies that "no woman shall come within a mile of my court ... on pain of losing her tongue" (1.1.120–24). Such lack of common sense, Shakespeare implies, harms not only the guilty, but anyone who out of bad fortune happens to cross their paths.

8. Anne Barton in her introduction to the play in *The Riverside Shakespeare* asserts that the men must "learn something that the women have known all along: how to accommodate speech to facts and to emotional realities, as opposed to using it as a means of evasion, idle amusement, or unthinking cruelty" (177). I find that while the men proceed artificially in almost any endeavor, the ladies hardly do much better: they taunt and deceive the men, impose penances as if they were spiritual advisors rather than equals in love-pursuit, and display what we might call thinking (versus unthinking) cruelty. Even Jaquenetta, a servant, places a fairly strict requirement on Don Armado, her social superior. The women impose on themselves a year of mourning, another kind of random vow. No one in the play proves particularly admirable, and all must learn to grow up. There the Princess must lead as she deals with her father's mortality, and we as audience must learn the weight and significance of a vow.

9. Other plays pose other kinds of problems. For instance, with *Pericles, Prince of Tyre, The Two Noble Kinsmen*, and *Henry VIII*, how much of them did Shakespeare write, and what parts?

Bibliography

Barton, Anne. Introduction to *A Midsummer Night's Dream*. *The Riverside Shakespeare*. Ed. G. Blakemore Evans, et al. Boston: Houghton Mifflin, 1974. 217–21.

———. Introduction to *Love's Labour's Lost*. *The Riverside Shakespeare*. Ed. G. Blakemore Evans, et al. Boston: Houghton Mifflin, 1974. 174–78.

———. Introduction to *Measure for Measure*. *The Riverside Shakespeare*. Ed. G. Blakemore Evans, et al. Boston: Houghton Mifflin, 1974. 545–49.

———. Introduction to *Troilus and Cressida*. *The Riverside Shakespeare*. Ed. G. Blakemore Evans, et al. Boston: Houghton Mifflin, 1974. 443–47.

Bevington, David. *How to Read a Shakespeare Play*. Malden, MA: Blackwell, 2006.

———. *Shakespeare's Ideas: More Things in Heaven and Earth*. Malden, MA: Wiley-Blackwell, 2008.

Boas, F. S. *Shakespeare and His Predecessors*. 1896. New York: Charles Scribner's Sons, 1900.

Charlton, H. B. *Shakespearean Comedy*. New York: Macmillan, 1938.

Chaucer, Geoffrey. *The Complete Poetry and Prose of Geoffrey Chaucer*. Ed. John H. Fisher. New York: Holt, Rinehart, and Winston, 1977.

Fox, Denton. "Introduction." *The Testament of Cresseid*. Ed. Robert Henryson. London: Thomas Nelson, 1968.

Frye, Northrop. *Anatomy of Criticism: Four Essays*. Princeton: Princeton University Press, 1957.

Frye, Roland Mushat. *Shakespeare and Christian Doctrine*. Princeton: Princeton University Press, 1963.

Garber, Marjorie. *Shakespeare After All*. New York: Anchor, 2004.

Girard, René. *A Theater of Envy*. New York: Oxford University Press, 1991.

Goddard, Harold. *The Meaning of Shakespeare*. 2 vols. Chicago: University of Chicago Press, 1951.

Grebanier, Bernard. *The Truth About Shylock*. New York: Random House, 1962.

Greenblatt, Stephen. *Shakespeare's Freedom*. Chicago: University of Chicago Press, 2010.

———. *Will in the World*. New York: Norton, 2004.

Gross, Kenneth. *Shylock is Shakespeare*. Chicago: University of Chicago Press, 2006.

Hartwig, Joan. *Shakespeare's Tragicomic Vision*. Baton Rouge: Louisiana State University Press, 1972.

Haydock, Nickolas A. *Situational Poetics in Robert Henryson's The Testament of Cresseid*. Amherst, NY: Cambria Press, 2010.

Henryson, Robert. *The Poems of Robert Henryson*. Ed. Robert Kindrick. Kalamazoo: Medieval Institute Publications, 1997.

James, Heather. *Shakespeare's Troy: Drama, Politics, and the Translation of Empire*. Cambridge: Cambridge University Press, 1997.

Knight, G. Wilson. *The Wheel of Fire: Interpretation of Shakespeare's Tragedy*. Cleveland: Meridian, 1957.

Lawrence, William W. *Shakespeare's Problem Comedies*. New York: Macmillan, 1931.

Leggatt, Alexander. *Shakespeare's Comedy of Love*. London: Methuen, 1973.

Lovejoy, Arthur O. *The Great Chain of Being: A Study of the History of an Idea*, New York: Harper, 1936.

Lyon, John. *The Merchant of Venice*. Boston: Twayne, 1988.

Maguire, Laurie E. *Studying Shakespeare: A Guide to the Plays*. Malden, MA: Blackwell, 2004.

Medcalf, Stephen. "Dreaming, Looking, and

Seeing: Shakespeare and the Myth of Resurrection." *Thinking with Shakespeare: Comparative and Interdisciplinary Essays*. Ed. William Poole and Richard Scholar. London: Legenda, 2007. 93–114.

Nuttall, A. D. *Shakespeare the Thinker*. New Haven: Yale University Press, 2007.

Roberts, Jeanne Addison. "Animals as Agents of Revelation: The Horizontalizing of the Chain of Being in Shakespeare's Comedies." *Shakespearean Comedy*. Ed. Maurice Charney. New York: Literary Forum, 1980. 79–96.

Schanzer, Ernest. *The Problem Plays of Shakespeare*. New York: Schocken Books, 1963.

Shakespeare, William. *The Riverside Shakespeare*, Ed. G. Blakemore Evans, et al., Boston: Houghton Mifflin, 1974.

Shippey, Tom. *J. R. R. Tolkien: Author of the Century*. Boston: Houghton Mifflin, 2000.

Smith, Hallett. Introduction to *The Tempest*. *The Riverside Shakespeare*, ed. G. Blakemore Evans, et al. Boston: Houghton Mifflin, 1974. 1606–10.

Snyder, Susan. *The Comic Matrix of Shakespeare's Tragedies*. Princeton: Princeton University Press, 1979.

Staley, Gregory A. *Seneca and the Idea of Tragedy*. New York: Oxford University Press, 2010.

Tennenhouse, Leonard. *Power on Display: The Politics of Shakespeare's Genres*. New York: Methuen, 1986.

Tillyard, E. M. W. *Shakespeare's Problem Plays*. Toronto: University of Toronto Press, 1949.

Updike, John. *Gertrude and Claudius*. New York: Random House, 2001.

Widdicombe, Toby. *Simply Shakespeare*. New York: Longman, 2002.

Wright, Louis B., and Virginia A. LaMar. *The Folger Guide to Shakespeare*. New York: Pocket Books, 1969.

Yaffe, Martin D. *Shylock and the Jewish Question*. Baltimore: Johns Hopkins University Press, 1997.

Index

Achilles 45, 47–48, 56, 59, 60, 61, 64, 65, 75, 209
acid character 42–50
Aeneas 25, 46, 59
Aeschylus 209
Agincourt 184, 214
Ajax 45–46, 56, 59, 63
alchemy 20–22, 205
allegory 11, 52, 66, 91, 95, 124–25, 167–68, 193, 201
All's Well That End's Well 2, 3, 5, 9, 66–89, 90, 91, 104, 109, 113, 208–211
Angelo 91–112, 211–13
anti-semitism 15
anti-stratfordians 4
Antony and Cleopatra 4, 5
Ariel 190, 192
Aristotle 4, 7, 8, 18, 44, 50, 144, 167, 189, 201, 205
As You Like It 210, 214

Bache, William 11, 12, 206, 216
Bacon, Francis 213
Barton, Anne 43, 90, 94, 136, 211, 217, 219
Bassanio 7, 16–40, 67, 79, 206, 207
Battle of Shrewsbury 181
Beardsley, Monroe C. 2
Beatrice 83, 109, 114–126, 194, 214
Benedick 114–26, 207, 214
Benoît de Sainte-Maure 51
Berowne 193–200
Bertram 208, 209, 210, 211
Bevington, David 2, 10, 42–43, 216, 219
Boar's Head Tavern 180
Boas, F.S. 2, 4, 219
Boccaccio, Giovanni 51, 52, 57, 206
Bottom 127–29, 132, 134
Byron (Lord) 157, 201

Caliban 190–91
Cassio 160–65

catharsis 3, 41, 44, 48, 49, 52, 57, 94, 101, 113, 137, 144, 165, 167–69, 176, 203, 205, 208, 209
Charleton, H.B. 193, 205, 219
Chaucer, Geoffrey 2, 12, 42, 44, 48, 50–53, 57–58, 71–73, 143, 191, 206, 208, 219
Christianity 10, 11, 16–18, 27, 30–40, 54, 64, 66, 77, 79, 81, 85, 95, 101–102, 116, 121, 125, 147, 160, 165, 167–68, 174, 179, 191, 207, 210, 216, 219
Claudio (*Measure for Measure*) 97–98, 101–108, 111–112
Claudio (*Much Ado*) 115–26, 214
Claudius (*Hamlet*) 8, 106, 146–58, 215
color symbolism 20–22, 207
comedy 1, 5, 7, 8, 9, 15, 38, 41, 42, 49, 50, 52, 209, 217
The Comedy of Errors 9, 194, 206
contemptus mundi 103
Cordelia 166–76, 210, 216
Coriolanus 200, 201, 210
Costard 194, 196–99
Cressida (Criseyde) 25, 28, 43–65, 70–75
Cymbeline 3, 9, 83, 87–90, 201, 207

Dante Alighieri 55, 104, 159
dark comedy 6, 93, 201, 205
deconstruction 15
De Quincy, Thomas 25, 216
Derrida, Jacques 7
Desdemona 159–66, 210
Dido 25
Diomedes (Diomed) 46–47, 53, 56, 60–63, 72
dissembling 23, 29, 36, 48, 56, 60, 67–68, 72, 84, 92, 96, 104, 108, 114–21, 124, 129, 133, 135–41, 143, 152–53, 160, 163, 165, 173, 187–88, 195, 199, 209, 211, 215
Doctor Faustus 2, 74, 107, 213
Dogberry 58, 115, 121–25, 128, 133, 138

Don John 115–23, 125, 158, 213
Don Pedro 59, 115–25, 214
Dryden, John 43
Dumas, Alexandre 203
duty 7, 12, 28, 39–41, 71, 91, 94, 96, 98, 99, 100, 103, 123, 125, 126, 128, 133, 142, 144, 160, 161, 169, 170, 177–80, 184, 186, 190, 201, 203, 206, 210

Eco, Umberto 44
Edgar 167–68, 173–75, 215
Edmund 40, 168–69, 173
Elizabeth I (Queen) 40, 48, 95, 150, 165, 211, 217
Epic 3, 5, 7, 9, 51, 55, 74, 84, 182, 208, 215
Euripides 126

The Faerie Queen 45, 54, 208
Falstaff 178–81, 186, 206
fear 18, 22, 24, 25, 44, 48, 51–56, 63, 70, 80, 92, 93, 96, 97, 100, 103, 104, 116, 119, 120, 128, 142, 145, 151, 158, 167, 168, 180
Ferdinand 189, 192
Feste 134–35, 137–38, 140, 142–43, 144, 215
First Folio 208, 215
Fluellan 184, 186
Fool (*King Lear*) 169–72, 176, 216
Fortinbras 147, 151–53, 158
Fortune (Fortune's Wheel) 52, 75, 141, 143, 150, 170, 182, 216
Fox, Denton 54, 208, 219
Freud, Sigmund 20
Frye, Northrop 9, 206, 219
Frye, Roland Mushat 10–11, 215, 219

Garber, Marjorie 6, 90, 91, 94, 95, 114, 205, 208, 209, 215, 217, 219
genre 1–4, 7–9, 12, 41–44, 48–50, 54, 69, 83, 90, 94–95, 101, 142, 144–46, 170, 177, 189, 192, 193, 200, 203, 205, 205, 206, 208, 208, *passim*
Gertrude 148–50, 152–58, 215
Giotto 151
Girard, Renè 6, 7, 120, 159, 219
Gloucester, Earl of 167–69, 172–76
Goddard, Harold 1, 15, 18, 20, 32, 49, 66, 91, 94, 126, 168, 178, 206, 209, 211, 219
Goldman, William 1
Goneril 93, 140, 172–73, 216
Gorboduc 140
Great Chain of Being 5, 6, 84, 90, 93, 158, 205, 208, 209, 211, 215, 217
Grebanier, Bernard 15, 219

Greenblatt, Stephen 7, 209, 211, 214, 216, 219
Gross, Kenneth 19, 206, 219

Hal, Prince/Henry V (King) 177–86, 216
Hamlet 5, 7–9, 35, 39, 47, 77, 106, 145–58, 171, 174, 176, 178, 187, 215
Hartwig, Joan 187, 205, 219
Haydock, Nickolas 48, 208, 219
Hector 43, 45–47, 56, 62, 63, 65, 75
Helen (of Troy) 45–46, 52, 55, 60, 62, 63
Helena (*All's Well*) 66–89, 208–11
Helena (*MSND*) 128, 133–34
Henry IV, Part 1 9, 177–81, 215–17
Henry V (play) 9, 72, 100, 112, 133, 181–86, 216–17
Henryson, Robert 44, 46, 48, 50, 52–58, 71, 75, 208, 219
Hermia 120, 128, 133–34, 214
Hero 11, 114–26, 214
Hippolyta 126–28, 132, 134
history play 3, 7, 9, 15, 42, 49, 70, 177–86, 206, 216–17
Holinshed, Raphael 167
Homer 75
Horace 2, 43
Horatio 145, 154–58, 215
Hotspur 178–81

Iago 140, 159–66, 215
Imogen 187–89
Isabella 97, 99–112, 207, 212–13

James, Heather 54, 208, 219
James I (King) 95
Jason 25
Jessica 15–40, 79
Joan 54
Johnson, Samuel 43, 86
Jonson, Ben 17, 43
Joyce, James 5
Julius Caesar 4, 210, 212

Katherine (Princess) 112, 182–84
Keats, John 3, 4, 57, 201–2
Kent, Earl of 167–70, 173–74
Kermode, Frank 209
Kindrick, Robert 52, 208, 219
King Lear 9, 39, 41, 59, 86, 91, 93, 138, 140, 145, 159, 160, 164, 166–76, 190, 201, 210, 215–16
Knight, G. Wilson 42, 219

Laertes 77, 148–49, 152–54, 158
LaMar, Virginia 48, 90, 135, 198, 206, 220
The Land of Cokaygne 43

Index

Lawrence, W.W. 3, 42, 90, 208, 219
Leggatt, Alexander 193–94, 214, 219
Lewis, C.S. 215
Loggins, Vernon P. 206
Lovejoy, Arthur O. 205, 219
Love's Labour's [or *Labor's*] *Lost* 10, 177, 193–200, 215, 217
Luca Signorelli 151
Lyon, John 32, 219

Macbeth 9, 25, 207
MacLeish, Archibald 2
Maguire, Laurie 216, 219
Malory, Thomas 191
Malvolio 135–36, 138–42, 215
Marlowe, Christopher 2, 7, 16, 74, 213
Matthew (gospel) 35, 90
Measure for Measure 2–5, 9, 11, 49, 76, 90–112, 205, 211–13
Medcalf, Stephen 167, 219
Medea 25
melodrama 200, 201, 205
memento mori 20, 39, 119, 208
The Merchant of Venice 2, 7, 9, 15–41, 64, 67, 69, 72, 79, 83, 84, 206–208
mercy 11, 15, 17, 25, 27–37, 54, 71, 85, 92–93, 99, 101, 103, 107, 109–112, 184, 188–92, 201, 211, 213, 214
Merry Wives of Windsor 9, 206
miasma 215
A Midsummer Night's Dream 9, 72, 113, 115, 126–36, 195, 196, 214, 214
Milton, John 64, 107, 116, 161, 166, 182, 213, 215
mimetic desire 6–7, 159
modern/Modernism 3, 5, 10, 16, 33, 43, 46, 64, 122, 129, 130, 153, 182, 183, 186, 209, 210, 211, 219
Much Ado About Nothing 9, 11, 58, 72, 209, 213–15

Nuttal, A.D. 2, 193, 203, 207, 208, 220

Oberon 126–29, 142, 214
Olivia 135–43
Ophelia 145, 148–50, 152–58, 215
Orsino 135–43
Othello 9, 158–67, 176, 206, 210, 215
Ovid 49, 62, 130, 139, 214

Pandarus 45–47, 74
Parolles 66–88, 209, 210
Pericles, Prince of Tyre 83, 207, 217
Phaedra 126–27
Plato 205
Plutarch 126

Poe, Edgar Allan 24
Poetics 4, 7–8, 44, 50, 144, 167
Polonius 35, 48, 77–78, 148–50, 152–58, 171
Pompey the Great 196–97, 212
Portia 19–40, 67, 79, 206, 207
Posthumus 187–88
postmodernism 2, 8, 12, 43, 209
The Princess Bride 1–2
problem comedy 1, 94
Prospero 93, 189–93, 217
Puck 128–29, 134, 214
Pynchon, Thomas 205
Pyramus and Thisby [or *Thisbe*] 25, 128–34, 196, 200

rash decision 5, 17, 25, 36, 72, 83, 86, 101, 113, 117–18, 120, 126–27, 130–31, 133, 141, 159, 161, 168, 175, 187–88, 194, 199, 210
Regan 93, 105, 140, 172
Reiner, Rob 1
Richard II 178, 184, 216
Richard III 140
ring 24–25, 28, 36, 38, 211
Roberts, Jeanne Addison 211, 220
Robertson, D.W. 208
Romance 3, 6–9, 15, 38, 41–42, 48–49, 55, 67, 69, 83–84, 93–94, 112, 136, 143, 177, 187–201, 205, 207–208, 215, 217
Romeo and Juliet 5, 132, 200, 210

St. Crispin's Day 185
Schanzer, Ernest 4, 5, 220
Seneca 126, 167, 220
Shaw, George Bernard 6, 114
Shippey, Tom 215, 220
Shylock 15–41, 80, 206–207
Sir Gawain and the Carle of Carlisle 43
Sir Gawain and the Green Knight 41, 191
Smith, Hallett 189, 220
Snyder, Susan 5, 220
Sophocles 209
Spenser, Edmund 45, 54, 208
Staley, Gregory 167, 220

The Taming of the Shrew 187, 189
Tasso, Torquato 191
Tate, Nahum 167
The Tempest 7, 9, 72, 94, 168, 189–93, 195, 201, 210, 217
Tennenhouse, Leonard 6, 206, 217, 220
Thersites 44–49, 58–62
Theseus 126–27, 129–30, 132–34, 196, 214
Tillyard, E.M.W. 4, 220
Timon of Athens 140, 200, 201

224 Index

Titania 127–28, 142, 214
Toby, Sir 135, 138–142, 214
Tolkien, J.R.R. 191–92, 215
tragedy 1, 5–9, 15, 42, 49, 52–53, 65, 69, 70, 83, 144–76, 177, 182, 187, 193, 200, 201, 203, 208, 210, 215–16
tragicomedy 42, 201, 205
trawþe 41, 50
Troilus (Troylus) 25, 43–65, 70, 72–74, 212
Troilus and Cressida 3, 5–9, 29, 42–65, 69, 70, 71, 74, 75, 83, 89, 208–209
Twelfth Night 9, 134–43, 168, 194, 210, 214–15210, 214

Ulysses (character) 45, 47–48, 56, 60–64
Ulysses (novel) 5, 220
Unities 7, 189
Updike, John 215

Venus 45, 51–53
Vincentio (Duke) 90–112, 211–12
Viola 109, 135–43, 215
Volpone 17
Vonnegut, Kurt 205

The Wedding of Sir Gawain and Dame Ragnell 43
Wendell, Barrett 208
Weregild 146
Widdicombe, Toby 205, 220
Wilde, Oscar 114
Wimsatt, W.K. 2
Wright, Louis B. 48, 90, 135, 198, 206, 220

Yaffe, Martin 18, 32, 220

www.ingramcontent.com/pod-product-compliance
Ingram Content Group UK Ltd.
Pitfield, Milton Keynes, MK11 3LW, UK
UKHW041950140426
5217IPUK00014B/727